THE MIND OF THE SOUTH: FIFTY YEARS

The Mind of the South: Fifty Years Later

Essays and comments by
BRUCE CLAYTON
ANNE GOODWYN JONES
MICHAEL O'BRIEN
ORVILLE VERNON BURTON
DON H. DOYLE
JAMES L. ROARK
LACY K. FORD, JR.
EDWARD L. AYERS
LINDA REED
JOHN SHELTON REED
BERTRAM WYATT-BROWN

Edited by
CHARLES W. EAGLES

UNIVERSITY PRESS OF MISSISSIPPI
Jackson and London

95 94 93 92   4 3 2 1

The paper in this book meets the guidelines for permanence and
durability of the Committee on Production Guidelines for Book
Longevity of the Council on Library Resources.

Library of Congress Cataloging-in-Publication Data

The Mind of the South : fifty years later / essays and comments by
   Bruce Clayton ... [et al.] ; edited by Charles W. Eagles.
      p.   cm. — (Chancellor's symposium series)
   Includes bibliographical references and index.
   ISBN 0-87805-580-0 (cloth). — ISBN 0-87805-581-9 (paper)
   1. Cash, W. J. (Wilbur Joseph), 1900–1941. Mind of the South—
Congresses.   2. Southern States—Historiography—Congresses.
I. Clayton, Bruce.   II. Eagles, Charles W.   III. Series.
F209.C3M56   1992
975'.0072—dc20   92-17130
                                                        CIP

British Library Cataloging-in-Publication data available

Contents

Acknowledgments

Sponsored by the Department of History and the Center for the Study of Southern Culture, the annual Symposium on Southern History now follows a schedule refined over seventeen years. Each symposium is in many ways a cooperative effort among many people at the University. Ginger Delk and Vicki Woodall, the History Department's indispensable secretaries, handled the chores of organizing a new mailing list, typing letters, and mailing brochures and posters across the country. A number of history graduate students joined the effort and helped the symposium run smoothly by performing many essential tasks. Colleagues in the History Department provided advice and assistance on matters great and small before and during the conference. David Sansing and Dale and Ann Abadie particularly helped make our guests feel welcomed. As he does so well, Bob Haws, the department chairman, made sure that we all did what we were supposed to do and had fun too. Dale Abadie, who is also the dean, helped with funding, and the chancellor, Gerald Turner, attended the first session and offered an official welcome to the university.

The audience for the symposium consisted of many from the university community and Oxford and others from Mississippi, but also many old acquaintances and new friends from as close as Memphis and as far away as California and Connecticut. In addition to their important presence, their comments and questions proved valuable.

Of course, the people truly indispensable for the success of the symposium were the participants. Not only did they prepare papers and comments of high quality, but they added to the stimulating, informal scholarly exchanges that took place before and after the formal sessions during the three-day symposium. A special word of thanks is due Don Doyle, who agreed at nearly the last minute to substitute for a scheduled participant who could not attend. In spite of the short notice, he made a major contribution.

The entire conference, however, depended on the Mississippi Humanities Council more than it did on even the participants or the audience, because MHC generously provided most of the funding for the symposium. The History Department appreciates the support of MHC and its executive director, Dr. Cora Norman.

The job of directing the symposium would have been much more difficult and much less pleasant without the help of all of these people. Even more important for the director, however, was the encouragement, support, and advice of his wife, Brenda. She was excited about the symposium from the start and played a significant role in its success. And we both appreciate the tolerance of our boys—Daniel and Benjamin—in allowing us to be away from them so much for three days.

Introduction

Fifty years after the publication of *The Mind of the South*, the annual Porter L. Fortune Symposium on Southern History focused on W. J. Cash and his classic work. The book's enduring significance warranted a critical reexamination of *The Mind of the South*. It has been continually in print for fifty years, and Alfred A. Knopf published a fiftieth anniversary edition in 1991. Unlike most scholarly works, however, the influence of *The Mind of the South* has reached far beyond the academy. C. Vann Woodward has suggested that "no other book on Southern history rivals Cash's in influence among laymen and few among professional historians."[1]

Praise and appreciation for *The Mind of the South* has been extensive. George B. Tindall, in quoting the *Atlantic Monthly*, has called *The Mind of the South* a "literary and moral miracle." Fred Hobson has hailed it as "a *tour de force*," which became by the 1960s "a sort of Southern testament," and Richard H. King has observed that it "is one of those unusual works that improves with rereading [because it] is exciting and audacious and still compels even when it cannot persuade." Daniel J. Singal has suggested that a major part of the book's significance derives from its avowedly revisionist interpretation of the southern past; it represented "a complete reversal of the vision of the region's history once offered by the New South writers" and delivered a "knockout blow" to the cavalier myth. Singal points out that Cash explicitly started his book "by disabusing our minds of two correlated legends—those of the Old and the New South."[2]

The praise for *The Mind of the South* has not, however, been universal. In 1969 Woodward wrote, "Time has dealt gently and critics generously with W. J. Cash and his book, *The Mind of the South*," but in the following twenty years the critics of Cash's interpretations of the South have come to dominate discussion of his book. For example, disputing Cash's emphasis on continuity in southern history, Woodward has argued that the South's history "would seem to be characterized more by *dis*continuity, one trait that helps account for the distinctiveness of the South and its history." Joel Williamson, censuring Cash's treatment of race relations, has called *The Mind of the South* "an artifact . . . that captures its own time superbly even as it sought to capture time past." And Michael O'Brien has charged that Cash "grotesquely overgeneralized" from his piedmont North Carolina experience to the rest of the South. In addition, scholars have repeatedly faulted Cash for ignoring women and blacks, for discounting the Civil War, for missing the great diversity even within the white male South, for neglecting southern religion, and for committing many other offenses.[3]

In spite of the criticism, however, *The Mind of the South* continues to exert a major influence on the study of the South. According to a 1990 survey of trends in regional history published in the American Historical Association's *Perspectives*, Cash remains the second most frequently cited author in Southern history courses; only C. Vann Woodward was cited more often. Even though Michael O'Brien has almost dismissed Cash's work as a "nuisance" and a "corpse," *The Mind of the South* just will not go away.[4]

At the symposium and in the papers that follow, eleven scholars grappled with Cash's still provocative and evocative ideas. In six lively and well-attended sessions, six papers analyzed W. J. Cash, criticized his arguments, and assessed *The Mind of the South's* reputation. Except for the opening session, a commentator responded to each paper and began a discussion that involved many in the audience. No unanimity resulted. Cash still has his defenders, and they vary in their reasons for appreciating his work; others continue to criticize *The Mind of the South*, though often while acknowledging its strengths.

In the opening essay, Bruce Clayton draws on his recent biography of Cash to provide the essential biographical background of

W. J. Cash. He sketches the contours of Sleepy Cash's life from his origins in the North Carolina piedmont to his tragic death in Mexico City. Supplementing his biography of Cash, Clayton then places *The Mind of the South* in historiographical perspective by examining the sources that probably influenced Cash. Clayton concludes his analysis, however, by arguing that "the strongest and most original parts of his book flow directly from his subjectivity, his passionate, deeply personal absorption in his subject."

In a provocative paper on "The Cash Nexus," Anne Goodwyn Jones draws on the theories of Antonio Gramsci regarding ideology and hegemony to analyze *The Mind of the South*. After seeing it as a text that questions the traditional divisions between history and literature, fact and fiction, she argues that "Cash's work is Marxist to the core, with overtones of Freud." Finally, Jones offers a feminist critique of *The Mind of the South*. In his commentary, Michael O'Brien acknowledges the originality of Jones's paper, but he remains unconvinced that Cash was a Marxist of the Gramscian school. He further maintains that Cash's politics and his prose were more conservative than Jones proposes.

In the third essay Vernon Burton contends that "Cash's ideas about the antebellum South remain crucial to his whole argument." Disagreeing with Cash's critics, Burton instead claims that "Cash was at his best" in analyzing the Old South. In a sweeping review of the historiography of the Old South, Burton finds Cash's influence continuing and widespread, and he points to many topics in the antebellum South that deserve further attention. In commenting on Burton's defense of Cash, Don Doyle remains somewhat skeptical both of Cash's originality and of Cash's influence of later historians. He finds that Cash's appeal rests more with his biting and provocative social criticism than with his historical analysis and influence.

James Roark assesses the merits of one of Cash's central arguments—his claim of continuity in southern history—by focusing on Cash's treatment of the Civil War and Reconstruction. After announcing his disagreement with Cash's continuity thesis and his agreement with what have become known as discontinuitarians, Roark carefully explains Cash's position. But he does more: he then suggests why Cash saw continuity in southern history. In his comment on Roark's paper, Lacy Ford agrees that Cash found too much continuity in the region's history, and erroneously expected more in the future, but that he perceptively identified and explained powerful myths in the southern mind.

Regarding the New South, Edward Ayers disagrees with Cash on nearly every topic, but he does not dismiss the book. Quite the contrary, Ayers praises Cash's boldly idiosyncratic style—his passion, his humor, his range, and his power. In a critique of current historical scholarship on the South, Ayers finds it rather dull and barren in comparison to *The Mind of the South* and other works of the 1930s. Ayers challenges historians to change their rhetoric, their poetics, and to emulate Cash's work, if not his prejudices. Linda Reed, in response, demurs that historical writing does indeed contain passion in the very selection of topics to be studied. In addition she maintains that historical scholarship also contains humor, though it may be increasingly difficult to find.

In the last paper John Shelton Reed, a sociologist, evaluates Cash's book as an analysis of southern history and culture. He grants all the shortcomings critics have found in *The Mind of the South* yet holds that the "residue is still impressive." In giving Cash a good rating as a social analyst, Reed finds Cash's explanations of southern individualism stronger than his accounts of southern romanticism. In his commentary after Reed's paper, Bertram Wyatt-Brown uses a more biographical approach to evaluate Cash's anti-feminism, and he relates it to Cash's view of southern individualism, which applied only to white males.

After three days the speakers and the audience reached no consensus about the merits of *The Mind of the South*. All seemed to agree, however, that it remains a book worthy of reading and serious consideration. The following essays should prompt further discussion and debate of Cash's classic.

C. W. E.

THE MIND OF THE SOUTH: FIFTY YEARS LATER

No Ordinary History:
W. J. Cash's *The Mind of the South*

BRUCE CLAYTON

Some time ago, a young historian, fresh from graduate school, asked me earnestly, "Where in the world did W. J. Cash get his information?" I was mildly discomfited by the question. Surely, I knew the answer. I had been researching Cash's life for several years and was finishing a biography of the man. But I answered by mumbling the names of some of Cash's sources—a couple of venerable historians, a sociologist or two, a few contemporary critics, and several well-known observers of the Old South. Walking away, I sensed why the question had seemed so odd. It was that innocent word information. *The Mind of the South*, W. J. Cash's one and only book, is a whirlwind of generalizations, sweeping assumptions, daring, risky contentions, personal and passionate arguments—all splashed on a huge canvas grandly called "the mind of the South." His book is not about information; don't go reading it for facts. It is a book of ideas, big ideas that roll thunderously over the quieter shores hugged by most historians. Cash, a down-at-the-heels newspaperman when the book appeared in 1941, wrote out of his heart, his soul. He borrowed here and there from historians and others, but the book is uniquely his own in the same way a William Faulkner or a Thomas Wolfe novel is their own. A writer, first and last—with no formal training in history—Cash was never in danger of producing a modest monograph, one gotten up, as someone once quipped, by taking obscure facts from many unread books and putting them into one unread book.

But where in the world did Cash get his ideas, his angle of vision, his special knowledge of the South? And his intellectual courage, where did he get that? And what accounts for the anger

3

in the man, his withering hostility toward the backwardness he
perceived in the South—its racism, its intolerance of dissent, its
inferior schools, its pious sentimentality, its violence? How had he
escaped being one of those "professional glad boys," as he called
them, those smiling optimists of the 1920s who wrote books called
The Advancing South? In some of this, of course, he was very much
a member of his generation that had taken a long step beyond the
always-confident assumptions of the New South creed. The answer is to be sought in his life—his time and place, his upbringing,
his response to it, his temperament, his education, his wide-
ranging reading that took him far beyond the South. In great part,
his life was a complex coming to terms with being a white, male,
Christian southerner and a simultaneous attempt to free himself
from all that that meant. So great a hold did his region have on him
that he spent his entire adult life wondering about the South and
trying to get its inner history down on paper. For Cash, the book
was an act of self-discovery, of exorcising demons, of settling old
scores, of trying desperately to say that southern history had to be
confronted—and escaped. No wonder he told his publisher that
his book rested "on a pattern into which I was born and which I
have lived most of my life." *The Mind of the South* was Cash's mind
writ large.[1]

Wilbur Joseph Cash's heritage and upbringing were tradition-
ally southern. He was born in 1900 in Gaffney, South Carolina, a
grimy but busy piedmont mill town where his father clerked in
the company store and nodded vigorously when boosters proph-
esied the coming prosperity. The Cashes were staunch Baptists,
proud to live in a church-going town, though Gaffney's hard-
drinking, violent element gave everyone pause. The family's taste
in literature ran to the Sunday supplements and the sentimental-
racist novels of Thomas Nelson Page and Thomas Dixon, the latter,
a celebrated native of nearby Cleveland County, North Carolina,
where the Cashes moved in 1912. In politics, Cash's parents were
no more likely to desert the Democratic party than to dissent from
its bullying racism. The Cashes were good country people, benign

but conventionally narrow in their social sympathies, at one with the region's assumptions and values.[2]

So, outwardly, was young, bookish "Sleepy" Cash, called that because of his squinting eyes. He thrilled to Dixon's romances, was a decent high school student, not a bad debater, tried to play football, thought about girls incessantly, chewed tobacco, could spit prodigiously, and fantasized about being a gallant Johnny Reb atop Cemetery Ridge on that July day in 1863. He was awkward, a bit odd, quite sensitive, forever locked in his feelings. He seemed always distracted, his mind elsewhere. As a youth, he slipped out with his buddies to drink beer and moonshine, appropriately called "busthead," delayed being baptized, and quarreled mildly with his parents about having to attend a nearby denominational college.[3]

But at Baptist Wake Forest College, Cash discovered teachers who bravely discussed Charles Darwin's theories, read H. L. Mencken and James Branch Cabell, the Virginian who wrote dreamy and forbidden books, and encouraged students to think. His teachers were Christians and, on the race issue, liberal paternalists, as was the embattled president, William Louis Poteat, a devout scientist whose robust championing of Darwin incurred the wrath of anti-evolution zealots. Cash idolized Poteat and luxuriated in the school's openmindedness. Soon Sleepy was a declaiming disciple of Poteat and given to saying that Darwin had it right, so did Nietzsche, Spengler, Conrad, and a host of modernist philosopher gods not worshipped in the piedmont. When he left school in 1923 Cash was a sassy Menckenite, eager to deride the barrenness of southern culture, religious fundamentalism, and traditional southern literature. He was on his way to becoming a cosmopolitan intellectual who dreamed of writing novels that would plumb the human condition and stand Dixon on his head.[4]

His dream turned to ashes. In the 1920s, he taught school briefly, worked off and on as a newspaperman, and failed disastrously at one attempt at love-making. He wrote fiction furiously— only to hurl his pages into the fireplace. Most of the time Cash lived at home—depressed, melancholic, haunted by failure, by fears that he was sexually impotent. He brooded about himself and ransacked Freud for answers. He continued reading. Conrad, Spengler, Hazlitt, Shakespeare, Cervantes, Theodore Dreiser, Willa Cather—they were his solace, his shield against haunting doubts and the raw, racist world outside his window. The Ku Klux Klan marched defiantly and often in the piedmont. Nearby Charlotte led the battle to ban Darwin and evolution from the schools and directed the virulent nativism and anti-Catholicism that swept the state during the 1928 presidential election. The benighted South, Mencken's "Sahara of the Bozart," contrasted rudely with everything Cash had come to hold dear.[5]

Meanwhile, others were making capital of the South's woes in magazines and newspapers North and South. A southern renaissance of self-criticism was on, with Mencken as cheerleader. His *American Mercury* published stories by Faulkner, Julia Peterkin, DuBose Heyward and critical dispatches from Emily Clark, Nell Battle Lewis, Howard W. Odum, and Gerald W. Johnson. Johnson, a fellow Tarheel and Wake Forest graduate, regularly sniped at Ku Kluxers, revivalists, timid southern journalists, and mill barons.[6]

In 1929, Cash joined Mencken's cheerful cynics with the first of eight articles, each a blast at some southern idol. Blow upon blow, Cash hammered out his repudiation of the demagogues of the Democratic party—just so many reactionary race-baiters; the Protestant clergy—just so many ignorant, cocksure holy men eager to put their thumb in the eye of freethinkers; and southern capitalists—just so many barons of greed exploiting those whom they pretended to cherish. Mencken and Johnson had said much of this already, but Cash so commandingly explored what he called "The Mind of the South," that Alfred A. Knopf invited Cash (just twenty-nine in 1929) to do a book on the southern mind.[7]

"In dreams begin responsibilities," a poet once said. Brimming with good intentions, eager to make a name for himself—so that he could return to his first love, fiction—Cash went to work, only to falter. He became depressed. Doctors prescribed rest. Ailments, perhaps imaginary, dogged him. He loafed. He drank. He fretted. At one point he blithely announced that he would do a biography of the writer, Lafcadio Hearn; then a novel seemed the thing to do. Early in the decade he managed to finish a large chunk of manuscript for Knopf, only to destroy it because it seemed "so hopelessly out of line with changes in my ideas and so unsatisfactorily organized."[8]

By 1936, soon after joining the Charlotte *News* as a reviewer and editorialist, he finished a large section on the Old South. Knopf responded with a contract and a critic's suggestion that Cash really needed to be more specific. Cash replied coldly that he was "painfully aware of the fault in the manuscript," but his book was no ordinary history. It was "one man's view—a sort of personal report—which must rest in large part on my imagination. . . ." Cash, the procrastinator, who in his correspondence with Knopf glided from obsequiousness to truculence to good old boy humor, knew what sort of book he had in mind. Writing it was another matter. He did not finish until mid-1940.[9]

The book appeared in 1941, alongside William Alexander Percy's *Lanterns on the Levee* and James Agee's *Let Us Now Praise Famous Men*. It was a good year for southern writing. It seemed like a very good year for Cash. Reviews were good. The Guggenheim foundation rewarded Cash with a grant to go to Mexico City and write his novel. Cash and his admiring bride (he had recently married) left North Carolina in the spring. But count no man happy until he is dead, said Herodotus. Tragedy descended. In Mexico City, Cash's chronic physical and psychological illnesses were exacerbated by severe digestive problems and a sudden intolerance for alcohol which had become more and more a part of his life. In an hallucinatory state—very likely an extreme form of delirium tremens—Cash hanged himself in a lonely hotel room far from his native land. He would never know that his book would engage generations of readers, causing more than one to wonder, fifty years later, how and why this unique, soaringly original history ever got written.[10]

Multiple strands of experience were woven into the mind be-

hind *The Mind of the South*. The strands are personal and intellectual and so intricately stitched that any attempt to disentangle
them runs the risk of distortion and oversimplification. Cash filtered everything he learned through his great intelligence, intense imagination, and complex psyche. When William James
argued that all ideas, even facts, are true or false, and worthy of our
attention only if they make some demands on our "passional na-
tures," he was describing W. J. Cash in minute detail. Cash's mind
was filled with what Michael Polanyi called "personal knowledge," abiding assumptions, deeply held convictions that guide
conscious thought.[11]

Many of Cash's mature contentions, such as those about violence, religion and literature, flowed directly from his youthful
and young adult experiences. He grew up in a violent section of
the South and came of age when lynchings were numerous and
grotesquely brutal. Demagogues like Ben Tillman and Coley
Blease, boasting about the white South's racial savagery, strutted
in the piedmont. Cash's observations in the 1920s and 1930s merely confirmed what he had learned as a boy: that his region was
inherently violent, particularly when race was at issue. In *The
Mind of the South* Cash recalled that in his boyhood well-known
lynchers swaggered through the streets, heroes to most adults,
and, to youngsters, "hardly less splendid than the most magnifi-
cent cavalry captain." Later, Cash heard university men boast of
having helped lynch Negroes. To confirm his observations and
document lynchings and other barbarities, Cash turned to writers
and scholars like Walter White, Arthur F. Raper and J. D. Chadbourn. Their books, and others rolling from the rejuvenated University of North Carolina Press, proved what his heart told him
was true.[12]

In addition, Cash, the secular intellectual who contemptuously
dismissed religion in *The Mind of the South*, reflected both his
immersion in and rejection of the Bible Belt mentality. He needed
no source, no three by five notecards, to censor religion for
obstructing new ideas and closing the southern mind, though
doubtless Poteat's championing of a more open-minded religious

consciousness worked subtly on Cash's mind. Even so, he was on his own contending that antebellum evangelicalism encouraged the spread of democracy. But it also helped isolate planters from the liberal tradition and imposed a self-denying Puritanism on an emotional, hedonistic people. "A sort of social schizophrenia" resulted that reinforced the region's "naive capacity for unreality." An unabashed anti-cleric, Cash lashed out at the clergy of the modern South for its role in the anti-evolution movement and for foisting a tribal god on headstrong southerners. Much of this was pure Mencken, but Cash had seen it all at first-hand.

A passion for literature and desire to write fiction imparted an unmistakable tone to Cash's book. He scorned the Page-Dixon tradition as irrelevant and applauded several of his contemporaries—Ellen Glasgow, Julia Peterkin, DuBose Heyward and Howard W. Odum—for their attempts to break free from sentimentality, particularly regarding blacks. Cash had more praise for Caldwell, Wolfe and Faulkner, though he doubted whether they were as good as their admirers said. Like many of his generation, he was too close to Faulkner to appreciate his achievement fully. Cash had read his contemporaries closely and swam in the same cultural currents, leading him to explore his generation's troublesome ambivalence toward the South. Like Caldwell and Faulkner, Cash faced the ugliness, the sordidness, the underside of life the New South generation had either denied or attributed to the lower orders of man. Like Wolfe, Cash created a panoramic, romantic, personal story, an epic of material and spiritual deprivation. Like Faulkner, Cash saw a South enmeshed in a negative history. When Cash turned his mind to his projected novel in 1941 he thought instinctively of returning to his "Old Irishman," his literary device for portraying the frontier southerner in *The Mind of the South*. That and his several other plots for novels steeped in history suggests that Cash was obviously intent on writing what Richard H. King has identified as the distinguishing genre of the southern renaissance: the father-haunted "family romance." *The Mind of the South* was a family romance and, above all, a writer's book.[13]

It was also a newspaperman's book. This skein of Cash's thinking is apparent in the warm, spirited style, his love of the vernacular, his "extravagance." His book has the air of a reporter's "scoop," something of a classy journalist's desire to dazzle the reader with attention-grabbing words and phrases: Tartuffe, gyneolatry, fair Athena, the lily-pure maid of Astolat, the Savage Ideal, and the proto-Dorian convention. Years in the crowded newsroom with crusty journalists who prized cynicism as much as a taut sentence, gave Cash a closeup view of the underside of a southern city, a Presbyterian one at that. Charlotte's high murder rates, its prostitution, bootlegging, slums, racial hypocrisy, and crusading journalism all found their way into Cash's book.[14]

During his years with the Charlotte *News* he reviewed scores of books, but only two works of history: Benjamin B. Kendrick and Alex M. Arnett's slender overview, *The South Looks at Its Past* (1935), and Paul Buck's *The Road to Reunion* (1937), an account of sectional reconciliation after the Civil War. Both books, Cash said, signaling his own forthcoming interpretation, exaggerated the "superficial" changes that had come over the South after 1877. Cash already knew that "The south retains the mind it framed for itself under the agricultural conditions of the early nineteenth century." He applauded Kendrick and Arnett for arguing that the Old South was rather different from legend and was not peopled by Cavaliers—a view Cash had already spelled out in his uncompleted manuscript. Actually, he read very little, and only sporadically, in scholarly writings and always with a selective eye, on the lookout for what he wanted. He ended up mounting a couple of academic hobbyhorses, and every single one hurt his book.[15]

For understanding the Old South, Cash's starting point, he relied mainly on traditional primary sources: Joseph Glover Baldwin, Daniel R. Hundley, Hinton Rowen Helper and the Yankees, Frederick Law Olmsted and Fanny Kemble. That all but Baldwin were basically hostile to the antebellum South and critical of the planter class in particular did not escape Cash who used their observations at will, and always to argue that the planters dominated the South. Hundley and Helper were his major sources for portraying planters as aggressive men on the make who became, once they had accumulated a few acres and some slaves, men of affairs, but who were, at bottom just so many *nouveaux*—an interpretation that found ambivalent expression in much of the scholarship of Cash's day.[16]

Because Cash included no footnotes or bibliography and made few specific references to historians, it is difficult to document fully whom he read. Moreover, given Cash's inimitable generalizing and the originality of his main arguments, tracking down every source would be tedious and irrelevant. But the occasional names Cash mentioned and the specific nature of some of Cash's themes and arguments make it possible to pinpoint some of his sources, to place the book in historiographical perspective, and to show how Cash was highly imaginative and, usually, independent in his judgments.

Consider Cash's use of G. W. Dyer's, *Democracy in the South Before the Civil War*, a short, informative book from 1905. Very likely Dyer, a southerner, was Cash's inspiration for attacking the Cavalier legend with such gusto. Dyer was one of the first to criticize the notions that Virginia's First Families sprang from adventuresome English Cavaliers, and that their descendants, the planter elite, everywhere constituted a soft, indolent leisure class too rich and proud to work. "Nobody of any considerable information," said Cash, still believed in the myth of the gentry's origins, but in his zeal to argue that most southern whites sprang from the same common clay, Cash went far beyond Dyer. To prove that the Old South was characterized by fluid social relations Cash borrowed Dyer's documentation that only one of Virginia's eight governors between 1841 and 1861 had been born a gentleman.[17]

Yet Cash rejected, as yet another version of the Cavalier legend, Dyer's argument that planters ruled politically on the basis of merit, and not slavery or some "puerile" psychological reason. Cash offered a gripping argument that the elite had so drilled its superiority into the psyche of the common whites that they intricately and mysteriously connected themselves once and for all

with their betters. Here was Cash's "proto-Dorian convention."
Because of slavery, and the common white's psychological needs,
color elevated the common white "to a position comparable to
that, say, of the Doric knight of ancient Sparta," Cash wrote. The
planters were admired and obeyed not because they were inherently good or capable, but because the lowly whites saw in their
masters—cotton patch Doric knights, in other words—examples
of what they might become. This belief was a fantasy that coddled
the ego of the common man and was thus integral to maintaining
the proto-Dorian bond. When Helper, Cash wrote, "and others
began at last on the eve of the Civil War to point out the wrongs of
the common white and to seek to arouse him to recognizing them,
they could get no response." Why? Because "the common white,
as a matter of course, gave eager credence to and took pride in the
legend of the aristocracy which was so valuable to the defense of
the land. He went further, in fact, and, by an easy psychological
process which is in evidence wherever men group themselves
about captains, pretty completely assimilated his own ego to the
latter's—felt his planter's new splendor as being in some fashion
his own."[18]

Cash found support for many of his ideas about the Old South in
William E. Dodd's *The Cotton Kingdom* (1921). Cash was obviously
taken with Dodd's insistence that the typical planter was a product
of the wilderness and that the entire Great South even by 1850 was
but a few steps beyond the frontier. Still, Cash doubted Dodd's
calculation that the "ruling class" numbered about "four or five
thousand of the great planters." Cash wondered whether the
South had more than five hundred "proper aristocrats." Dodd
pointed to the hedonism of an outwardly religious people—a
paradox Cash put at the heart of the southern mind. Dodd's view
that the planters artfully cultivated an easy familiarity and democracy of manners with the poorer whites in order to keep their trust,
win their votes and thus stay in power—is Cash's proto-Dorian
bond in a milder, embryonic version. And the germ of Cash's
searing argument about the savage ideal can be found in Dodd's

frontie

temperate summing up of the social and intellectual hegemony of the planters. Since they "were the articulate element in society and the small farmers and landless groups were hardly in a position to assert any contrary views, it was not difficult to make the lower South socially solid. No newspaper of any importance, no college or university professor, no prominent preacher, and no politician of any party offered effective resistance."[19]

But Cash chose what he wanted from Dodd and Dyer and used his boundless imagination and penchant for stunning generalizations to go far beyond what either wrote. Cash would have none of the notion that the Old South truly valued education. "The majority of the colleges were no more than academies," Cash wrote, and even the University of Virginia sank into a "hotbed of obscurantism and a sort of fashionable club, propagating dueling, drinking, and gambling." Cash never shared any of Dodd or the New South's romantic identification with Jefferson as the "true southerner" and the notion that Calhoun and other reactionaries had corrupted the true South into a defense of slavery and state's rights. Antebellum culture, said Cash, "was a superficial and jejune thing, borrowed from without and worn as a political armor and a badge of rank."[20]

Of course, no one of any considerable learning, as Cash would say, could escape his generation's infatuation with Frederick Jackson Turner's frontier thesis, a view particularly attractive to southerners. To Dodd, U. B. Phillips, and Howard W. Odum, the South's reigning sociologist in Cash's day, the frontier was at the heart of the southern experience and put the plantation and planter in perspective. Cash did Dodd and the rest one better by portraying the Old South, Reconstruction and the rise of industry as three rolling, unsettling frontiers. And by finding the source of violence and brutality and other ugly, unpleasant features of southern life Cash rejected the Victorian assumptions inherent in Turner.

In this and more Cash was aided by Odum's influential works, *An American Epoch* (1930) and *Southern Regions of the United States* (1936). From the late 1920s Cash was an ardent admirer of Odum's writings. In his best and, for Cash, most accessible book, *An American Epoch* (1930), Odum elaborated upon a sense of southern culture as an enmeshing whole with distinctive culturally-shaped, regionally definable folkways and mores. Like historians, Odum sensed the interconnectedness of the past and the present. Odum and his disciples, Rupert Vance and Arthur Raper, stressed the importance of the frontier and the plantation for understanding both the Old and the New South. In all of this, Odum and the Chapel Hill regionalists doubtless left their mark on Cash. But their ambivalences about the South, and Cash's assertive, single-minded point of view on issues such as the frontier and the planters, make it hazardous to say that Odum or anyone's influence on Cash was very great. In *An American Epoch* Odum devoted an entire chapter to praising the "The Glory That Was the South," only to reverse himself in the next and to point to a socially insensitive, class-conscious "unthinking aristocracy," given to hard drink, rioting and dueling.[21]

Cash never had any of Odum's ambivalence toward the frontier or the planters—those swash-buckling, masters of psychology, those proto-Dorian masters. Cash had a sneaking, even robust secularist's admiration for frontier types like Andrew Jackson, a real southern cap'n if there ever was one, and Abraham Lincoln. But to Cash the frontier rewarded "cunning," "hoggery and callousness," "brutal unscrupulousness and downright scoundrelism." The frontier produced not a refined minority of Virginians to civilize the Black Belt but a hollow aristocracy—whose boots, like Faulkner's Thomas Sutpen, were still dirty from the mud of the frontier—painfully aware of its lack of refinement and true culture. Cash's mind was shaped less by Odum and the Chapel Hill regionalists than Freud. Consequently Cash confidently argued that, at bottom, the planters were a guilt-ridden, self-made elite with a discomforting awareness of their deficiencies deep in their "subconsciousness." Hence their loud bragging and boasting, their tendency to unreality, and their various "defense mechanisms" created to protect their "egos" against Yankee slurs.[22]

Did Cash read U. B. Phillips, the greatest southern historian of his time? Probably. And if so Cash learned, as several generations learned from the lively pages of *American Negro Slavery* (1918) and *Life and Labor in the Old South* (1929), that slaves were lazy and docile, though sullen and mean if mistreated, as they were occasionally, Phillips admitted, and that the typical planters were hard-working, racial paternalists who, after subduing the Virginia frontier, had taken culture and refinement to tame the new frontier, the lower South. Never quite free of the cavalier myth, as Daniel Singal has shown, Phillips could not resist portraying planters as "courteous and charming men and women" who represented "the highest type of true manhood and womanhood yet developed in America." Growing more reactionary and apologetic about the South with each passing year, Phillips concluded his masterpiece, *Life and Labor in the Old South* saying, "The scheme of life had imperfections which all but the blind could see. But its face was on the whole so gracious that modifications might easily be lamented, and projects of revolution regarded with a shudder."[23]

Almost all of this, Cash rejected. No matter what Phillips and the best historians of his day were saying, Cash was uncompromisingly critical of slavery. It was "inescapably brutal and ugly" and "rested on force," said Cash citing Harriet Beecher Stowe, not Phillips. The so-called paternalism and various apologies for slavery, so attractive and convincing to historians in Cash's day, were nothing more than an attempt to glorify something inherently ugly. "Mutilation and the mark of the branding iron were pretty common," Cash wrote, along with forced miscegenation, all covered with an apologia intended to deceive everyone, even themselves. The South "must prettify the institution and its own reactions, must begin to boast of its own Great Heart. To have heard them talk, indeed, you would have thought that the sole reason some of these planters held to slavery was love and duty to the black man, the earnest, devoted will, not only to get him into heaven, but also to make him happy in this world." Given his view of southern whites as naive and impetuous, haughty and callous in their scramble for position on the frontier, Cash could not for a moment accept Phillips's notion that slavery was a civilizing force for blacks. Moreover, Cash sensed that slavery was a complex set of social interactions in which each race entered into the other, silently shaping and molding the other.[24]

And yet in his account of Reconstruction Cash reiterated, in his own fashion, the prevailing racial myths. Lamentably, Cash followed rather completely the scholarship of William A. Dunning and his disciples, W. L. Fleming, J. W. Garner, and J. G. de Roulhac Hamilton, white males who elaborated on the racist myths of the prostrate South, suffering the indignities of debauchery and rampant corruption at the hands of carpetbaggers, scalawags and freedmen. Cash read Fleming's *Civil War and Reconstruction in Alabama* (1905), considered by Dunning the "most comprehensive" of his students' work. But after applauding the unsentimental attitude of the Dunning masters, Cash pointedly contested Fleming's argument that the Black Codes were not intended to re-establish servitude. Cash appears to have overlooked W. E. B. DuBois's *Black Reconstruction* (1935), an attack on the racist assumptions of the Dunning school. But DuBois, whose book was based primarily on the very literature he was attacking, had no standing as an historian, certainly not among white southerners in the 1930s when "the orthodox story of southern Reconstruction was fully rounded out and accepted almost without question." Very likely Cash read Claude G. Bowers's *The Tragic Era* (1929), a spirited, national best seller in 1929 when Cash was still planning his book. Bowers's popularized account is "as violent and extreme as the fiction of Dixon and [D. W.] Griffith." What irony! Cash breathing life into the myths that animated Dixon.[25]

Even here, Cash was driven to be his own historian. He nowhere speaks of "Negro domination," though he implies it and his slangy racist imagery and sophisticated literary technique of showing a mood by taking on the persona of the white southerner leaves him open to charges of racism. That technique, however, was central to his psycho-sexual method of trying to get inside the white South's psyche that, Cash believed, experienced Reconstruction as rape. The "rape complex" consisted of interlocking myths and fantasies in the white mind, triggered by the death of slavery. Since the white South had identified itself with white woman—the crucial link in the proto-Dorian bond—it followed that freeing the Negro, to say nothing of any political power blacks may have exercised immediately after the war, raped the "mind of the South." Once politically freed, went the subterranean terror, what was to stop blacks from desiring complete equality, meaning, of course, sex, the not-so-hidden but tacit truth in the southerner's obsessive warnings against "social equality."[26]

Cash is implying much more, suggesting that the rape complex pointed to a proud, boasting white anxiety-ridden male-dominated culture that subconsciously regarded itself as feminine, which, from the perspective of the times, meant an inferior, weak culture always in danger of being thrown on its back and ravished. Thus did Cash employ a daring sexual argument, rich in symbols and stunning metaphors, that, ironically and quite unintentionally, reexpressed racist myths and stereotypes. At no time did he suggest, as had the New South generation, that Reconstruction justified the white South's harsh treatment of the Negro after 1877. That bestiality Cash documented with a fury that makes his absorption in the myths of Reconstruction pale.[27]

In tracing the rise of the cotton mills Cash was an uncritical borrower. He accepted the New South litany that the sorry plight of the postbellum whites pricked the consciences of the landed gentry, touching off a new dynamic *noblesse oblige*. The Old South's cap'ns became captains of industry with a heart and, saluting progress and southern pride, built schools and factories to rescue whites from poverty and the shame of falling as low as Negroes. Such was the view rolling from the propaganda mills of the textile industry, a view Sleepy had heard many times in his father's kitchen, and from the pulpit, lectern and editorial office. Such was Broadus Mitchell's view in his widely-praised book *The*

Rise of the Cotton Mills (1921), whose thesis Cash appropriated wholesale and lauded as a "celebrated monograph." Gerald W. Johnson and others had endorsed and popularized Mitchell's view, a judgment that would stand until C. Vann Woodward destroyed it in the late 1940s. More irony yet! In praising the altruism of the mill owners, Cash had been seduced by another incarnation of the Cavalier Myth.[28]

And then, perhaps sensing his transgression, Cash reversed himself and lashed out furiously at the numbing conditions of the mill hands' lives: long hours, sweatshop conditions, low wages, child labor. Cash's workers appear tragically old before their time with "dead white skin, a sunken chest, . ." the women "stringy-haired and limp of breast at twenty." Cash, moved by deep feelings for the common people, recorded what he had seen and what he had read by the child labor reformers of his youth, Alabama's Edgar Gardner Murphy and North Carolina's Alexander J. McKelway.[29]

Cash's understanding of Populism, an embarrassing outburst of radicalism to New South's partisans and usually passed over in silence, rested mainly on the major work of the era, John D. Hicks's *The Populist Revolt* (1931). Like Hicks who concentrated on the West and stressed the reformist mentality of the angry agrarians, Cash saw southern Populism as "essentially only a part of the national agrarian movement," representing "an outburst of farmer interest against the great cities of the East rather than a class movement within the South itself." Perhaps had he paused in 1938, as he scribbled feverishly on his book, to read C. Vann Woodward's stunning biography of Tom Watson, Cash might have taken Watson and southern populism more seriously and reconsidered his emphasis on the pseudo-Populist, Ben Tillman. Tillman had towered ominously over Cash's youth, and Cash may very well have read Francis Butler Simkins, *The Tillman Movement in South Carolina* (1926). Even so, Cash's conviction, flowing from his abiding personal knowledge, that the South's ever-present, dynamic racism—

that ancient proto-Dorian bond—was exploited by the Democratic Party to destroy Populism, still breathes with freshness.[30]

Cash's major arguments revolve around his basic assumption that race was at the heart of the southern experience. Racial consciousness in whites, their resolve to keep blacks in their place, their willingness to sacrifice everything, if need be, to maintain white supremacy controlled the mind of the South—such was Cash's primary axiom. It formed the foundation of his celebrated and much debated thesis that southern history was characterized by the twin realities of unity and continuity. If one ignores Cash's sophisticated, modernist argument that an irrational racism had consistently blinded whites to an awareness of class and all but obliterated class consciousness—which Cash saw lurking beneath the surface of southern history—Cash's arguments lack substance or force, whether one is talking about the proto-Dorian convention, the Savage Ideal, Reconstruction, or the failure of Populism. Perceptive critics of Cash have tended, quite rightly, to concentrate on his overarching theses of unity and continuity, but both arguments rest his abiding conviction that race was the fault line running through all of southern history.[31]

Cash's "personal knowledge" of racism flowed from his experiences as a youth and as a newspaperman. The centrality of race was in turn reinforced by historians, from Dunning to Phillips; by social scientists, from Odum and Raper to northerners like John Dollard and Hortense Powdermaker; by journalists from Jonathan Daniels to Gerald W. Johnson; and by writers, from Dixon to Faulkner. Phillips spoke for the first half of the twentieth century when he declared that the white South's resolve to keep the black man down was "the central theme of southern history."[32]

Cash could know this because he was a deeply introspective intellectual who had tried to detach himself from myths. In this he was a product of modernism, his mind an amalgam of Freud and Nietzsche and Marx and Conrad, Odum and Mencken. Cash's reasoning turned on the axis of modernism: self consciousness, the awareness that thought is always bounded by race, class, biology, time. True, Cash could utter flippant, ill-considered stereotyped slurs about blacks and virtually everybody else—mill-billies, rednecks, preachers, teachers, women—but his deepest modernist convictions impelled him toward an emancipation from the fundamental, cherished assumption of his region: that whites knew blacks, knew what they really wanted, and knew that they had been happy in slavery and content with segregation. Cash argued forthrightly that whites *did not know blacks*. When Cash looked at the Negro, he saw a mask of mystery and rebuke—a rebuke to centuries of southern boasts and illusions. He understood, aided by black writers, particularly W. E. B. Dubois's *The Souls of Black Folk*, that blacks hid their feelings behind a veil. But what was behind that mask, asked Cash, what was going on behind that servile grin? "What was back there, hidden? What whispering, stealthy, fateful thing might they be framing out there in the palpitant darkness." It would be a grave mistake to underestimate, as scholars have, the significance of Cash's refusal to believe with his generation that he understood the Negro.[33]

Consider just one incident in the life of W. T. Couch, a white liberal justly proud of his reputation as an advanced thinker on the race issue. As director of the University of North Carolina Press in the 1930s, he published many seminal and liberal books on race and in 1936 persuaded the editorial board to abandon its policy of refusing even to read manuscripts by blacks. Several years later, Couch invited Rayford Logan to edit a symposium of writings in which blacks of all viewpoints would state their beliefs and "indicate what the Negro wants and what he ought to have." But when every contributor stated a desire to see segregation ended, Couch was shocked, almost beyond belief. Surely, he told Logan, your fellow blacks want segregation; Logan was to persuade them to revise their essays. But to no avail. Couch grudgingly agreed to publish *What the Negro Wants* (1943) but not without a cautionary introduction from his own pen. Several of Couch's fellow white southern liberals hastened to agree with him and to assure him that he had told the truth.[34]

Cash would have understood Couch's reaction. But Cash would have also understood the black writers' demands. *The Mind of the South* is a radical criticism of the white South's failure to confront itself or the Negro. And Cash, the loner, the questioner, the intellectual who brooded about everything, and worried himself sick about Hitler and compared Ku Kluxers to Nazis and feared that the white South might capitulate finally to a version of fascism, knew that any master class's confident knowledge of what its underclass wants is a subtle and hence powerful way of exercising social and personal control. And when the masters sincerely believe their own myths they make themselves even more powerful—and blind to their own self-interest. More than one civil rights leader in the decades after Cash wrote battled the white South's confident notion that it knew the Negro best. All of white America could have done—and could do—with a bit of W. J. Cash's courageous humility.

Many hands went into the making of *The Mind of the South*—some of those hand prints are clear, easily discernible; others, vague and barely visible. Many other prints are still undetected. But Cash's fingerprints, starkly visible on every page, are the major ones and, finally, the ones worth tracing carefully. Cash wrote as an insider—from inside himself and his subject. Thus, the strongest and most original parts of his book flow directly from his subjectivity, his passionate, deeply personal absorption in his subject. *The Mind of the South*, as W. J. Cash used to say of books he admired, was "written in blood." We will probably never see such a book again.

The Cash Nexus

ANNE GOODWYN JONES

The current mood of celebration surrounding Wilbur Cash and *The Mind of the South*—the new edition, a symposium at Wake Forest University, and this symposium—should not obscure the uncertain, indeed the troubled status, of the text itself. To start there is no clear agreement about what sort of text it is: the 1969 Vintage edition called it "sociology," the 1991 edition has placed it in "history/American studies," and since its publication in 1941 there have been repeated calls to see it as "literature." My hunch is that *The Mind of the South* is still taught primarily in history courses, and it will certainly stay there if my literature students at Florida have any say in the matter.[1]

These uncertainties about placing *Mind* suggest more than changing marketing strategies, or scholars splitting straws. As uncertainties that derive from academics' as well as publishers' desires to place texts, they point to historical and philosophical questions about disciplinary differences and boundaries. And as uncertainties that derive from the language of Cash's text, they suggest a reading of *Mind of the South* as a deliberate challenge to the conventional meanings of those differences and boundaries.

Peter Novick has called the "dividing line" between history and fiction "the most sacred boundary of all" for American historians, and the (related but separable) debate over "whether history was an art or a science" a "hoary squabble."[2] *The Mind of the South* from the start has been read in terms of these debates. The earliest responses to *Mind* set the tone by claiming a rigid dichotomy between history and literature and placing *Mind* in one, whether as a success or a failure to meet that discipline's demands. C. Vann Woodward led the movement to read *The Mind of the South* as literature in his initial (1941) review of *The Mind of the South*. He wrote that "these problems [the 'imponderables and the intangibles of southern history'] are more amenable to the methods of the novelist than to those of the historian, and Mr. Cash has fortunately chosen a literary and imaginative rather than scholarly approach." If this was faint praise, Woodward would soon damn Cash, for, of course, he went on to produce a series of critiques of Cash as an inadequate historian. It is evident that Woodward's argument in 1941 depended on an assumption of clear disciplinary and generic boundaries separating ("rather than") history from fiction and scholarly from imaginative methodology and labor. That seems to have been the case for literary scholar Louis D. Rubin, Jr., as well. Rubin reinforced Woodward's line in a 1954 essay; instead of praising *Mind* as art, as Woodward does, however, he damns it as history by comparing a passage of Woodward's own historical writing to a passage from Cash. Rubin concludes, sardonically, that "when it comes to rhetoric and ornament Mr. Cash has got it all over a scholarly historian like Professor Woodward. Of course, . . . Professor Woodward . . . document[ed] his remarks with some careful, painstakingly research [and] pages of example, quotation, and citation, whereas Mr. Cash without further ado plunged ahead toward more vivid, unfootnoted, unproven brilliance."[3] Rhetoric and ornament are disparaging terms in this context because, Rubin implies, Cash uses their "art" to disguise bad history—that is, insufficient data. While Woodward the historian pushes *Mind* politely into literature, then, Rubin the literary scholar shoves it back into history—bad history, but history—and neither wants to claim it as a legitimate heir to his own disciplinary discourse.

Thus the possibility of arguing that *The Mind of the South* actively questions the dividing lines between history and fiction, and between art and science, instead of mindlessly failing to meet standards, was foreclosed early on by the imposition of traditional assumptions. But the contemporary intellectual environment invites raising that possibility again. I will argue that *The Mind of the*

South's status was and would remain uncertain and troubled precisely because it interrogates the very boundaries that enforce such disciplinary placements as Woodward and Rubin assumed and imposed—and that remain by and large in effect, at least *vis à vis The Mind of the South,* today. I will argue further that Cash's "mind"—in ways that are strikingly similar to Antonio Gramsci's understanding of ideology as "hegemony"—is a theory that moves on the border between history and literature because it provides an explanation for the relations between reality and representation, conventionally the domains respectively of history and literature. I will move from there to argue that *Mind* is not only about, but also enacts "ideology"—that, in short, the strange and undecidable form of the text is a function of its verbally "acting out" its double theoretical base in both history and literature, reality and representation, or what Cash more frequently calls "fact" and "rhetoric." Finally, I will argue that *The Mind of the South,* read as an ideological production as well as a theory of ideology, should be critiqued as such, specifically from a feminist position.

Among historians, there appears to be no consensus even today about the usefulness of *The Mind of the South* as history. Michael O'Brien has wittily summed up the arguments against it:

> *The Mind of the South* ignores the colonial history of the South, scants the Old South, and misunderstands the new South. It barely mentions slavery and is more or less racist in its characterization of blacks. It neglects women, except as totemic objects of Southern mythology. It diminishes the existence of class conflict in the Old South and insists upon its relative impotence after the War. It misunderstands the nature of aristocracy. It overstresses both the unity and the continuity of Southern history. It has very little grasp of political history and has no coherent explanation for the Civil War. It is provincial in its emphasis both upon white males and upon the Piedmont of North Carolina as the archetypal South. It exaggerates the guilt of Southerners over slavery. It shows little understanding of the formal ideas of generations of Southern intellectuals. Its view of Reconstruction is primitive. It overestimates the static quality of agricultural society.

So the corpse is riddled [O'Brien concludes], and it would require a necromancer to piece together the shattered bones, torn sinews, and spilled blood.[4]

Nothing daunted, O'Brien moves on to "attempt to breathe life into the corpse," revivifying in the process his own argument that *The Mind of the South* "can be seen as a quasi-Hegelian book," an argument which in certain respects comes closer than any other to my own.[5] For now, let me observe that almost every criticism in this list of charges against Cash rests on what could be called the assumptions of historical positivism or "objectivity": that is, assumptions that the past existed in some knowable way independent of historians' constructions of it; that the truth of the past exists or can exist somewhere (thus that claims about the past are falsifiable); and that we can get to the truth if we have adequate information and the correct methodology. This view of history is apparent in the structure of O'Brien's sentences: a repeated subject-verb-object construction connects an object "out there" in the past ("political history" or "women") to the subject (*The Mind of the South*) with a verb ("ignores," "scants") that suggests a failure of representation. It is thus implied that accurate, complete, and presumably transparent representation of the historical "object" (the past) is possible. By this view of history Cash, with his omissions, distortions and obsessions, did not even approach adequacy. He cavalierly ignored vast amounts of information and dismissed the need for documentation, not only avoiding accuracy and completeness but suggesting that he did not value them. Worse, he allowed his historical narratives to drift into blatant fictions such as that of the Irishman at the center, making up history, in effect, out of the whole cloth. Thus he confused the boundary between fact and fiction on which history's identity rests, even calling attention to his own inventions, and thus making it impossible to read his language as a transparent window into the past. As for Woodward and Rubin, so in O'Brien's summary: Cash is still too much the artist, too little the historian.

On the other hand, literary scholarship has been concerned

with Cash's "art" and has largely ignored the history. Atypically, a suspicious Louis Rubin wrote in 1954 that "one begins to spot something awry with *The Mind of the South* from the very beginning. The style shows it, as style has a way of doing. It is a facile style, an elusive one which glitters, reflects sunlight brilliantly, and yet hides as often as it illumines. . . ."[6] Since then, discussions have not made much of the connection between manner and matter. Richard King analyses Cash's "story-telling act," narrative stance, diction, and interior monologue;[7] Michael Dean goes further to argue that because Cash's style is that of a Southern storyteller, it "renders the subject in the manner that best suits it."[8] Bertram Wyatt-Brown locates Cash's rhetoric in conventions of legal writing and Victorian fiction.[9] Despite their sensitivity to the language in the text, to its rhetorical strategies and its style, such analyses stop short of thinking in detail about the relation of Cash's "style" to his "history." Dean, for example, forecloses the question with the claim that "Cash's mastery of style overshadows any controversy about his historical conclusions." And Fred Hobson writes that *"The Mind of the South* cannot be approached as good history. It contains, *rather* [my emphasis], a personal truth, an imaginative truth, charged with the power and the integrity of the individual vision."[10] Thus he implies that a "personal truth" can, perhaps must, be divorced from "good history." But such a reading prevents asking important questions about the relation of history to art. For example, in *Mind of the South* Cash argues that the history of southern storytelling is a history of perpetuating unreality. Can we then simply praise Cash as a good southern storyteller, and the text as appropriately told? His own premises cast suspicion on such praise, and thus undermine literary analyses that depend on separating the "history" from the "art."

The split between these two positions—one might call them the camps of "fiction" and "fact," where fact is uninteresting to the fiction-lovers, and fiction is, to the factually minded, nearly a lie—is a form of the split between the New critical literary theory and the positivist historiography (Peter Novick calls it "objectivity

reconstructed"[11]) that were the dominant assumptions of each
discipline from the 1940s to the 1960s. (The New Criticism was
popularly understood to focus attention on the internal workings of
the individual work of art, suppressing its relation to history and
biography; positivist historiography was understood to focus attention on the historical object of knowledge in order to eliminate
bias—"art"—in its representation). This split between modes of
interpreting *The Mind of the South* is arguably a function less of
Cash's intent—which, in the spirit of the 1930s, seems to have
been to challenge just such divisions—than of the vestigial remains of those dominant positivist and New Critical assumptions.

In fact, the uncertain status of *The Mind of the South* is precisely
what constitutes its interest to contemporary thought. Insofar as
the quarrels over *Mind* have been signs of difficulty with generic
boundaries, they offer us now the opportunity to examine our own
implicit theoretical and disciplinary commitments. Moreover, instead of being read as failed history or failed fiction, *The Mind of
the South* can now be read as a form of theoretical discourse,
neither history nor fiction. In it Cash participates in the interroga-
tion of genre and of epistemology that was common to modernism
in the arts, and in the challenges to and defenses of objectivity that
characterized the period's histories. More precisely, *The Mind of
the South* needs to be rethought not as a torn corpse but as a textual
nexus in which facts and fictions are linked, re-membered, by
means of a theory and practice of ideology. It is thus a text *about*
ideology's work—about the mind of the South—that produces a
theory of ideology and that itself works on the reader *as* ideology.

The opposition between fact and fiction, the conventional
domains of history and literature, resembles another opposition
that comes out of Marxist discourse and that preoccupies Cash
throughout *The Mind of the South*. That is the opposition between
material conditions in the South, which Cash occasionally calls
"the logic of circumstances," and southern ideology, which Cash
calls "mind." This opposition is roughly analogous to that between
Marx's "base" and "superstructure." For Cash, the "logic of cir-

cumstance" increasingly is allied with what he calls "fact," while "mind" from the very outset takes on the qualities of fiction, at times even fantasy. "Fact" comes to be allied for Cash with a materialist analysis and a politics of change; "fiction" with an idealist analysis and resistance to change. But this opposition is never very stable for Cash; and even when it is temporarily fixed, Cash's preference for fiction or for fact is never entirely predictable. Ultimately, Cash's theory challenges the very distinction itself: "mind" becomes not the opposing term to "circumstances," but a term that represents the relation between circumstances and ideas, the border between fact and fiction.

Few critics have taken Marxist thought as a way of understanding Cash's text, despite what seem its obvious debts to Marxist discourse. Instead, the conventional wisdom is that Cash was an "amateur Freudian," analyzing mind apart from conditions. Even those who have come closest to Marxist readings, such as (again) Louis Rubin in 1954, have hurriedly, perhaps anxiously, concluded that Cash's analysis is "not Marxist." Bruce Clayton makes a move away from this split by claiming that Cash "relied unobtrusively on a core of Freudian ideas and an economic argument with overtones of Marx and Charles Beard."[12] I want to reverse this claim, to argue that Cash's work is Marxist to the core, with overtones of Freud. To introduce this, I will look at some similarities between the lives and ideas of Antonio Gramsci and Wilbur Cash.

Gramsci and Cash wrote, unknown to one another, during the decade of the thirties. Gramsci was in Turin where he had been imprisoned by the Fascists, later to die of illnesses contracted there; Cash was in North Carolina, where finally, in his thirties, he moved out of his parents' home and established a foothold on an adult life, only to become obsessed with Fascism and to die believing Nazis were out to destroy him. Gramsci's understanding of "hegemony" and Cash's final understanding of "mind" seek in remarkably similar ways to understand what they saw as disjunctions between material conditions, or "facts," and cultural (mis)-representations of those facts, or "fictions." "Hegemony" and "mind" are by definition sets of representations that (mis)interpret fact and thus can be called forms of cultural fiction. But because one can perceive facts only through representations of them, the predominance of "mind" over fact emerges, as does the more radical possibility that mind constructs fact.

All writers—even those who take ideology as their subject, such as Cash and Gramsci—are subject in turn to construction by ideology. Reading a text "symptomatically," looking at its less overt figures, can enable us to read its own unconscious, or at least its less obvious, ideological investments. When a text contains such glaring omissions as women's subjectivity, this technique becomes a way to carry out a gender analysis and a feminist critique. I will conclude with such a reading of both Cash and Gramsci.

In *The Ideology of Slavery,* Drew Gilpin Faust uses the term "ideology" to refer to proslavery thought in the antebellum South; she calls it a "formal ideology with its *resulting* social movement [my emphasis]."[13] This notion of ideology assumes a direction that moves from ideas to social structures. Marx and Engels argued against this view first in *The German Ideology* (1870), seeing formal ideas as the product, not the producer, of an economic base, and "ideology" as the false consciousness that binds us to economic realities. Marxist thinking about the relation of conditions to ideas has never entirely left its grounding in materiality. Nevertheless, the understanding and definition of ideology have changed considerably. With Althusser, ideology has come to mean today a system of representations and material practices—including but not limited to formal ideas—that works to maintain the dominant relations of production in a society by providing the medium through which people "live [their] relation to the real." These representations and practices make life feel natural and inevitable, rather than a function of complex political and economic structures. Ideology in this sense actually constructs human beings; it gives us the meanings without which experience would be impossible. In Althusser's words, "ideology is the relay whereby, and the element

in which, the relation between men and their conditions of existence is settled to the profit of the ruling class."[14] This process
works by addressing unconscious fears and desires; it works
through feelings as well as thoughts.

Althusser's focus on ideology as "relay" and "relation" is very
similar to the meaning of "mind" for Wilbur Cash. Cash acknowledges from the outset that he is not addessing mind in the sense of
a formal set of ideas. Instead, he is writing about a "fairly definite
mental pattern, associated with a fairly definite social pattern—a
complex of established relationships and habits of thought, sentiments, prejudices, standards and values, and associations of ideas
. . . common . . . to white people in the south."[15] Like Althusser,
Cash here assumes that "mind" includes both feelings and
thoughts, conscious and unconscious activity—in short, subjectivity in its totality. Like Althusser, Cash will show that "mind" or
ideology is constructed through material practices. In fact, he
represents this in scenes of ideological practice. Here is one such
moment in an antebellum "common white man's" life: at public
gatherings

> there would nearly always be a fine gentleman to lay a familiar
> hand on the [common white man's] shoulder, to inquire by name
> after the members of his family, maybe to buy him a drink . . .
> and to come around eventually to confiding in a hushed voice
> that that damned nigger-loving Garrison, in Boston— . . . in
> short . . . to send him home glowing with the sense of participa-
> tion in the common brotherhood of white men.

Finally, like Althusser, Cash points in two directions, to superstructure and base, "mental" patterns and "social" patterns, joining them with the perhaps deliberately vague term "associated."
(This vagueness will allow him later to represent the relation—
i.e., "mind"—concretely, as a variety of complex interpenetra-
tions of conditions and mental patterns.)[16]

Cash's method of analysis will follow a precise and predictable
pattern. His focus is consistently on the "common white man."
Methodically, each time a new issue is broached, Cash begins with

the material conditions, usually the economic conditions. He draws what would seem a likely conclusion from those conditions; almost always the conclusion is the development of class consciousness on the part of common white men, and the consequent possibility of a better life. Then he notes that class awareness did not occur, and seeks a reason why it did not. Time and again, the reason he finds is the power and persistence of "mind." "Mind," like Althusser's ideology, keeps common white men in subjection to the interests of the ruling class.[17]

Thus *The Mind of the South* can be read as a systematic and careful study of the ways ideology works to maintain the power of the ruling class. Cash's rhetorical strategy did not refuse Marxist discourse—his diction is peppered with terms like "ruling class," "revolution," "the proper laws of industrialism," "class consciousness," "the illusion of opportunity," "lack of social and economic focus"—but it did not elaborate Marxist theory as an explicit set of premises. Instead, *The Mind of the South* is a series of historical *representations*, frequently in the form of invented narrative, whose effect is to make the reader aware of ideology at work. As such, it is far from a certain form of positivist history, with its focus on information and objectivity. But neither is it fiction as conventionally defined, for *The Mind of the South* carries truth claims that such fiction can escape: it is, for Cash, about historical reality. For Cash, as for other southern modernists like James Agee, the boundary between history and fiction is false. Because experience, especially in the South, is constituted by ideology, which is to say by an inextricable conjunction between material "fact" and imaginary "story," the *representation* of experience (in "history" and in "fiction") incorporates that conjunction, challenging the convention of disciplinary distinction. Further, as sets of representations of ideology at work, history and fiction are themselves—*The Mind of the South* itself is—a form of ideology. When we read *The Mind of the South*, then, we are subject to ideological interpellation.

This is not to say that Cash—perhaps in an anticipatory parody of post-modernism?—reduced all the world to text, and then claimed all texts to be equally (non)truthbearing, though his logic would seem to lead in this direction. On the contrary, Cash agonized over the splits in the southern mind that allowed social, political, economic, and racial realities to be mystified and obscured by dominant southern myths. The point is that he did not work for an elimination of myth (or fiction) and its replacement by objectively reported "fact"; for Cash, the solution did not lie in a simple turn to objectivity. Instead, he sought a rearticulation of the relation between "fact" and "fiction"—a new ideology, with more progressive effects than the old, grounded in a more congruent relation between reality and representation.

Thus Cash managed to articulate, in the strange and troubling form of *The Mind of the South*, what was in 1941 a new theory and practice of ideology. It was a theory that went beyond the thinking of contemporary Marxism and anticipated the work of Louis Althusser. And it took a form that was then—and may still now be— illegible as theory. But it was a form that Cash devised to evade and destroy the stranglehold of the mind of the South, with its deadly separations between fact and fiction, its capacity to deny reality and live in fantasy.

Cash may have anticipated Althusser's interest in the unconscious interpellation of the subject, but his work and life have closer affinities with the work and life of his contemporary in prison in Italy. Althusser's work was to come considerably later in the game, after Jacques Lacan had paved the way by theorizing a subject whose capacities for control and rationality were deeply compromised. It is Gramsci's work on the theory of ideology that can best help us to see how Cash's odd text may be read in a new, enabling way, as a challenge to older ideologies and an effort to implant a new one.

During the painful period of composition (and inability to compose) that for Cash constituted the 1930s, Antonio Gramsci, in prison in Turin, worked out a more explicitly articulated set of ideas that related culture to the economy in strikingly similar

ways. Gramsci's contribution to the development of a Marxist
theory of ideology can be quickly summarized. Gramsci grew
uneasy with the then current notion that economic structures
determined superstructural events; he rejected this as "econo-
mism," but at the same time rejected the idealism of Hegel and
particularly Croce. Aware nevertheless of the nearly autonomous
power of a society's pervasive dominant ideology to shape perception and thus behavior, he retheorized ideology to account for this
power. His term "hegemony" represents the realm of a society's
frequently unconsciously held assumptions, values, feelings, beliefs—the society's "common sense," the sense of what is natural
and inevitable. "It is with Gramsci," writes Terry Eagleton, "that
the crucial transition is effected from ideology as 'systems of ideas'
to ideology as lived, habitual social practice—which must then
presumably encompass the unconscious, inarticulate dimensions
of social experience as well as the workings of formal institutions."[18]

It is precisely this effort to understand both the formal institutions and the "unconscious" of the South that leads Cash to his
capacious notion of "mind." We have already seen how Cash
defines "mind" as lived daily practice that mystifies class relations.
The kinship patterns of Cash's southerners, to take another example, allow them to identify "up" across what would otherwise be
class barriers. Thus, Cash writes, a "community of feeling . . .
unconsciously dominated you and kept class awareness from penetrating below your surface and into the marrow of your bones."

There are other components of Gramsci's theory that reappear
in Cash. Gramsci's "hegemony" serves the interests of the ruling
class by constructing a broadly accepted mentality that allows
virtually everyone to read the desires of the dominant class as their
own. Thus hegemony works through consent, or, in Eagleton's
painful phrase, "people . . . invest in their own unhappiness". As
with Gramsci, Cash's "mind" works through consent. Identifying
with "the thing called the South . . . [the common white man]

found in the prescriptions of his captains great expansion for his ego—associated the authority yielded the master class, not with any diminution of his individuality, but with its fullest development and expression." The planter class cooperated by "assuming their own interests as the true interest of the common white also."[20]

Edmund Jacobitti locates the intellectual history of Gramsci's concept of hegemony in the notion of rhetoric: Isocrates, Aristophanes, Horace, and Cicero saw "poetic explanation" as the "way unsophisticated and ordinary men, those who do not 'understand' hegemony, explain events—from *inside* the events, as participants."[21] For Cash, as for Gramsci, "rhetoric" becomes the hegemonic mode of explanation, the way of explaining from "inside." In Cash's South rhetoric takes an extra twist. Not only does it produce (and exhibit) consent but it does so through a willful disclaimer of realism, rather than through the more familiar strategy of claiming realism. Thus southern politics became as Cash read it a form of self-conscious "theater" which "caught the very meanest man up out of his own tiny legend into the gorgeous fabric of the legend of this or that great hero. . . . But the only real interest [served] . . . was that of the planter."[22]

For Gramsci, hegemony works by coercion as well as consent.[23] The ruling class inevitably controls the police and the army; it will use these if consent begins to break down. For Cash as well, coercion emerges when consent breaks down. Cash writes that the "wholesale expropriation of the cracker and the small farmer" after Reconstruction seemed to be—surely he intended the pun—"a capital development. . . . For here was an end for these people of the independence and self-sufficiency, the freedom from direct exploitation and servitude, which had been so primary for the preservation and growth of the old frontier individualism, for the suppression of class feeling, and the binding of the South into its extraordinary unity of purpose and outlook." That is, with the coming of direct exploitation of the cracker, the survival of the earlier system of indirect exploitation by means of constructing

consent under the names of "independence" and "self-sufficiency"
and "individualism" is endangered, because it is exposed as a set of
enabling fictions. This threat of hegemonic collapse, however,
only brings out, from the ruling class, "that power to coerce which
had been the baron's all along," the "force for the exercise of
compulsion." This move from consent to coercion will happen
again in the mills.[24]

Consent is in a sense un-will-ing, for we do not realize hegemony is there; "in fact," writes Jacobitti, "we may say that to realize
it *is* there is to destroy it."[25] For Gramsci, once one becomes aware
of hegemony, it loses some of its power. Thus a possibility opens for
change, specifically by deliberately and consciously fighting the
hegemony or "fictions" of the ruling class with an alternative
hegemony. Gramsci's prescription for revolution thus entailed first
a sweeping effort to gain control of ideology. Once the people were
convinced of the rightness of the revolutionary model, once they
had accepted intellectual leadership from the revolutionary group,
that group could achieve political and economic dominance as
well. In particular, Gramsci developed the notion of the "organic
intellectual," an intellectual who came from the masses, understood their concerns, and could speak their language. This "organic intellectual" could find ways to make theory comprehensible
and acceptable to the people, hence enable theory to have practical results. "Traditional" intellectuals, on the other hand, served
the ruling class and of course saw no need to connect their thinking
to material conditions, since its very function was to mystify them.

Cash too was concerned about the possibility of change; indeed,
more than once in *Mind of the South* he entertains the possibility
of revolutionary change. But his thinking seems to have been less
sanguine than Gramsci's, and for several reasons. Like Gramsci,
Cash was drawn to the power of intellectuals. Modernism's forays
into the South (as he saw it) constructed for Cash a space for
detachment, hence for becoming aware of "mind." As he put it
in a different context, "something which had been essentially un-
thinkable before suddenly began to be more thinkable." In this
process, "fact" plays a new and crucial role. The new university

teachers, many educated in the North, can look at "facts." Sociological and fictional works of the Southern Renaissance are coming to terms with the "facts" of southern life. Because intellectuals could now (from the detached, alternative position enabled by "factual" knowledge) see the operation of hegemony, they could plausibly help it to dissolve and reformulate in newer, more progressive ways. However, Cash saw little hope for this. In an interesting repeated figure, he writes that the "intellectual leadership . . . was almost wholly unarticulated with the body of the South," the head apparently drifting in free fall and the body entirely unconscious, one supposes because there are no strong structural links between them, no neck. This suggests a failure of "organic intellectuals" to connect to the organism, for whatever reasons. Certainly, too, Cash lacked an organized and supportive political party; whereas Gramsci thought in terms of the Communist Party as the location for intellectual leadership, Cash had only the Democrats. But Cash also saw the problem of the South to be fundamentally tragic, sentenced to the death his decapitated figure implies. For in the South, even members of the ruling (not the intellectual) class remained—incredibly—mystified by (their own) ideology to the extent that they subverted their own economic interests. Spinning off even from the most fundamental connection to material reality, then, the South's hegemonic discourse put it on a trajectory of doom. Habits of extravagance, of preferring voluptuous words to difficult deeds, and of denying the pain of recognition with the pleasure of verbal play, characterize Cash's mind of the South in every class. The "capacity for unreality" means massive cultural denials, such as the denial of the realities of cross-racial relatedness, and the accompanying willingness to submit to a rhetoric of unreality. When the dominant class itself insists on unreality, when it does not even know when hegemony is and is not serving its own interests, there are no longer, to use Gramsci's terms, "two peoples"—one conscious and the other not.[26] And the entire South is headed for self-destruction.

One might think this would make revolution easier for Cash to envision; after all, power should flow to Cash's new intellectuals, who have consciousness and detachment, thus the capacity to analyze, to plan, and to take advantage of the ruling class's blind-nesses. This was not the case. One might speculate that for Cash the grip of the savage ideal was so pervasive among the people who had a stake in change, its imprint even on the "organic intellec-tuals" he saw emerging so deep, that he could not envision a space within which such people could gather and organize. Moreover, his notion of hegemony, more than Gramsci's, attended—like Althusser's—to the power of unconscious demand and desire over the power of the ego, reducing his confidence in deliberate politi-cal action.[27] Finally, even while some of Cash's harshest criticisms of the South came for its privileging of the word over the deed, easy talk over difficult actions, fiction over fact, Cash himself was of course not immune to words' charm. The temptation to think—more radically—that perhaps words do or can constitute reality would have been appealing, especially given his work as a counter-hegemonic writer. Cash saw himself most fundamentally as a novelist, even while he counted himself among those organic intellectuals whose analytic detachment and respect for fact might enable change from within. Thus to move to that more radical (and in the context conservative) position on language would repeat the very problem he aimed to correct, changing only the names of those with ideological power. In the search for tools for change, Cash relied finally not on a collective revolution but on his own ideological text: *The Mind of the South*, with its deliberate rear-ticulation of the relation between fiction and fact.

Perhaps his sense of the frailty of this tool and of the impos-sibility of a collective movement for change fed the despair, as well as the fears about Nazi power, that were part of Cash's process of dying. But if Fascist ideology in some sense contributed to killing Jack Cash, there is no doubt that it killed Antonio Gramsci. Gramsci and Cash actually had quite a bit in common. Both were frail, sickly, bookish boys; Gramsci had a hunchback from infancy. Both grew up with a strong awareness of the power of religion to shape perceptions and behavior. Both came to political awareness in college, both wrote on Babbittry, both wrote their texts (as I will argue shortly) in a sort of code, both suffered mental collapse, both spent their professional lives as journalists.[28] Most interesting in the present context, both were southerners. Gramsci was born in Sardinia and, though he moved to Turin and identified himself with urbanity, took as a continuing concern what he called the Southern Question. Although it may be coincidental, again there are striking similarities to Cash's southern question, though the solutions and the stakes for the two men differ.

The history of the Italian South differs, of course, in many critical ways from that of the American South. It has never been a separate "nation," as the American South has been, and ideology in southern Italy did not have the unifying and stabilizing (perhaps petrifying) force that it did in the American South. But there are intriguing similarities. Gramsci's South, like Cash's, was primarily agrarian, faced similar problems of hurtful protective tariffs and self-destructive farming practices, and served northern capital. Yet in Northern ideology, it occupied the space of the Other. To the North, Gramsci wrote, "the South is the ball and chain [of Italy]; the Southerners are biologically inferior beings, semi-barbarians, or total barbarians, by natural destiny; if the South is backward, the fault does not lie with . . . any . . . historical cause, but with Nature, which has made the Southerners lazy, incapable, criminal, and barbaric—only tempering this harsh fate with the purely individual explosion of a few great geniuses, like isolated palmtrees in an arid and barren desert." Gramsci's North may not call it the Sahara, but the similarities to Mencken's American South are plain. Like Cash's demagogue, the traditional intellectual in Gramsci's South was "democratic in [his] peasant face, reactionary in the face turned toward the big landowner and the government." In fact, a savage ideal prevents dissent in the Italian South as well, where Gramsci writes there is "no intellectual light, no programme, no drive towards improvements or progress," and the occasional "southerners who . . . pose the Southern Question in a radical form have . . . grouped themselves around reviews printed outside the South."[29] Gramsci's ideas of hegemony and of the organic intellectual have deep roots in his early experience and identification as a Southerner, just as do Cash's ideas of mind and intellectual awareness.

If the Southern incapacity for analysis and capacity for unreality kept southerners from even minimal awareness of the patterns that structured their lives, how was Cash to accomplish his task? How could he move his readers from fantasy to reality, rhetoric to analysis, hegemony to detachment, without alienating them from the start with an unfamiliar discourse? Cash's strategy was to construct a counter-hegemonic discourse that draws on the techniques of southern hegemony. It speaks in a voice that southerners as he understood them could recognize and understand. It is a voice that addresses the reader personally, that chivalrically anticipates the reader's reservations and lays them to rest, that offers at times a modest self-deprecation, at other times the tones of authority. This is not "truly" the voice of Cash, as Michael O'Brien has already argued; it exposes neither his stakes nor his history. It is a constructed voice whose purpose is to melt the reader's defenses, to open a way for more unfamiliar, analytical, modes of address, for a new hegemonic discourse.

A close reading of the "Preview to Understanding" exposes the conflicts Cash faced in constructing this narrative voice. Cash claims initially that narrative will be his method of explanation: "to understand [mind], it is necessary to know the *story* [my emphasis] of its development," he writes. But given Cash's own analysis of the southern "mind" (much of which he had already written by the time he wrote the "Preview"), with its love for story of any kind, for exaggeration and play, for the most outrageous lies, Cash's narrator now has a contradictory task, for his very purpose is to wean his reader from such habits. Cash enacts this contradiction in the Preview. Immediately after we learn that "to understand" we must "know the story," Cash recounts the legends of the Old and New South, legends that he says "bear little relation to reality." How then will we get at "reality"? If Cash is use to use narrative as explanation, as he has claimed, he will have to counter story with story. This will raise the question of how to determine the truth of conflicting stories.[24] Perhaps flinching from this difficulty, Cash makes a move to science as explanation: "To get at its nature [that is, the mind of the South] we shall have first of all to examine the question of exactly what the Old South was really like." This is the last sentence of the Preview; thus with the language of science— "examine," "exactly," "really"—Cash appears to offer a conclusive alternative (and for the South a subversive epistemology), the "argument from fact." But for reasons already suggested, Cash could not sacrifice fiction for fact, subjective rhetoric for objective history, at least for very long. Indeed, the repressed returns even as Cash writes out his desire for science. The last word, literally, belongs to "literature": it is the word "like"—"what the Old South was really like." The discourse of science concludes in the discourse of literature; fact falls into simile. By ending with "like," Cash hints that even the most exacting scientific representation will depend upon figurative language. "Exactly what the Old South was like" thus represents, in little, the large problem Cash faced of the impossibility of settling on either fiction or fact; it is what I mean by my title, "The Cash Nexus." The pun is meant to suggest a nexus that, unlike Marx's more material one, connects fiction and fact, literature and history, through the notion of mind.[30]

In fact Cash has already dramatized this difficulty, in the previous paragraph. The first half of the paragraph begins "these legends . . . bear little relation to reality" and restates this claim in various "realistic," non-metaphorical, even anti-metaphorical sentences, such as "it was another thing than this." Midway through the paragraph, though, he takes on the question of what the South *is*, and Cash's voice breaks into metaphor: "a tree . . . with its tap root in the Old South; [an English church whose] exterior and superstructure are late Gothic . . . [but whose crypt has stones] cut by Saxon brick made by Roman hands."[31]

Does Cash know what he is doing in the Preview? Is he deliber-

ately reflecting upon the power of language itself to construct
reality, on rhetoric as hegemony? Perhaps. Such awareness is at
least suggested by the phrase with which, within the paragraph,
Cash makes the shift from "realism" to metaphor. That phrase is
"one might say." "One might say" the South is like a tree, etc.,
Cash writes. An apparently innocuous cliché, this phrase actually
raises questions about authorship and language that will preoc-
cupy Cash through the volume, though never in overtly theoretical
terms. *Who* might say? *Might* under what conditions? And, most
important, what would the effect of "saying" be? If hegemony
(mind) means the power of representation to mystify material
conditions, could Cash himself have the power through language
alone to construct an alternative South? Cash toys with this possibility at various points in *The Mind of the South*, calling attention
to his own act of writing in phrases like these: "Such are the curious
uses to which words may be bent . . . that we can say of Progress
[that it was beating back one frontier while creating another], " or
"It [change] rises up and becomes manifest *in the very telling of the
story*" (my emphases).[32]

If Cash borders on self-reflexivity here, his manipulation of an
organizing metaphor for *The Mind of the South* seems still more
deliberate. That metaphor—the Trojan horse—address the issue
of the relation between story and fact. The Trojan horse is of course
the wooden horse of Homer's epic story that, hollowed out, filled
with Greeks, and presented to the Trojans as a gift, allowed the
Greek army entrance into the enemy Troy. Cash is intrigued
enough with this figure to use it several times. It appears first in
the context of a discussion of the effect on the southern mind of the
shift from the "laws of agriculture" to the "laws of the machine."[33]
Southerners were, Cash writes, "as innocent of the existence of
such laws as the Trojans were of the Argives crouching in the belly
of the wooden horse on the day they drew it within the gates of
Ilium." Later, discussing the hopeful signs that the modernist
"mind" has filtered into southern universities, he writes "cunning
Odysseus had ineluctably been fetched within the gates with the

Trojan horse and could not be forever kept shut up." Thus the
"breach had been made in the savage ideal . . . the modern mind
had been established within the gates, and . . . here at long last
there was springing up in the South a growing body of men . . .
who deliberately chose to know and think rather than merely to
feel in the terms fixed finally by Southern patriotism. . . ."[34]

I would argue that this metaphor encodes Cash's hopes for his
own text. Disguised—by means of its rhetorical strategies—as a
gift, *The Mind of the South* could, once "opened" and read, give
birth to a new and alien way of thinking, accomplishing the political end of restructuring not only the mind, or hegemony, of the
South but its political economy as well. *The Mind of the South*
would be the subversive agent, in short, of hegemonic revolution.
The chances for widespread acceptance of an overtly Marxist
analysis of the mind of the South, even in 1941, were minimal. In
Mind, Cash comments sardonically on the southern hatred for the
"Red Peril," yet he covers himself with explicit disavowals of
Marxist affiliation. Instead, Cash coded his ideology as "history,"
planting it in this Trojan horse of a book to spring out behind the
defenses of his readers under other names than Marx.

Elsewhere, Cash's metaphor seems to retreat further from conscious control. Contradictions appear when one explores this metaphor in the light of Cash's invention of the proto-Dorian bond, a
bond of racial pride that simultaneously solidified white supremacy and mystified class difference. Cash chose to represent this
bond, which he abhorred, in the language of Greece as well: the
Dorians were Greeks. If the enemy for Cash is Troy, why represent
it here as Greek? This confusion may represent the difficulty Cash
faced as an organic intellectual, a southerner trying to revolution-
ize the South that made him. It is not surprising that he would
conflate enemy and ally in his metaphors; at one moment his heart
is with the South, and at another it is set against it. In Cash's
words, "a thinker in the South is regarded quite logically as an
enemy of the people."[35] Perhaps Cash's conflicting metaphors
underline the chagrin of these words.

Certainly as an "organic" intellectual, Cash inevitably found
the divisions and contradictions about which he wrote inscribed
throughout his own subjectivity, in and on his own body. And
inevitably they appear as well in the body of his text. Gramsci
would have understood this. He wrote: "To think that such
[organic] intellectuals . . . can break with the entire past and
situate themselve totally upon the terrain of a new ideology, is
absurd. . . ."[36] There are strategies for reading the "unconscious"
of a text that can come into play here. A "symptomatic reading" of a
text looks to the signs of rupture or fission in an otherwise apparently unified and coherent text. Such a reading—which emerges
from psychoanalysis and deconstruction—locates sites of stress
and uncertainty that may undergird and challenge the overt claims
of the text's more deliberate design. It is based on the premise
argued earlier that ideology (of which textual production is a part)
addresses the subject on many levels of subjectivity, conscious and
unconscious. In a history (even this odd one, *The Mind of the
South*), metaphors can be especially telling, for the writer's attention is typically engaged at another level of consciousness, farther
from primary process than in fiction, developing a rational argument.

It is in this area that we can locate a feminist critique.

Of all the ideological interpellations that the South produced,
Cash seems to have been least aware of the call of patriarchy—less
aware, for example, than he was of his participation in the ideology
of racism. Patriarchy works like any other ideology, by making
traditional gender patterns feel natural and inevitable. Although
Cash was able to see upon occasion that womanhood was a cultural
construction,[37] he almost invariably accepted as natural the characteristics of southern manhood. It would be surprising, though,
to find Cash wholeheartedly accepting any inscription from the
mind of the South, even those closest to his own sense of himself.
Thus I would suggest that Cash's "difficulties" with his own sexuality should be read not as signs of failure and weakness (no doubt

the way Cash thought of them) but as signs of his unconscious engagement with the contradictions of southern manhood. Cash's lack of detachment, analysis, and awareness in the arena of gender was, in short, contradicted by his hostility to the demands of the savage ideal (which included those for manhood).

Those contradictions appear most palpably in Cash's textual representation of the men who succeed and the men who fail in the South, whether on the frontier the wilderness made, the frontier the Yankee made, or the frontier produced by industrialization. Here, Cash surprisingly locates the secret to success not in material conditions but in the essential "character" of a man: either he is aggressive, strong, determined, and energetic, or he is passive, weak, vacillating, and lethargic. The first sort, like his Irishman at the center, will make it into the "aristocracy"; the second will gradually "drift" into small farming, tenantry, or, later, mill labor. This can happen even between brothers.[38] Cash's diction tells the story. His model Irishman "piled, grubbed, hacked, stamped, drove, bruised." The successful brother "carve[s] out" success; the other "fail[s]" or is "timid and unambitious" or is the "weakest and least competent."[39]

Two things are striking about this analysis. First is the deviation from the methodology that characterizes Cash's analysis elsewhere, the move from material conditions, to the plausible ideological effects (class awareness), to the actual hegemonic conclusion (class mystification). Instead, this analysis depends on a distinction unaccounted for either by biology (the gene pool) or by social and economic conditions (since all begin under the same conditions). It is a deviation that remains unanalyzed, and perhaps unconscious. A second clue to the ideological basis for this understanding of masculine success and failure appears in its vastly oversimplifying dichotomy: one is either energetic or lazy, a success or a failure. Such rigid dichotomies typically align themselves with and may be produced by a rigid system of gender that "naturalizes" sexual difference into a vastly oversimplified opposition between male and female. It is not difficult to imagine how the imposition of such oppositions on one's own body would produce, for a man, a scene of sexual impossibility, where no sexuality counts except "success" or "failure," acting like a "man" or becoming the unnameable other. Arguably, in fact, it is not the production of gender that is at issue in such thinking, but the preservation of the space between the oppositional terms. Transferring that space between man and woman to the putative gap between success and failure, blinded by gender ideology himself, Cash cannot consider the ways in which he might be entering and inscribing a discourse not only of patriarchy but of patriarchal capitalism which demands aggression and strength of its men, passivity and weakness of its women.

Nor can he see the similarities between his positive representations of successful masculinity and his ambivalent but finally negative position on individualism. The hegemonic discourses of male sexual "success" and class success dovetail in the very language of a passage like this one describing the less successful men: ". . . vague ambition, though it might surge up in dreams now and then, was too weak ever to rise to a consistent lust for plantation and slaves, or anything else requiring an extended exertion of will [from] those who, sensing their own inadequacy, expected and were content with little." Cash suggests that for him gender is prior to class; if you "outshoot" or "outfiddle" your neighbor, even if he has more slaves, you are "essentially as good a man as he"; I suspect that, as David Leverenz has written in another context, "class dynamics become subsumed in gender ideologies" for Cash at this point.[40]

Certainly at this point, the detachment that elsewhere allows him to construct an entire project whose basis is the exposure and analysis of hegemony vanishes, and Cash's text becomes homologous with the system it aims to deconstruct. Perhaps it was his own stake in capitalist manhood; perhaps it was simply habits of thought and perception; perhaps it was the lack of a critical discourse and community that took gender as its subject. Whatever the case, I will conclude by suggesting the ways in which even this ideological investment in some intersection between patriarchy and capitalism became unstable for Cash, within the text as well as the life.

Had he had access to Gramsci's terminology, Cash would probably have called the Nashville Agrarians "traditional intellectuals." The Agrarians' project was marked by misogyny in its particularly Southern forms. The most distinctive example is the apparent reverence for white women, a reverence that, as William Taylor noted long ago in *Cavalier and Yankee*, barely conceals suspicion and contempt, and thus serves to bind (white) woman by "consent" in her ideological place. Cash called this "gyneolatry." As Lillian Smith showed, this reverence for white women's purity is inseparable from the construction of black women as sensual and amoral. A second sign of Southern misogyny is the habitual appropriation of the ideologically feminine—whether it is the association with the natural, the beautiful, or the penetrated—to serve the ideological construction of manhood. In this move, Southern manhood effectively claims a virility that is enhanced, not "feminized," by its appropriation of the feminine. A final link in the chain of southern gender ideology is the (mis)representation of "actual" women. The Agrarians rendered "historical" women, whether a character's wife in *I'll Take My Stand* or Edna St. Vincent Millay in a book review, with astonishing deprecation and hostility; for the most part, however, women are simply ignored.[41]

Cash has been accused, and rightly so, of ignoring women and African-Americans, among others, in his construction of the mind of the South.[42] Nevertheless, his position in the political landscape of the South in the 1930s was far to the left of the Agrarians. The crucial difference between them is that Cash longed for change in the direction of diversity, equality, and liberty, and the Agrarians longed for change in the direction of unity, hierarchy, and particularism. Thus while the Agrarians' views on womanhood and women are coherent with their larger project, and consistent with the savage ideal of gender, Cash's are incoherent and confused. Contradictions and conflicts were bound to result when a man who opposed class and race privilege could reinscribe it in the scene of domesticity.[43]

Let us turn again to the figure of the Trojan horse. In that figure, Cash focuses most obviously on the men who spring out, fully armed, to do battle with the Trojans. But the ground for that figure is the horse itself, which in a sense gives birth to the soldiers. When we look closely at the text, we can see that Cash has in fact reversed figure and ground, writing the entire scene as a scene not of grown men and battle but of a fecund woman (very fecund indeed) giving birth. In describing "Progress" as "truly revolutionary" in potential, he has already written that "it quite definitely carried in its womb the potentiality—the logical necessity, even— of eventual revolution from our own special view point." Two pages later we find the first reference to the Argives "crouching in the belly of the wooden horse." Cash may well have identified himself and his text with the horse figured as a woman in labor as fully as he did with the armed soldiers going to battle. My best support for this hunch appears in Cash's sole allusion to the "author" of the story of the Trojan War. If my argument about the importance of this metaphor to an understanding of the book is correct (or at least persuasive), then this would be in effect a self-representation of the author who brought the Argives of modernism, even Marxism, to the South. Here is the passage: "If one gets out into the countryside . . . one is pretty sure to come upon . . . an old woman— with a memory like a Homeric bard's."[44]

But even if Cash does identify with the feminine here, it could be argued that this is only an example of a masculinist appropriation of female experience. More conclusive for me at least are Cash's sympathetic, even identificatory representations of actual women who, in Teresa de Lauretis's words, are "transmitting and transforming cultural values."[45] They appear only when he reaches the twentieth century and tells the story of union organizing. The subjectivity of the nineteenth century Irishman's wife, for example, is ignored, though her hands show the workings of ideology by signifying first farm labor and then aristocracy. And he never enters the subjectivity of a black woman. But in the twentieth century we do get the story of the young woman labor organizer who goes to a strange city and is met by the town brass with warnings to go home for fear she will be hurt. Calling their bluff, she asks—sweetly, no doubt—whether this means the men who are addressing her can't protect her. Of course they must say they can; she stays, and does her work. Cash tells the story of her intelligence and courage with obvious admiration.

Cash may have been drawn to this story for several reasons. This nameless woman uses southern ideology to her own and the union's advantage. Her position in many ways resembles his own: determined to effect change in the South, she manipulates the southern mind instead of simply, and hopelessly, confronting it. A union organizer in the guise of a southern lady and a radical cultural analyst in the guise of a good old boy telling stories are for Cash comrades in arms, hunched within the belly of a hollow wooden horse.

Despite such hopeful moments, and although he notes the ideological bases of "gyneolatry" and the proto-Dorian bond of white supremacy, Cash never queries the material conditions of white women or black people and their possible eventuation in counter-hegemonic minds. To do that, to be fair, he would have had to write southern women's and African-American history.

Gramsci shared Cash's near-blindness to hegemonic gender. For Gramsci, the question of domination remained contradictory. Although his final vision seems to have been of a classless society unified by truly voluntary consent, Gramsci's theorizing of hegemony assumes that the route to the ideal end must be won by gaining hegemonic dominance for the working class. He thought of ways for the workers to gain control, to achieve equality; one plan, for example, was to subject the Southern agrarian peasants to the leadership of the industrial workers in the North. This apparently uncritical acceptance of dominance appears in the domestic scene as well. Gramsci's son Delio had decided to read *Uncle Tom's Cabin*, and Gramsci wrote this letter from prison to

his wife about the correct way to interpret the book for their
son:

> I really doubt if you are very well equipped to do it yourself
> . . . it seems to me that you put yourself in the position of a
> subaltern and not of a commander (not only in this matter but in
> others too). What I mean is that the position you adopt is not that
> of a person who can criticise the ideologies from an historical
> point of view, dominating them, explaining them, and justifying
> them as an historic necessity of the past. It is rather that of a
> person who when put in contact with a particular world of
> sentiments and ideas may feel himself either attracted or re-
> pelled, but will always remain in the sphere of sentiment and
> immediate passion.[46]

The interpenetration of gender and Marxist ideologies is, I
hope, obvious in a term like Gramsci's "dominating." Although
Gramsci is careful to represent his wife not as a "natural woman"
but as a "person" who "adopts" a "position," he seems unaware of
the force of hegemonic gender that might subvert such efforts
at self-representation on her own part, and equally unaware of
his own rather dominating writing style. Despite his attention
throughout his work to the subjectivity of the marginalized, then,
"dominance" is hardly a problematic term for Gramsci here. Like
Cash, he was habituated to and privileged by the patriarchal sex/
gender system; imprisoned, ill, and suffering, he still had his
confidence in his writing and his sister-in-law, Tatiana, to provide
him with books and a sounding board for his thoughts.[47] One can
only wonder what Gramsci—and Cash—might have produced
had they found a place from which to analyze patriarchy.

Gramsci would probably not have seen Cash as quite the people's hero and organic intellectual I am presenting here; indeed,
he might have called him a liberal and a reformist, anathema to a
devoted Communist and revolutionary theorist. After all, Cash did
think of politics as a space in which conflict *could* be resolved—
he simply saw that it wasn't happening that way in the South. Nor
did Cash ever theorize a practicable method for change; perhaps

he was so overwhelmed by his increasing awareness of the power of traditional southern hegemony as to doubt the possibility of change by any means. But whatever their differences, they came from similar roots and came to strikingly similar terms in which to think about the cultures that had constructed and would finally kill them both. And if the Cash nexus shows the impossibility of dividing history from literature, fact from fiction, and conditions from ideology, other southern writers—most obviously James Agee, whose *Let Us Now Praise Famous Men* appeared the same year as *The Mind of the South*—were coming to similar conclusions, and could be read in similar ways.

Commentary / Michael O'Brien

Anne Jones presents us with an unwonted Wilbur Cash. One is accustomed to think of the Carolinian in company with the likes of Thomas Wolfe or James Agee, to think of him in disordered press rooms, or sitting rapt and frustrated before an old battered typewriter, or lying stupefied with whisky in a bedroom of his parents' home. This Cash is an old familiar, comforting, crumpled. But Jones's Cash is quite another thing, spanking and modern, with no Panama hat but a smart French suit, a glass of lucid Montrachet in his hand, the keys of a new Citroen in his pocket, talking sinuously of hegemony and fissures in a text. Is this plausible? Or, rather, since I would not wish to stand condemned as a positivist by speaking baldly of matters of fact, is this persuasive?

Any canonical author has to be read variously by differing generations as the price of survival. We live in a theoretical age, in which the inscriptions of ideology matter greatly. If Cash is to survive, a bargain must be struck between him and a different generation of Southerners, to whom Althusser might matter as much as, more than, Jonathan Daniels. It is to Jones's credit that she understands the necessity for this renegotiation. She has struck the most original note of any I have heard in this long year of anniversary.

What does this renegotiated Cash look like? He is a Marxist, parallel to the school of Gramsci. He is aware of genre and the subversive power of language. He is political, close to revolutionary. He is a theoretician, who challenges positivism. He is a son of the patriarchy, an admirer of energy and virile success.

Is Cash a Gramscian? If we define the essence of Gramscianism as, first, the broadening of the scope of Marxism by infusing it with Croce's Hegelianized idealism and, second, the elaboration of a sociology for the social influence of intellectuals and ideology, the answer might be yes. If we loosen that definition further and define Gramscianism as a meditation on the relationship between material conditions and *mentalité*, the answer is yes; Cash was interested in a similar meditation and came up with some cognate reflections. In this loose sense, a parallel between Gramsci and Cash helps us to locate Cash in the philosophical spectrum, to see that he stands more in the camp of people like Gramsci than, say, Swedenborg. But is the parallel worth more than this gesture of identification? I doubt it. I particularly doubt Jones's contention that Cash was "Marxist to the core." For the kinds of Marxism with which she attempts to associate Cash—those of Althusser and Gramsci—are not themselves central to the materialist tradition of Marxism, but heresies from or improvements upon it, depending on your standpoint. There is so much Hegelianism at *this* Marxist core, that to locate Cash there leaves his analytical status less, not more clear.

Even at the level of personality and character, the parallel of Gramsci and Cash is unconvincing. While it is true they shared sickly childhoods, in adult life they could not have been more different. Gramsci was lean, ascetic, unsentimental, ruthless, and prepared to make sacrifices for his creed. He led protesters at the gates of FIAT, commanded a great political party, was incarcerated because Mussolini feared the power of his mind. His ideology was rooted in the cool judgement that is concerned with action. Wilbur

Cash was tubby, hedonistic as far as he could manage it, prone to crying with emotion, was the sort of person who goes to watch a labor strike not lead one, and probably could not have drowned a kitten let alone a capitalist. Wilbur Cash did not know the meaning of action, and (perhaps to his credit) did not have a mind that anyone needed to fear.

Moreover, Cash was a Southerner and Gramsci, I think, was not. It is true that he came from Sardinia, which some including Gramsci have included under the category, "Mezzogiorno," which in Italian implies South because it means midday, the time when the sun shines. Sardinia, however, held an ambivalent status in the regionalisms of Italy, half facing towards Naples and Sicily, half facing the Piedmont with which it had been politically united under the House of Savoy before unification. Mostly, Sardinia the island faced inward, with little sense of identification with Italy, with an idiosyncratic history and political economy strongly marked by its long association with Spain.[1] Of that ambivalent status, Gramsci was aware. His 1926 essay on "Some Aspects of the Southern Question" bears its traces. At one point he includes Sardinia in the South, though in the same breath he makes a distinction: "The South can be defined as a great social disintegration. The peasants, who make up a great majority of its population, have no cohesion among themselves (of course, some exceptions must be made: Apulia, Sardinia, Sicily, where there exist special characteristics within the great canvas of the South's structure)." Later he elaborates on the distinctiveness of Sardinia: "The only region where the war veterans' movement took on a more precise profile, and succeeded in creating a more solid social structure, was Sardinia. And this is understandable. Precisely because in Sardinia the big landowner class is very exiguous, carries out no function, and does not have the ancient cultural and government traditions of the mainland South."[2]

But Gramsci himself was at great pains to shed any identity with the island. He faced towards Turin, where he went to university, where he worked and agitated. Certainly Gramsci was sensitive to

the problem of the Mezzogiorno and his 1926 essay made a marked
contribution towards reordering attitudes towards the social and
political problem of the South. But, if one examines the rhetoric of
that essay, the conviction grows that Gramsci was no Southerner.
Throughout he speaks of the South and southern intellectuals as
the other, as someone else, a phenomenon to be understood and
challenged. He, Gramsci, is not a southern intellectual, shows no
interest even in claiming the status of an expatriate from the South.
His identification, the moments when he talks of himself or, more
commonly, of "us" are those when he speaks of "the Turin Communists." Thus he talks of Piero Gobetti serving as a link between
the Turin Communists and the Southern intellectuals, between
"us" and them.[3] And it was this same Gobetti who, from that
mediating position, was to observe that Gramsci "seemed to have
come from the country to forget his traditions, to substitute for the
diseased inheritance of Sardinian anachronism an enclosed and
inexorable effort towards the modernity of the city dweller."[4] So,
on the whole, I am inclined to relieve Cash of the keys to that new
Citroen, and allow that, at best, he might have taken the odd spin
in an old Alfa Romeo, though far less often than he rode in a
Chevrolet.[5]

What about the Montrachet? Would Cash be at home in the
cafés of Les Halles, gazing towards the externalized plumbing of
the Beaubourg Centre? What was Cash's understanding of genre
and language? Was or is his book "a nexus in which questions of
fact and rhetoric are inseparably linked through the mediation of
ideology"? The problem is that any text is such a nexus. *The Mind
of the South*, the *Prison Notebooks*, *Alice in Wonderland*, the
Manhattan telephone directory, all can answer present if we ask, is
there a nexus in the room? That does not diminish the usefulness of
Jones's insight, only its particularity. If, however, we ask a historical
question, did Cash *intend* to subvert language and genre? I am
inclined to answer yes to genre, no to language. I do think Cash
intended to muddle the line between genres; he wrote history,
sociology, journalism, fiction, sermon, all in the one book. I doubt

he did this in full analytical self-awareness, sitting down and saying to himself, "Today I shall deconstruct genre." But I think he had his story to tell, this rhetoric he painfully loved, and the discretions of genre did not bother him, had to be swept aside if the story and the rhetoric were to be expressed.

As to language, I think Jones misreads *The Mind of the South*. I doubt that Cash had any sense that language, words, metaphor, were subversive and unstable. On the contrary, I think his text cries out that words are to be trusted. Indeed they may have been the only thing Wilbur Cash did trust. Which is not to say he did not understand that reality was fluid, often indistinct, full of shadows and ambiguity, but I am convinced he felt that words could capture it, that reality in all its nuance could be expressed in language. He knew it was difficult, he found it in fact agonizing, but his agony did not reside in the sense that the venture was impossible, only in the fear that he might prove inadequate, as he had on that night with the coed.

Was his language political and revolutionary? Certainly he offered a swinging condemnation of his culture and, on the whole, has spoken more to Southern liberals than to conservatives. One finds little of Cash in the literary criticism of the neo-Agrarian school, in Cleanth Brooks, Louis Rubin, C. Hugh Holman, and Lewis P. Simpson. Donald Davidson gave the book a fierce review on its publication.[6] Richard Weaver in 1964, it is true, expressed agreement with Cash's contention that "the Southern mind is one of the most intransigent on earth," but only cautiously to celebrate the fact.[7] Yet reform—let alone revolution—ought to be an act of creation, as well as destruction. Cash knew what he did not like, but had little precise idea of the social order that might emerge if his demolitions were successful. He admired critical thinking, but more for the excitement of the process, less for the ends. So, while I agree that he had a vision that was "in the direction of diversity, equality, and liberty" because he thought to inhabit such a world would be more interesting and less constraining, I do not think one can find in his writings a description of that world.[8] Would blacks be equal, unsegregated? Would women be freed from the role of the belle and the matron? Would society be agnostic? Would science be unfettered? Who knew? Certainly not Cash. And, to be fair to him, given his belief in the power of the savage ideal, it would have been wasted energy for him to have speculated and planned for such a world. It was not going to happen.

The trouble is, some of it has happened. Did Cash help this? Woodward has firmly said, no, *The Mind of the South* has incapacitated subversion and must be retired to the back benches of Southern thought if the business of change is to go forward. On this point, I think Woodward was right. Cash has been most admired by those of modest political agendas and of conservative epistemologies. He has had little to do with the single greatest transformation in Southern life since 1941, civil rights, and absolutely nothing to do with that other—far less complete—motion, feminism. The various conferences held this year have made the fact abundantly clear, that Wilbur Cash has almost nothing to say to blacks and women. For them, he is part of the problem of Southern culture, not—as his admirers think—the solution. Jones's paper reinforces this impression, explicitly by identifying his patriarchalism, implicitly by generously inscribing on his illegible theory a few inscriptions that postmoderns might sympathetically read. It is a generosity that I doubt too many of her feminist contemporaries share.

But Jones addresses something more subtle than explicit politics, language. I agree with her that Cash's prose and his politics are seamless, but I read both as more conservative than she does. Was his prose modernist? Perhaps, in some of his themes. But the rhetoric? Cash has always reminded me more of Charles Dickens than T. S. Eliot, more of *Little Dorrit* than *The Four Quartets*. *The Mind of the South* is a great Victorian narrative, with choking sentiment, brooding melancholies, much conversation with the "dear reader," lots of weather and landscape. Like Dickens, Cash followed the aesthetic counsel that one should never let the pace slacken, never underestimate the power of death and mourning, never use one adjective when three will do. Whatever else it is, *The Mind of the South* is a tear-jerker. One reason he is less read today than in 1965 is that all the sad young men, who once came anxiously out of small Southern towns into the timid new world of an urban South, do not come in such numbers now, needing Cash to comprehend their predicament.

Once, of course, Cash was often read to offer a model to prose. Bruce Clayton still feels the dignity and inspiration of this *exemplum* and states his case in the *coda* of his biography.[9] But I suspect the biographer grows idiosyncratic in this admiration, because the norms of Southern prose have drastically changed since 1941. How many recent Southern writers write like Cash? Marshall Frady, perhaps. Who else? This is not because, as Clayton implies, Cash was a *real writer* and others are mere pigmy academics, stumbling around with their pedantries. The recent South has many prose stylists fully the equal of Wilbur Cash. One of them, John Shelton Reed, is at this conference. Rather, it is that recent Southerners do not *want* to write like Cash. The tone now is leaner, more ironic, less evangelical. How many in this audience would urge an aspirant Southern author to model himself or (even more problematically) herself on Cash? He has gone the way of Thomas Wolfe. The South of Cash's prose is, for his successors, an interesting place to visit, but not somewhere they want to live.

The Burden of Southern Historiography: W. J. Cash and the Old South

ORVILLE VERNON BURTON

No history of the American South should be able to withstand an attack by Eugene Genovese on the Old South, C. Vann Woodward on the New South, and Joel Williamson on race relations. Indeed, how can any work on the southern mind survive an assault such as Michael O'Brien's:

> [It] ignores the colonial history of the South, scants the Old South, and misunderstands the New South. It barely mentions slavery and is more or less racist in its characterization of blacks. It neglects women, except as totemic objects of Southern mythology. It diminishes the existence of class conflict in the Old South and insists upon its relative impotence after the War. It misunderstands the nature of aristocracy. It overstresses both the unity and the continuity of Southern history. It has very little grasp of political history and has no coherent explanation for the Civil War. It is provincial in its emphasis both upon white males and upon the Piedmont of North Carolina as the archetypical South. It exaggerates the guilt of Southerners over slavery. It shows little understanding of the formal ideas of generations of Southern intellectuals. It overestimates the static quality of agricultural society.[1]

And most of us could add our own litany of protests to Cash's shortcomings.

This was not always the conventional wisdom. When written, *The Mind of the South* was considered a classic.[2] At its thirtieth anniversary Richard King wrote, "W.J. Cash's *The Mind of the South* remains the definitive book about the South. . . . it is the book with which serious students must come to terms if they are to

59

begin to understand the South."[3] Yet, even then it was already
becoming apparent that Cash had gone out of favor and could
muster few defenders. At least part of the rejection began with
a famous session at the Southern Historical Association annual
meeting in 1969. There C. Vann Woodward formally presented his
critique of Cash, published that year in *The New York Review of
Books* and revised for inclusion in 1971 in *American Counterpoint.*
Eugene Genovese, one of the commentators at the session, supported Woodward's criticisms and wondered "just how and why
the whole profession could be anesthetized for so long." The
following year Genovese presented his own critique in *The World
the Slaveholders Made.*[4] These two scholars have so influenced
historiographical developments in southern history that Cash has
remained out of favor. O'Brien summarized that, except for Bertram Wyatt-Brown, Cash has few disciples: "So the corpse is
riddled, and it would require a necromancer to piece together the
shattered bones, torn sinews, and spilled blood."[5]

I have been called many things in my life, but never a necromancer; nevertheless, I disagree with O'Brien. And although
Woodward (who incidentally encouraged readers not to ignore
Cash) warned that "[i]n America, historians, like politicians, are
out as soon as they are down,"[6] I think W. J. Cash at fifty, like
another flabby heavyweight, George Foreman, is making a come-
back.

C. Vann Woodward made us aware of the "burden of Southern
history," but scholars also face a burden of southern historiography
on the American South. In no other field are historical works so
shaped by previous writings.[7] In southern history, interpretative
works fit into patterns of focusing on another book within a historiographical tradition, thus, the continuing dependence and interest in W. J. Cash.[8]

Historians are currently taking another serious look at the man
whose book has remained important, whether as interpreter or
straw man, for references to the American South. In fact, in this
golden anniversary year, Cash is hot! A new major biography,

papers or sessions at several historical associations, and at least two conferences are devoted to Cash. Yet I have to notice that this renewed interest seems focused on Cash's postbellum South. An exciting conference at Wake Forest pretty much ignored Cash's antebellum South.[9] Debate and study of *The Mind of the South* center on Cash's theme of economic and social restructuring that took place in the South from 1877 to 1940, the rise of mills and mill towns, increasing urbanization, labor unrest, ossification of race and class relations. I too have been more intrigued with the postbellum South, at one with the white South I knew in the 1950s and 60s in the South Carolina piedmont near Cash's own home.

Nevertheless, Cash's ideas about the antebellum South remain crucial to his whole argument. As Cash wrote to Blanche Knopf: "My thesis is that the Southern mind represents a very definite culture, or attitude toward life, a heritage, from the Old South but greatly modified and extended by conscious and unconscious efforts over the last hundred years to protect itself from the en-croachments of three hostile factors: the Yankee mind, the Mod-ern Mind, and the Negro."[10] Cash's biographer, Bruce Clayton, states that Cash had two major contentions—both regarding the antebellum South. One was continuity of the Southern mind from the Old to the New South. The second was that the fabled plant-ers, the so called aristocrats, were nothing more than upstart farmers carving homesteads out of the frontier. These ideas have certainly affected subsequent historiography; even if historians ignore Cash, they still are playing off his ideas and insights.

The view scholars take of old South society and culture predeter-mines their assessment of causes of the Civil War. Furthermore, and most important for Cash, scholars cannot make assumptions about continuity and change based upon studies of the postbellum South only. The foundation of Cash's thesis concerning the conti-nuity of Southern history rests upon his characterization of the na-ture of antebellum southern society. As Cash so elegantly phrased it, "The South, one might say, is a tree with many age rings, with its limbs and trunk bent and twisted by all the winds of the years, but with its tap root in the Old South."[11] If Cash was wrong about what made the Old South distinctive, then his argument for the continuity of this Old South is fatally flawed.

In explaining the old South, Cash was at his best. In this section he was much more the journalist as historian rather than the journalist as observer, participant, and prophet. But before assessing Cash's interpretation of the antebellum South, certain perspectives need clarification. First, Cash virtually ignored women, African-Americans, Native Americans, and any influences of those cultures. Women, slaves, and freed African-Americans appeared only as white males perceived them. He did not deal whatsoever with the horror of rape and exploitation of black women. Some might try to rationalize that Cash was less overtly racist than many of his time. But W. E. B. DuBois had published *Souls of Black Folks* in 1903; C. Vann Woodward, only nine years younger than Cash, had published *Tom Watson* in 1938.[12] Cash's neglect of African-American influence in an analysis of the southern mind is not excusable. Also inexcusable are such pronouncements as "the Negro is notoriously one of the world's great romantics and one of the world's great hedonists. . . . in the main he is a creature of grandiloquent imagination, of facile emotion, and, above everything else under heaven, of enjoyment."[13] Yet, to truly understand Cash, this statement has to be read in the context of his argument that the relationship of the southern black and white was "nothing less than organic." While no less racist, and perhaps even more so, Cash juxtaposes the hedonist quotation beside the following quote: "Negro entered into white man as profoundly as white man entered into Negro—subtly influencing every gesture, every word, every motion and idea, every attitude."[14] What Cash wrote and thought he knew about blacks was actually to help him make his point about whites. When Cash talked about the southerners, he meant the white male southerner. Cash's greatest failing was his inability to understand that the South was inevitably the history of blacks as well as whites, and of blacks and whites interacting.

Second, the picture of this white southern male is a negative

one. To Cash this southerner was exceedingly simple and individualistic. Unrealistic, romantic, sentimental, and hedonistic, he also
was violent and intolerant of dissent. Cash managed to include a
few good traits, such as southern manners (the celebrated southern hospitality in which a southerner is polite to you up until the
point he is mad enough to kill you). White southern males were
loyal and duty bound; and, of course, the heralded Confederate
fighting man was a great warrior, but lousy soldier.

Bertram Wyatt-Brown has written eloquently about Cash and
the savage ideal and sense of honor.[15] Other scholars, notably Carl
Degler, who argued, "Race in the South, as in the nation, has
always overwhelmed class," also have accepted Cash's arguments
about racial solidarity and the proto-Dorian convention.[16] This
convention of white supremacy is pivotal to Cash's argument.
White unity on the race issue, like U. B. Phillips's theme of
southern history as the desire to keep the South a white man's
country, prevented class consciousness and unified white southerners in a defensive, intolerant, siege mentality.

Although he gave Turner's frontier thesis and its resulting democracy a negative twist, Cash appropriated the frontier thesis for
the South, and, of course, any frontier is limited in the number of
its aristocrats. Harvey Jackson has answered the charge that Cash's
thesis applied only to the Carolina piedmont; Jackson found evidence for Cash's planter in the black belt of Alabama and argues
that Cash's frontier analysis is sound.[17] Daniel Singal, the historian
of modernist thought in the South, has contended of *The Mind of
the South* that "Surely the great significance of that work lay in the
knockout blow it delivered to the Cavalier myth."[18] Cash's thesis
was quite an attack on the southerners' spurious aristocracy, that
those who became the elite were aggressive land-grabbers who
accumulated their wealth by fraud, created an economy based on
cotton, and used the political and economic structure to serve
themselves. Most white southerners, he argued, were rather
small farmers slowly clearing land in the wilderness. These poorer
whites, often kin to the planters, ranged from yeomen to neo-

frontiersmen, some of whom had been pushed off the land that could produce cotton. Cash underscored a paternalistic relationship between antebellum planters and yeomen and racism as the key to explaining why oppressed whites in the postbellum South did not challenge the economic domination of the southern ruling class. Cash maintained that the South retained its frontier mentality, emphasizing individualism and discouraging class conflict or government intervention or control of any kind. Moreover, he argued, whites could always strike out for a new life on a new frontier.

In many ways one could describe Cash's work as a book of stereotypes, and like all stereotypes, the book is reductionist; it homogenizes and simplifies. Yet, by depicting radical individualism in the context of close knit communities, Cash captured— even if he did not explain—the South's contradictions. One of the earliest settled parts of the United States, the South remained one of the nation's last frontiers. With an agrarian heritage and deep love for the land, the South from the Civil War on has had the highest proportion and the largest number of landless farmers. Justly renowned for its gentleness, the South's extravagant hospitality is only outdone by southern violence and lynchings. The South received a less diverse influx of immigrants than the rest of the nation, particularly after the American Revolution, yet its ethnic polarity is high. The South prides itself on its individuality, yet no region has been so cursed with conformity of thought and behavior. Only the South tried to leave the Union in open revolt, but today the South is the seat of superpatriotism. While New England was founded to be a religious "city upon a hill," the South was the most secular section of the nation during the colonial and revolutionary eras; now it contains the Bible belt, the seat of religious conservatism, as well as a languorous hedonism. Cash wrestled with these palpable contradictions, and therein lies the book's appeal.

Cash's influence on the subsequent historiography is ubiquitous. Wyatt-Brown has correctly pointed out that, like Woodward, "Cash is simply part of a southern scholar's intellectual frame of reference, and it is impossible to not deal with him."[19] Joel Williamson has contended, "After 1941 if anyone needed to say something, almost anything, about the Southern ethos, one simply cited Cash and moved confidently and comfortably on."[20] And Jack Roper has observed, "Cash's *The Mind of the South*, while itself deeply flawed, has stood up as a work that demands a response by anyone attempting to explain the South."[21]

Indeed, to read Cash is to read almost every scholar who has written on the American South. Many of Cash's undeveloped insights predated later interpretations: Francis Butler Simkins in *The South Old and New;* William R. Taylor's mirror portraits in *Cavalier and Yankee;*[22] Charles Sellers, Kenneth Stampp, and James McPherson on southern guilt; George Fredrickson's *herrenvolk democracy;* Grady McWhiney and Forest McDonald's Celtic heritage thesis; David Hackett Fischer's Celtic influences and folkways; Bertleson's Lazy South; Richard Maxwell Brown and Sheldon Hackney on violence; Steven Hahn on nonslaveholders' exclusion from economic development; David Brion Davis on slavery dying out in the rest of the world at the time the South embraced it; Joel Williamson's and Winthrop Jordan's Freudian analyses of southern racism; Mills Thornton on the diversity of opinion among southerners except on slavery; Drew Faust's argument that southern intellectuals had no acceptance or appreciation in the South; John McCardell on a distinct antebellum southern identity; Edmund Morgan on the colonial scarcity of labor and the development of racial slavery. Cash's "hell of a fellow" conjures up images from Rhys Isaac's dancing colonial Virginian to the more modern "Smokey and the Bandit," where Burt Reynolds tells Sally Fields that what he does best is "show off," or Billybobbus rednexus in Doug Marlett's Kudzu comic strip. How can one ever classify all these and many more on Cash and the South?[23]

Cash is referenced in two superb historiographical volumes, both essential reference items for Southern historians. For the literature before 1965, historians must read *Writing Southern*

History; for the literature from 1965 to 1983–85 (years covered vary
with each essay), *Interpreting Southern History* is a must.[24] That
Cash is still considered relevant in these books is an achievement
unto itself. Few books are referenced as many times and in as
many different subject areas as *Mind of the South.* (For those of
you who expected a quantitative analysis, references to the antebellum South are still about the same proportion, down slightly
from 37.5 to 33.3 percent for antebellum South from 1965 to 1985).
In the earlier historiographical study, Cash is more central to the
interpretations of the antebellum South. "Jeffersonian Democracy
and the Origins of Sectionalism" linked Cash with William E.
Dodd, Clement Eaton, Vernon Parrington, and others who argued
that Jeffersonian liberalism declined as Calhoun's conservative
doctrine replaced that ideology.[25] "Plantation and Farm: The Agricultural South," used Cash to illustrate historians' arguments for
the lack of class consciousness among planters and nonslave-
owners.[26] "The Mind of the Antebellum South" contrasted Cash to
Clement Eaton's *The Mind of the Old South,* which demonstrated
a "more diverse and impressively detailed" southern mind.[27]

   In the more recent work, Drew Faust lumped Cash together
with six other historians who oppose Genovese's view of the proslavery argument as a natural extension of slavery in an anti-
bourgeois premodern South.[28] Randolph Campbell, in discussing
Eugene Genovese, footnoted Wyatt-Brown's insight that while
Genovese earlier had critiqued Cash's argument that white southerners lacked class consciousness, by 1975 Genovese's description
of yeomen planter relationships had come to sound very much like
Cash.[29] Thus, the major interest in Cash today appears to center
around Cash's argument about the lack of class consciousness in
the old South; Eugene Genovese is the fulcrum on which Cash
now rests.

   In 1978 in the introduction to *Class, Conflict, and Consensus,* I
grouped the historiographical interpretations of the white antebellum South into four coherent groups. At that time, I thought
that the most popular view was that the southern economy was

essentially capitalistic, that planters were rational economic men who responded to market forces, and that Eugene Genovese was the foremost challenger of this dominant view.[30] Since 1978, Genovese's ideas of the American South have become the dominant interpretation. Writing from a sophisticated Marxist perspective, Genovese emphasizes the sources of irrationality inherent to any slave system, including the one that developed in the American South. His early work came close to characterizing the southern social system as flawed feudalism.[31] His later development of ideas on paternalism and reciprocity as the standard of human relationships adds further to his influential interpretation of the antebellum South. Joined by Elizabeth Fox-Genovese, who had argued that the southern household and patriarchal system differ from those elsewhere in the United States, Genovese has particularly influenced a younger generation of writers on the old South, such as Steven Hahn, who has carried forward Genovese's Gramscian and hegemonic interpretation to the upcountry Georgia yeomen, Cash's man at the center.[32]

Basically, Genovese and Cash have different emphasis in their investigations; whereas Cash focused on the relationship of blacks and whites,[33] Genovese admires the critique of the pro-slavery theorists who denounced the developing capitalist economy and society in the antebellum North. As an anti-capitalist, he is fascinated by the planters and their paternalism, which he sees as vastly preferable to the excesses of factory exploitation in the North at that time. By stressing the reciprocal obligations of "lord" and "servant," Genovese deemphasizes the inferiority paternalism ascribed to the slaves—a tendency consistent with Genovese's accentuating class over race.[34] He accepts the rhetoric of the planters and credits the high standards they set for themselves as revealing their quality. Cash, on the other hand, called the ideals of the slaveholders "romantic fictions."[35] Yet, several students have pointed out to me (usually after reading Wyatt-Brown) that a closer look at some important topics shows agreement, often missed, between the two authors. They are in basic agreement on slaveholders' hegemony, southern intellectual life, and southern personality. Genovese, as a Marxist, emphasizes social divisions and a growing class consciousness in the antebellum South, but he and Cash agree that nonslaveholders willingly followed the leadership of the slaveholders because of kinship ties and social interaction. Genovese includes an important Cash-like example of Joshua Venable (a poor farmer reminiscent of Cash's own Wash Venable) and his planter cousin Jefferson Venable. Genovese also develops the economic relationships among whites. He believes that a majority of planters helped their yeoman neighbors: bought their agricultural produce, ginned and marketed their small cotton crops, rented slaves to them, charged fair prices, and not only were not exploitive, but, in fact, saved them from exploitive merchants. In contrast, Cash thought only a minority of planters behaved this well. Genovese improves on Cash by differentiating, where Cash did not, between upcountry and plantation-belt yeomen. Both agree that the dominance of the planters resulted in a rigidly stratified system that in the long run was oppressive.

Cash curtly dismissed the possibility that the South had an intellectual tradition.[36] Genovese is less abrupt; his critique of George Fitzhugh is lengthy and sympathetic before he states his basic agreement with Cash. Genovese summarizes intellectualism in the antebellum South by saying that it failed to "produce a science or a art of its own."[37] (Now that Genovese and Fox-Genovese are writing on southern theologians, the next installment may more strongly defend the antebellum southern intellectual tradition.)[38]

On the character of the white southerner, both Genovese and Cash agree on honor, violence, graciousness, and impulsiveness. Yet, if there is so much agreement, why does Genovese debunk Cash? Genovese does not disagree with Cash about the Cavalier Myth; he claims that by 1830 the myth had become reality. Genovese, furthermore, points out that all aristocracies are self-made. Therefore he takes the planters at their word that they created and believed in a distinct world view that saw slavery as a positive good.

Genovese blames Cash for disseminating the idea that planters had a guilt complex. Cash wrote that the Old South "was a society beset by the specters of defeat, of shame, of guilt . . . a society driven by the need . . . to justify itself in its own eyes and in those of the world." This is unacceptable to Genovese, and the scholarly community is divided on the guilt thesis.[39]

Today, James Oakes is the leading challenger of Genovese's interpretation of the Old South. Oakes, in the tradition of his mentor, Kenneth Stampp, is the leading proponent of the planter capitalist school.[40] In *The Ruling Race*, James Oakes scrutinizes the southern slaveholding class and draws attention to the majority of small and middle-class masters as opposed to large planters. Like Cash,[41] Oakes believes planters craved wealth; Oakes depicts the southern slaveowners as a highly acquisitive, capitalistic class characterized by great social and physical mobility. The masters' concern for economic advancement resulted in harsh conditions for the slaves. The slaveowners subscribed to an egalitarian and democratic ethos based on white supremacy. Oakes finds paternalism and capitalistic liberalism mutually exclusive; he rejects Genovese's paternalistic interpretation of slavery.

Cash argued that a true southern "aristocracy" could only develop in the oldest parts of the South. He located this small elite of planters in tidewater Virginia, the surroundings of New Orleans, and in parts of the Carolina and Georgia lowcountry stretching from Georgetown to Charleston and Savannah. Only this elite and the very best of the planters in the younger parts of the South showed the paternalistic attitude of feudal lords towards their slaves.[42] Oakes follows Cash's argument. Oakes suggests that only a few masters pursued paternalistic ideals. These slaveholders concentrated in the oldest settled regions, the "perimeter," of the South. In other parts of the South, paternalists were found mostly among masters with a military background and among former New Englanders of federalist convictions. Ironically, however, whereas both Cash and Genovese view the South as distinct, Oakes discounts significant differences in the political and social principles, or as one student called it, "mind-sets" of North and South.[43] Oakes sees the North and South as sharing the same political heritage—except that slavery muddled it somewhat in the South. Oakes strongly supports Cash's ideas about lack of class consciousness in social mobility and marriage patterns. Edward Ayers, in a recent review of Oakes's latest book, noted about the Genoveses and Oakes: "as both sides have more fully articulated their positions, some of the distinctions between them have begun to blur."[44] This is true as well for the work of Wyatt-Brown and Genovese, although Wyatt-Brown is explicitly drawing upon Cash for a model. And thus it is with all historical debate: to reduce a given argument to simple statements is to rob it of its complexity.

Community studies and an interest in republican political ideology have breathed new life into an interpretation that developed at about the time that Cash wrote. Frank Owsley, one of the agrarians of whom Cash disapproved, and Harriet Owsley and their students were deemphasizing the influence of both planters and slaves; instead they viewed southern society as shaped by the yeomen. Owsley and his students, unlike Cash, believed the frontier experience had a beneficial influence on democracy, much like that Turner had set out in his famous thesis. Similar to Cash, Owsley denied any class conflict among antebellum whites.[45] In their ongoing reinterpretation of southern herdsmen, Forrest McDonald and Grady McWhiney reinforce both Owsley's and Cash's conviction of the importance of the southern plain folk. Arguing that Celtic ancestry bequeathed a spirit of independence, clannishness, and racism, McDonald and McWhiney argue that nonplanter whites had no class consciousness.[46] A number of scholars have used social science techniques and local studies as microcosms and have generally emphasized, like Cash and Owsley, the importance of the "man at the center." In terms of social structure and family, scholars have found that Cash's emphasis on family and kin networks has been upheld.[47] In addition, a number of studies have applied republicanism to the South, and these studies have focused on the southern plain folk. If they found class issues, these scholars have generally argued that southerners found other ways to express those interests than through traditional class conflict. Cash's conundrum of why nonslaveholding whites would wage a Civil War for slavery's preservation takes on new meaning in the context of republican political theory.[48] Interestingly, however, some of the recent works that emphasize republican theory likewise emphasize southern whites and therefore fall prey to the same criticism that has been levied at Cash; they do not look at black southerners, nor do they acknowledge racism in the South.[49]

Somewhat similar to Owsley and Cash, David M. Potter advances yet another interpretation of the Old South when he categorizes the region as a "folk culture." Potter notes the persistence of cultural patterns in the South in which "relations between the land and the people remained more direct and more primal" than in industrial cultures, and patterns "retained a personalism in the relationships between man and man which industrial culture lacks." Inspired by anthropological insights, Potter sounds much like W. J. Cash who described the Southerner as "a direct product of the soil" and argued that "doctrines of race served to minimize the potentially serious economic divisions between slaveholders and nonslaveholders."[50] Potter's emphasis on family and community suggests local studies, but also Wyatt-Brown's explanation of the antebellum southern society as a "family-centered, particularistic, ascriptive culture." Recommending a typology to understand the American South, Wyatt-Brown, like Cash, tries to show "how all parts of southern society functioned to form a social whole." Like Cash, he emphasizes continuity, arguing that "the main thrust of southern life was the preservation of its traditions."[51] With the emphasis on what holds society together, Wyatt-Brown has found a white solidarity very similar to Cash's proto Dorian convention. Yet, all interpretations that downplay class conflict in the South, including Cash's, are consistent with Eugene Genovese's argument that local aristocrats' paternalism muted friction.

The debate on Cash and class conflict has enjoyed a long tradition. Newer is the currently thriving area of southern intellectual history.[52] Discussion of intellectual history brings up a dilemma for any reviewer of W. J. Cash's *The Mind of the South*, that is defining the term *mind*. Although it is most easily comprehended when it refers to one individual such as *The Mind of Frederick Douglass*,[53] historians successfully have applied the term to groups of people who have similar thought patterns and beliefs or to a particular epoch or region, such as Perry Miller's *The New England Mind*, Joseph Dorfman's *The Economic Mind in American Civilization*, Norman Pollack's *Populist Mind*, Henry Steele Commanger's *American Mind*, Arthur K. Moore's *Frontier Mind*, and Rush Welter's *The Mind of America, 1820–1860*.[54] Southern historians have particularly benefitted from Lewis P. Simpson's *Mind of the American Civil War* and Clement Eaton's *Mind of the Old South*.[55] Some of these works study the "average" mind, but the books generally refer to intellectual history and the recounting of intellectual accomplishments of the regions. Woodward criticized Cash because *Mind* was not intellectual history and suggested different titles—Temperament, Feelings, Mindlessness. O'Brien faulted Cash as a detriment to southern intellectual history and referred to "*Zeitgeist*" and "the Southern idea." Dewey Grantham described it as "character," Richard King as "attitudes and feeling." Several years later King wrote that Cash's "mind or perhaps better 'spirit' *(Geist)* was inseparable from social context."[56]

Some of these attempts to rename Cash are reflected in the two encyclopedias of the American South. Both the *Encyclopedia of Southern History* (1979) and the *Encyclopedia of Southern Culture* (1989) have one article on Cash, but whereas *History* has three other references to Cash, *Culture* has no fewer than thirty-eight.[57] *Writing Southern History* (1965) includes two essays on the "Mind" of the South, but *Interpreting Southern History* (1985) has none. The earlier volumes reflect the decline in interest in traditional intellectual history from the 1970s through the mid-1980s and also help explain the neglect of Cash. But the *Encyclopedia of Southern Culture* with its many citations of Cash shows another context in which mind can be understood.

Cash himself was not concerned with traditional intellectual history, but instead was interested in a "fairly definite mental pattern, associated with a fairly definite social pattern—a complex of established relationships and habits of thought, sentiments, prejudices, standards and values, and associations of ideas, which, if it is not common strictly to every group of white people in the South, is still common in one appreciable measure or another." Cash could not have read E. Le Roy Ladurie's *Montaillou,* but Cash's *Mind* was what we today think of as Mentalité.[58] Mentalité, a commonly shared cultural outlook of a social class or ethnic community (here I think of George Tindall's ethnic southerners), is in part a reaction to the common environment and economic and political structures. Somewhat disconcerting to historians, mentalité appears to be ahistorical. It emphasizes culture, continuities, and patterns; it deemphasizes change.

Some early reviewers hinted that Cash was breaking new ground with *Mind.* Agrarian critic Donald Davidson noted "His work is not of the substance, but of the spirit. He is writing poetically and should be answered poetically."[59] More recently, sociologist John Shelton Reed has suggested, more for the contemporary and modern South, but perhaps with equal insight into the antebellum period, that dismissing journalists' works as impressionistic is a mistake, "mere academic snobbery." Reed believes that Cash was "one of the greatest of the journalists" whose *Mind of the South* "at its best is brilliant and sensitive ethnography."[60] Ray Mathis wrote, "The profession's analytic side is repulsed by the book's simplifications, but on the other hand, historians' continuing penchant for the synthetic or religious function has not permitted *The Mind of the South* to be discarded."[61] It has certainly not been discarded; the kind of cultural history that Cash wrote is making a tremendous impact at this very time.[62]

The Mind of the South, as you might know, is categorized as sociology not history. Now, a sociologist's nightmare is a fact that destroys a theory. At the University of Illinois, I was officially appointed to the sociology department as well as history, so I wanted to find out the difference between sociologists and historians. After intensive research I concluded that a sociologist is simply someone who writes about ideas without doing the historical research and work. A historian, on the other hand, is someone who does the research and work without the ideas. Cash, telling about the South, was full of ideas, but we historians must provide the facts and the details.[63]

We need, for instance, more details on environmental studies. Cash was influenced by the environmental determinism of his day when he noted the emotional and sensual perspective of the South. In the 1930s the idea that climate influenced intellectual and physical activity was a popular one; and, according to then prevailing theories, people's brains functioned best when the outdoor temperature was about 40 degrees Fahrenheit. Environmental determinists optimistically predicted great things for Alaska. Of course, no one knew that southerners, especially so many Texans, would migrate to Alaska. (The folks I worked with in Daniel Construction Company headed off to work on the Alaska pipeline; and, true to Cash's frontier thesis, many began life anew on that frontier.) In the South, however, intellectual energy was thought to be at a minimum. In 1942 (the year after Cash's book was published), a book of advice was given to all New Deal Work Progress Administration employees as they traveled throughout the United States. In one sequence, Howard Martin of Illinois had this to say about his foray into the South: "In plain English, you get lazy. I noticed it. The first two weeks I was there I ate oranges with enthusiasm. Then I got too tired to peel an orange and always bought tangerines. The skins pull off with about two motions. Then I got too lazy to handle the tangerines, and ate kumquats the rest of my stay."[64] What more can one say?

Cash's interest in the environment, folklore, and folkways has again come before the public in such work as David Hackett

Fischer's *Albion's Seed*. With interdisciplinary insights, this book seems to agree fully with Cash's Celtic roots thesis.[65] Another environmental and cultural geography study, less well known, is Terry Jordan and Matti Kaups's *American Backwoods Frontier*, which traces the heritage of the backcountry, the Carolina piedmont that Cash wrote about, not to the Celts, but to Finland! Jordan argues that the Finns through the Swedes in the Delaware Valley had "first effective settlement," a cultural phenomenon that shaped the attitudes of latecomers. (Actually, Jordan presents an excellent argument on the importance of contact and mixing with indigenous Americans and makes clear the need for more study.)[66] Partly in jest, one cannot help but think that with Jordan's book we will have to contend with indigenous Americans, the Celts, now the Finns and Swedes, and who all else?

Seriously though, historians of the American South can benefit from geography, folklore, and other disciplines. The impact of various ethnic groups, especially those groups that settled together in communities, still needs to be studied. Daniel C. Littlefield's identifying, mapping, and plotting of ethnic origins of Africans in the American South is an important model for the study of other ethnic groups in unraveling the mystery of the culture and folkways of the American South.[67] The colonial South, with the exception of the Chesapeake, has never received the intense scrutiny in community studies that benefitted our understanding of New England and the middle colonies. Studies of spatial mobility and persistence to determine who moved, who stayed, and who became the leaders of various communities still need to be done. Issues of kinship, inheritance, intermarriage among planter and yeomen families, and endogenous marriage all need to be carefully investigated. Most issues of the new social history have not yet been fully explored, and, even with the exciting work being done in women's history, as well as the interest in the urban South, we have only scratched the surface.

With so much interest in class among scholars today and with Barbara Fields's warning that historians have not studied racism historically, scholars of the antebellum South need to find ways to explore systematically the factors that constitute racism and the quantitative and qualitative changes over time. It may be that Cash's proto Dorian convention has a "transhistorical, almost metaphysical, status that removes it from all possibility of analysis and understanding,"[68] but scholars must attempt it nonetheless. Models of cultural domination that scholars of literature are now debating might be useful in approaching racism and class, as well as for further exploring one of Cash's truest insights, the defensive reactions of the South to the perceived threats of the outside, especially the Yankee after the 1820s. Cash's frontier and the southerner resemble the anthropologist's "other," and studies of the literature of the period just might present the image of the white southerner not as the romantic noble savage, but as more the product of the "wild," much like Cash's suggestion that the frontier entered into the being of the white southerner.

Despite the huge literature already written on the Old South, we do not have agreement on the nature of the society itself, even on basic definitions of capitalism, speculators, or aristocracy. Much of our social history has been based on limited understanding of sociological theory. Scholars still lack carefully developed criteria to define social or interest groups in the South. Studies of economic development make clear that the problem is not interpreting isolated economic data, but assessing the impact of economic issues on the development of society.[69] The effect of economic development on the South remains controversial. While labor and economic historians have provided us with new insights into the development of postbellum textile mills, the workers themselves, and the emergent town middle class, we need work on the nascent industrial development of the antebellum South, and especially we need the insights of labor historians concerning the rural labor force.

Also desperately in need of study is the Southern legal system, both the actual laws and the way people reacted to them. Authority and violence have been contradictory themes in the South.

Southerners have been viewed often as violent and outside the law, but in contrast to this stereotype, both Wyatt-Brown and Edward Ayers argue that one of the first things the frontiersmen built was a courthouse, the very symbol of authority.[70] We need to understand which groups in the society benefitted from the interpretation and implementation of law. Especially in relation to Cash, the law is a gauge of class interests.[71]

Although Cash's stereotype of the hedonist/Puritan rings true, the religious side of the South received scant treatment in *The Mind of the South*. Scholars of the antebellum South are now beginning to take religion seriously in some very exciting work, exploring what religion meant to black, white, and indigenous peoples in the American South, and how that meaning changed with the development of the plantation society over time.[72]

Although the Civil War and Reconstruction are both somewhat outside the scope of this essay, it is worth noting that Cash's depiction of those periods was so stereotypical of his period and so abominable that scholars have not deigned to debate his interpretations. The Civil War and Reconstruction, including the homefront to the battlefield, speak to class and race, as well as to both the Old and the New South. We do not even know who sacrificed what, who fought, who stayed the entire four years, who deserted, who managed through political connections to serve in the relatively safe state home guards. Even southern casualty rates are estimates based upon Union casualty estimates. Where better to understand a society than in the crucible of war? What happened to the southern commitment to individualism and localism in those four years, and what does that tell us about the antebellum society from which the Confederacy emerged? Indeed, instead of the dichotomy of change or continuity, scholars need to separate out those things that persevered, such as family and landownership, and those that changed, such as black and white southerners' world views. George Rable recently eschewed the dichotomy of continuity or change as too simplistic; the Civil War, he writes, wrought "change without change."[73]

While it is fun telling others what they should be researching, this specific charge would make a book unto itself, and ultimately, each generation must write its own history. Thus every topic is open to new questions and new methods of investigation, if not synthesis. Cash's essay resurrects the crucial question for historians of the South: Does a South exist anymore, or did it ever, as a distinct culture and society? While the South is generally considered a homogeneous region, an increasing number of regional and local studies suggest significant differences *within* the South. Moreover, themes discussed in Cash, and in this essay—planters, plain folk, slavery, secession, women, religion, as well as class, racism, sexism, paternalism, hegemony, honor, and violence— may or may not be peculiar to the South.

Ultimately, a "mind of the South" makes sense only in the comparative context of differences from a "mind of the United States." Few Southern historians have anchored a perspective beyond the South to explain how the South differs from the non-South. For future study we need to compare South and non-South over time.[74]

Over the years there has been a major turnaround in my students' reaction to Cash and the image of the American South. When the southern civil rights movement was still in the public memory, students agreed with Cash's assessment of the South as the nation's depository of evil qua racism. Students today, and the general public, have the opposite perception of both the South and the nation.[75] Recently, a black leader in my community made the following comment: "Champaign is unique in that it is unable to come to grips with the racial tensions in the city. . . . It is unable to come to grips and realize it could elect a black man for its mayor." He continued, "If it was a Southern city, it would be more willing to deal with this racism."[76] Cash gives the impression that racism is an exclusively southern problem, when in reality the racist mind of the South was, and increasingly is, the mind of the nation.

In conclusion, I would like to quote C. Vann Woodward on

Cash. "The man really had something to say, which is more than most, and he said it with passion and conviction and with style. Essentially what he had to say is something every historian eventually finds himself trying to say (always risking exaggeration) at some stage about every great historical subject. And that is that in spite of the revolution—any revolution—the English remain English, the French remain French, ... That was really what Cash, at his best, was saying about Southerners, and he said it better than anybody ever has—only he rather overdid the thing." [77]

Commentary / Don H. Doyle

A paper by Vernon Burton, or even a conversation with him, is always an experience I take delight in. At times I feel like I am listening to one of those apocryphal "hell uv a fella" front-porch philosophers he talks about in upcountry South Carolina, whose stories tumble forth like a mountain stream, moving unpredictably and recklessly at times through shoals and over waterfalls and then spread out grandiloquently to flood a huge expanse of land.

His main purpose in this paper is to assist in what he sees as a rehabilitation of a once revered guide who inspired him and others when he was a neophyte about to enter the profession of history. Cash's reputation and standing in the profession, he fears, has now fallen on hard times as intellectual winds have shifted and new political values have changed the way we read Cash, making what once seemed fresh, provocative, iconoclastic, and wise to seem now narrow, reactionary, offensive, or, worse, just irrelevant.

I, too, read Cash in one of my first graduate seminars in American history, with George Fredrickson, at Northwestern. It was one of those classics that one just had to read to lay a foundation for further study in the history of the South. It was a book that I returned to frequently over the years, as often to argue with as to find support for whatever point I was dwelling on. Last year I took my old copy from Fredrickson's seminar, now yellowed and falling apart, over to Rome, Italy, with me during a six-month tour as a Fulbright lecturer. It was one of the few books I brought to consult and, perhaps, assign in connection with a course I taught at the University of Rome on the history of the South and Faulkner's fiction. I realized just last week when I was madly rummaging through packed boxes looking for my old copy of Cash that I had left it behind with some graduate students at the University of Rome who were hungry for books in southern history. As I've thought about Cash these last few days I've wondered whether this is not the single most appropriate book for a foreigner to read about the South; it is at least arguable that it is, which, in itself, may justify the time we are devoting here to this book.[1]

Had Cash made a similar impact in the field of literary criticism (or perhaps some other field in the humanities) it is likely some of us would be talking about this book as belonging to "the canon" of scholarship in our discipline—the revered, sanctified, and essential articles of faith or dogma for all those who enter our profession, or at least the sub-field of southern history. Vernon Burton, according to his testimony, first saw the light and was converted to his calling because of the teachings of St. Wilbur—or, as he tells it, initially in reaction to his teachings. He is naturally concerned that this prophet, whose canonization was—just twenty years ago—secure and beyond reproach, has been rejected, censured, even excommunicated by a new crowd with new standards for canonization in Clio's reformed and enlightened church.

What is most disturbing to this believer is that the new tests by which St. Wilbur has been examined and found wanting are not heretical doctrines, but ones that he, Vernon Burton, also espouses. They are that African Americans and women must be included in the history of the South, and that the discrimination and oppression, which they and poor white male southerners suffered, ought to be, at least, acknowledged, along with the contributions each made to southern history and culture.

Vernon Burton does not answer Cash's censurers by making excuses for his blind spots or prejudices—these were "inexcusable," he admits. Other white scholars were enlightened on the issue of race, at least, even in those benighted times in the South. Cash's sins of *commission* is what he says about blacks were more egregious than his sins of *omission* with regard to women, but still inexcusable. If Cash is in error on race and gender, his position on class is more difficult to pass judgment on. Cash, is said to have negative views of white male southerners, but his argument that poor whites did not harbor class resentments against the wealthy planters is not entirely at odds with at least some of the views about planter class hegemony that remain afloat in contemporary scholarship.

Whatever inexcusable blind spots and prejudices must be admitted, and however these may have marred the final product, Vernon Burton argues, Cash deserves a place in the pantheon of luminaries because of the many disciples who have followed in his path. That many of these followers are indebted to Cash without even realizing, let alone acknowledging, their debt makes it all the more important that someone else point out the lines of persuasion. In his effort to demonstrate the pervasive influence of Cash's book on the decades of historical writing over the past half century, the links between Cash and a large and assorted menagerie of historians and research subjects become, I sometimes felt, strained and twisted. "Cash's influence on the subsequent historiography is ubiquitous," he opens his argument. "Indeed, to read Cash is to read almost every scholar who has written on the American South," he goes on. When I got through reading this paper and its footnotes, I wondered if there had been anything written on the South that did *not* owe credit to Wilbur J. Cash for its inspiration or influence. I would say of Burton's argument here what Woodward said of Cash's, that he has a valid point to make about Cash's book as an influence in popular and scholarly understanding of the South over the past half century, but by claiming so much influence for Cash on subsequent research and writing I fear he "rather overdid the thing."

There are two problems with his argument for Cash's influence:

For one, though other historians have written about subjects Cash wrote about, it does not follow that Cash's book inspired, influenced, or in any way affected their thinking. Eugene Genovese, James Oakes, Frank Owsley, Forrest McDonald and Grady McWhiney—to recall just a few who are said to have followed in Cash's path—are indeed dealing in different ways with issues that Cash examined (the nature of the planter class, the plain folk), but I am not convinced that Cash is the starting point for their work, or that Cash is the reference to which each historian writing on these and other issues had to come to terms with before saying anything new.

Where Cash seems to be cited most often these days is in the tireless discussion of the continuity or discontinuity of southern history, and more specifically on matters dealing with southern social and political leadership. But most of the contributions to this debate draw on empirical evidence, usually from geographically focused case studies, and these do not require refutation or even reference to Cash's impressionistic or anecdotal case for continuity, except for the obligatory graceful quote about the hooves of Jeb Stuart's cavalry pounding behind the rumble of textile mills.

Another problem with Vernon Burton's argument about Cash's influence is that not every subject or theme brought up in Cash's book was original with him. Owsley and the Vanderbilt school had been working on studies of the plain folk in the 1930s, well before Cash placed his "man at the center" before readers. As for Cash's interpretation of the planter class, I suspect he owed much to southern writers of fiction in the 1930s. William Faulkner's novel, *Absalom, Absalom!*, published in 1936, depicted a memorable antagonist, Thomas Sutpen, who came from poor white stock in Virginia and arrived in Yoknapatawpha with wealth of questionable origin in slaves and gold coin. There on the Mississippi frontier he "tore violently" from the land a big house and plantation upon which to found his would-be dynasty. Margaret Mitchell's version of this ambitious planter, in the character of Scarlet O'Hara's father, Gerald O'Hara, certainly had made a popular impression on readers and movie viewers a few years before Cash's book was published. But there were also several historians whose work on the planters and yeomen provided material for Cash to build upon. U.B. Phillips was strongly influenced by Frederick Jackson Turner's ideas on the centrality of the frontier to America's history and had published his books on *American Negro Slavery* in 1918 and *Life and Labor in the Old South* in 1929, well in advance of Cash's book. William E. Dodd, *The Cotton Kingdom* 1919, Thomas Jefferson Wertenbaker, *First Americans* 1927, and others had also been at work for some time analyzing the social structure of the Old South, the role of the yeomen, the nature of the planter class, and other subjects that Cash would take up.

What was original about Cash was a coherent synthesis delivered with a felicitous style and vivid anecdotes and with a powerful, provocative argument. His book captured the attention of a much wider audience than most professional historians were capable of reaching. An essayist or journalist like Cash can often carry off this trick of synthesizing and interpreting history for a large audience precisely because they ignore the evidence that historians insist upon, the very "details" that Vernon Burton is calling for in his plea for more research along the path that Cash trod.

What was also original with Cash was his acerbic wit and his iconoclastic attack on so many of the self-serving myths with which southerners had enshrouded their past. Both virtues made Cash more influential among lay readers and impressionable students than among historians, I suspect. In the end, Cash's book must be understood not as history or sociology, but as social criticism.

It was that bold, irreverent tone of Cash's book that I suppose must have aroused the young Vernon Burton years ago, and it is the same style and tone that can—he argues—still provoke undergraduate students today. This brings me to another of Vernon Burton's claims regarding Cash's value as a teaching device—not only as a straw man to excite opposition, but also as a highly relevant guide to the South, a provocative introduction to its history and sociology. This position is advanced as something of a corollary to the argument for Cash's lasting impact on historical scholarship. I have assigned chapters of Cash to students in a seminar on southern history and Faulkner, and, of course, I've borrowed from him while preparing lectures, but my experience with student reactions is too limited to say much about Cash as a teaching device for today's students. I was impressed with the comment of my colleague, David Carlton, who teaches southern history at Vanderbilt and uses Cash more frequently:

> My experience at teaching Cash leads me to think he's starting to get decidedly musty in the eyes of my freshmen, who simply don't get bowled over by him the way I was when I first read him as a college freshman. His Menckenesque picture of an oppressive, obscurantist, small-town South, however attractive to small-town intellectuals like myself, hardly jibes with the urban-suburban world of multiple 'life-styles' that these kids inherit; the ghosts of racism are pretty invisible to people who are comfortable with class. When you think the South is one big suburb (and Tara, as the *New York Times* pointed out last Thursday, looks in most eyes far more like an affluent suburban dwelling than it does like anything Margaret Mitchell actually had in mind), Cash's tales of millhands and small-town Babbits scarcely seem 'southern' at all.

He added that the book may work in Illinois "because he [Vernon Burton] teaches people who'd be disappointed if the South weren't exotic; I teach people who are embarrassed by it, and prefer the South to be something more upscale."

As I thought about this last comment it occurred to me that this may be a good argument for continuing to use Cash; that is, to remind young, affluent southerners like those we teach at Vanderbilt and other colleges across this region, that the South was not always one big affluent suburb—if they think it is now. It may be worth reminding our students that one of the forces for change over the past half century that has brought such remarkable change to this region, for better and for worse, was Cash's book, a book that assailed the mind of the South as it existed in the past and, in the process, assailed the minds of its readers.

"So Much for the Civil War": Cash and Continuity in Southern History

JAMES L. ROARK

Like love and marriage, a horse and carriage, Cash and continuity go together. Although you can have one without the other, no one has proclaimed the South's unbroken past and its unyielding folk mind more insistently than Jack Cash. So smoothly does his Old South flow across the nineteenth century and into the twentieth that he insists that the term "New South" is a misnomer. In reality, there is only "one South," he argues. "The extent of the change and the break between the Old South that was and the South of our time," Cash declared Twain-like a half century ago, "has been vastly exaggerated."[1]

I must admit that when I first heard my assignment for this conference my immediate thought was to slip this noose. Change and continuity, continuity and change—how shopworn and tired a formulation. Fifty years after Cash, sophisticated historians surely could frame analysis of the Southern experience more subtly and imaginatively. Hadn't the debate grown sterile, even simpleminded: rupture or persistence—choose one. My friend and colleague Dan T. Carter concluded several years ago that it might "be better to forget the whole dichotomy of change and continuity except as a mental filing system for temporarily arranging historical data in our minds."[2] Clearly, the task requires a more fine-grained and discriminating analysis, one that identifies precisely what changed and precisely what remained the same.

But, no. Southern historians seem psychologically disposed to argue one way or the other. Besides, Jack Cash made a choice, and coming to grips with him requires that we choose. Cash's gift was the big picture and the *longue duree,* together with a clear point of view. Thus, at the risk of matching Cash hyperbole for hyperbole, of slipping back into a kind of Manichaean "either-or" historiography, and, most importantly, of irritating some who have argued continuity more persuasively than Jack Cash, let me stake out my position among the discontinuitarians.

The size of this band has risen and fallen and risen again since the 1951 publication of C. Vann Woodward's *Origins of the New South,* which still reigns as the sovereign text of discontinuity. The Civil War and Reconstruction meant a sharp break in Southern history, Woodward argues. Defeat and emancipation destroyed one society and gave birth to a new one. While Redemption ended the radical experiment of Reconstruction, it did not restore to power a reactionary planter elite. Instead, Redemption marked "a new phase of the revolutionary process begun in 1865. Only in a limited sense can it be properly called a 'counter-revolution.'" Redeemers were new men with new ideas who "laid the lasting foundations in matters of race, politics, economics and law for the modern South."[3]

During the late 1960s and 1970s, advocates of rupture in the Southern past were on the defensive. Disappointed in the aftermath of the civil rights movement and painfully aware of the sticking power of what Cash called the "proto-dorian" consensus and the "savage ideal," historians joined the North Carolina journalist in questioning whether anything of significance had changed in the South since the early nineteenth century. Liberals and radicals clasped hands with conservatives and insisted that the institutions and values of the Old South retained their vitality in the New. To be sure, they disagreed about the worth of the Southern tradition, but they united in proclaiming the tradition's unbrokenness.

In the 1980s the pendulum of historical opinion began to swing back. Critical perspectives changed again, and historians began to measure just how far the South had travelled, rather than how far it had to go. Under the assault, continuity's defenders fell back.

Today, Woodward remains where he has been for more than 40 years—at the head of the attack—but at his side are younger warriors—the most prominent of whom are James McPherson and Eric Foner, whose interpretations of the Civil War and Reconstruction as revolutionary experiences, while not uncontested, now hold the high ground in our historical understanding.[4]

Cash's case for continuity rests largely on the persuasiveness of Book Two, his analysis of the years from 1860 to 1890. His Civil War, unlike the one the South actually experienced, is very brief. It takes just a few pages in a book that runs to more than four hundred pages. The reader hardly has a chance to get comfortable when Cash announces—"So much for the Civil War"—and turns to an only slightly more extended discussion of Reconstruction, the chief effect of which, he says, was "to hammer home the war's work. . . ."[5]

At first glance, Cash appears to argue that the war's work was revolution, for he draws a vivid picture of a ravaged landscape and a decimated social and economic order. Conditions and institutions antebellum Southerners considered "primary" had "vanished," he says. Rather than self-defeating concessions, however, Cash's images of chaos and destruction amount to little more than a literary device. His strategy is to sketch what appears to be revolutionary upheaval, then to explain why appearances are so deceiving. White Southerners emerged from the war, he argues, fiercely determined "to hold fast to their own, to maintain their divergences, to remain what they had been and were." The Yankees, enraged by the South's unwillingness to change, vowed to finish the job. Unscrupulous carpetbaggers, unsavory scalawags, and laughable freedmen connived to fasten the Republican party and its policies on the South. But their foolish meddling only succeeded in making the Southern mind "one of the most solidly established, one of the least *reconstructible* ever developed."[6]

Cash insisted that not a single vital feature of Southern culture took a direct hit. The romanticism and sentimentality, the ethics of leisure and hedonism, the conflicted religiosity, the weakness for rhetoric and disposition to violence, the individualism and social irresponsibility, the political complacency, the paternalism and upper-class control, the "savage ideal" and "proto-dorian" consensus—they all survived intact, indeed, strengthened. The war disciplined rather than debilitated what Cash calls "the ancient pattern." Under the whip of adversity, Southerners got right again with their primitive faith, the "supernatural and Apocalyptic." Years of trauma etched even more deeply the lines of "Southern unreality." Nostalgia and sentimentality reigned, the legend of the Old South blossomed, and the entire region slipped into "Cloud-Cuckoo Land." Yankee devastation restored a primitive economic frontier which once again rewarded pioneer virtues—gouging, cheating, and a single-minded devotion to business. Sloughing off the thin skin of gentility, planters reembraced their "old, primary, simple, back-country heritage" of rugged, rapacious individualism. The "Virginians"—Cash's term for the region's genuine aristocrats—fell by the wayside, but most of the antebellum elite avoided tumbling out of the ruling class.[7]

According to Cash, the war and its aftermath restored social solidarity and revived upper-class hegemony. Wartime service in the military reinforced both the common man's "habits of following and of obedience" and the gentry's right of command. White supremacy, moreover, ran like a skewer through the various classes of whites. The region's first social principle remained the conviction that it would remain "a world in which the Negro was still 'mud-sill,' and in which a white man, any white man, was in some sense a master." Hypnotic fixation on race helped dissolve old class distinctions and to weld common whites to the ruling class. As a consequence, the Democratic party drifted even farther from class realities and the plight of the masses.[8]

Nevertheless, Cash explains, economic changes still threatened traditional social and political relations. Yeoman whites fell into the maw of the cotton economy. The descent into tenancy and share-cropping signaled "an end for these people of the independence and self-sufficiency, the freedom from direct exploitation and servitude, which had been so primary for the preservation and growth of the old frontier individualism, for the suppression of class feeling, and the binding of the South into its extraordinary unity of purpose and outlook." Planters wrestled with problems of their own—among them, Cash tells us, the breakup of the great plantations—but they assumed responsibility for their white tenants and croppers, fashioning what Cash dubs "genuine paternalism." Common whites recognized that the gentry had cushioned their fall, and they were grateful. In the rural South, therefore, "the old scale of values, so far from being overturned by the new conditions, would be once more strengthened and confirmed."⁹

But plantations could absorb only so many whites. To provide the others with a "sanctuary" that offered both employment and protection from equality with blacks, the elite ("old Confederate captains for the most part") launched the cotton mill campaign. On the surface a capitulation to Yankee civilization and "Progress," the movement in reality "flowed straight out of that past and constituted in a real sense an emanation from the will to maintain the South in its essential integrity." It was only a "revolution in tactics," Cash claims, a zigging and zagging compelled by new economic and social circumstances. The plantation origins of the mill owners, the paternalistic ethos of the mill villages, and the rural background of mill workers assured that the factories and towns that rose in the Piedmont were old wine in new wine skins. Factories and cities would eventually modernize the Southern mind, Cash concedes, but by 1940 modernity had not yet subverted "the ancient social order."¹⁰

Sealing it all and placing it almost beyond remedy was the "savage ideal," that rage for conformity that "paralyzed Southern culture at its root." What little tolerance the Old South had nurtured withered and died as Southerners declared war on Yankee ideas. In essence, Cash says, the South had "drawn a ring about itself, as narrowly coincidental as might be with the past." So effective was the insulation that "Southerners in 1900 would see the world in much the same terms in which their fathers had seen

it in 1830. . . . ." Thus, he concludes, the Yankee victory in the war
was "almost entirely illusory," the South's adoption of Yankee
"Progress" merely a "new charge at Gettysburg."[11]

At about this point in Cash's argument, you may remember,
Woodward threw up his hands and cried: "How could he? How
could any historian?"[12] Indeed, how could Cash believe that the
upheavals and eruptions that punctuated Southern history from
secession in 1860 to the Mississippi Plan in 1890 were merely
ephemerae, historically no more than mosquito bites? How could
he provide such astonishing insights into the antebellum South
and the twentieth-century South and be so blind to what came
between?

In part, Cash's view reflects the power of the Dunning and
Progressive Schools of Reconstruction, the prevailing interpretations in the 1930s. But Cash did not just mouth conventional
truths. For example, while he shared the revulsion of the Dun-
ningites and Progressives for Northern radicals, he knew better
than to argue that the white South accepted defeat and stood ready
to do justice to emancipated slaves. Cash believed in "negro
incapacity" as much as the next white historian, but his compas-
sion compelled him to depict the viciousness of white violence,
and his sensitivity to class relations led him to expose the elite's
role in the guerrilla campaign against freedmen. Most important,
Cash parted company with orthodoxy on the matter of continuity,
for unlike Cash, established opinion declared the Civil War and
Reconstruction a sea change in history.[13]

The question remains, then, how could Cash derive uninter-
rupted continuity from what others labelled revolutionary change?
We know that Cash formulated his definition of the Southern mind
principally from what he observed at close range while growing up
in his native Piedmont North Carolina. That is, he derived the
South's mind from living with the natives, what an anthropologist
might call fieldwork. Not surprisingly, his Southern "mind" took
on a distinctly ethnological cast—a cluster of folk traits and cultural values.[14] Cash's "mind" might better be called viscera. His

definition of Southern identity was at once too narrow and too broad, one that dismissed too much and ignored too many, but it did have the advantage of defining the South in terms of its most resistant features. Lodged in the gut, this "mind" did not respond easily to "transient" historical experiences.

But the best explanation of Cash's conviction of continuity lies in chronology. As a number of critics have observed, Cash wrote near the end of the South's longest and most stable era. His emphasis on persistence reflected what appeared to be true.[15] To Cash, the South had "always marched away, as to this day it continues to do, from the present toward the past."[16] From the present toward the past, that was how he wrote his history—backwards. He identified the elements that to him comprised the modern Southern personality and searched back across time to find the antebellum origins of each. His assumptions, purpose, and method made it impossible for him to recognize the Civil War and Reconstruction as the pivotal epochs they were; instead, he was compelled to see them as connective tissue. Cash was right, of course, that ligaments joined the antebellum and postbellum eras. He proved beyond a doubt that the South did not cease to be the South. But his demonstration does not add up to an unbroken, continuous Southern past. Cash found what he wanted to find. No, more accurately, he found what he had to find.

The briefest glance at *The Mind of the South* reveals the intensity of Cash's quest. Sickened by certain features of his native region, he came close to defining the South by its pathology. A wonderfully gifted writer, he could have chosen to tell his tale in a ironic vein and thus distance himself from his painful task. Instead, he chose sarcasm and engaged Southern culture at close quarters. Convinced that the past had extraordinary power, he fought on every page to break its spell. Obstinately pessimistic, he nevertheless dared hope that honest history might prove therapeutic. Confronted with hard truths, Southerners might yet heal themselves.

Presentism among historians—academic and nonacademic—is

hardly rare. Neither is depression about the present. But more often than not it is upheaval—not inertia—that drives historians into the past in search of answers to what has gone wrong. One thinks of another man—Henry Adams—who observed American life from the vantage of Boston and Washington rather than from Boiling Springs and Charlotte, but who, like Cash, was alarmed by his savage world and projected his dismay backwards. Adams completed *The Education of Henry Adams* in 1907 when the pace of change in the North was dizzying and apparently accelerating. *The Mind of the South* appeared in 1941 when the author viewed his homeland from the perspective of the longest unbroken era in its history. One man wished that old ways had never disappeared, the other feared that they never would. One was driven to distraction by change, the other by persistence. One wished history had flowed smoothly, the other yearned for a watershed. Both, however, were on a mission—personal as well as cultural—and history was made to deliver.[17]

Of course, scholars since Cash have been no more successful in escaping their own times. If we see farther, it is not only because we stand on the shoulders of giants, but because we look through lens ground in our time, not Cash's, lens that to us seem clearer and sharper. Since Cash's death, our understanding of the three decades that followed secession has altered almost beyond recognition. New sources, changing definitions of history, evolving methodologies, different assumptions about African Americans, and much more have combined to recast our view.[18] There is no orthodoxy, but historians have revived Charles and Mary Beard's conception of these turbulent and wrenching decades as "The Second American Revolution." In its new formulation, the concept has at its center emancipation and the profound upheavals it inaugurated.[19] For all the apparent resemblances to slavery days, the South of 1900 was a very different place.

Today, scholars are likely to view the War for Southern Independence principally as a struggle to preserve slavery and Reconstruction as a contest to define the meaning of freedom. At one point,

Cash casually mentions that the region's "foundation stone had been torn away in the abolition of slavery," but he does not develop the metaphor.[20] If he had, he might have realized that without foundations structures tend to collapse. Instead, Cash discounted slavery by viewing it as a sub-category of a more potent reality—white supremacy. The essence of Reconstruction, then, lay in Southern whites' successful counteroffensive against the Republican effort to tamper with race relations. Thus, Cash could argue that the South had "lost the war but won the peace." But victory did not restore slavery, the bedrock of antebellum Southern society and culture. Cash was right to emphasize the whites' heightened regional self-consciousness and stubborn determination to resist change, but at issue was their capacity, not their desire, to remain the same. Even before Appomattox, the old order had come apart.

It seems now that the Civil War was not the unifying, healing experience Cash portrayed. It was the bloodiest event in American history. The struggle took the lives of some 620,000 Americans, more than a quarter of a million of them Southerners. One of every four of the South's white male population of military age died in the conflict. Southerners were three times more likely to die than Northerners. Southern soldiers died at the hands of Yankees and also at the hands of men who months before had been their slaves. Of the 190,000 black Union military men, some 130,000 were former bondsmen. The Southern home front was not spared. As the conflict evolved into total war, civilian casualties mounted, eventually numbering some 50,000 individuals. The full consequences of the South's astounding mortality have not been calculated, but when the reckoning is done it is unlikely to confirm Cash's restorative war.[21]

Rather than close the fissures in Southern society, the war increased discord among whites and widened divisions. Fighting to defend slavery aggravated class tensions and alienated substantial numbers of nonslaveholders from the Confederate cause. Recent studies of North Carolina by Paul Escott and Wayne Durrell and of Tennessee by Stephen Ash and Philip Paludan have documented social disintegration within the Confederacy.[22] At times, lower-class resentment spilled over into actual violence. Planters proved poor citizens of the Confederacy, and their selfish commitment to their own class interests helped erode traditional accommodations among whites. Yeoman soldiers may have idolized their captains, as Cash argues, but back at home farm women and children who went hungry in sight of planter plenty did not swoon in admiration.[23] According to Roger Ransom's recent study, slavery and the divisiveness it spawned proved decisive in the Confederacy's defeat.[24]

For the South, then, the Civil War meant ghastly mortality, vast physical destruction, massive economic loss, and unprecedented social turmoil, but the truly revolutionary element of the war was the freeing of some 4,000,000 slaves. Where practical, African Americans took an active part in their own liberation. Maids and cooks, field hands and carpenters claimed freedom and tipped the balance of power from the "big house" to the slave cabins. Typical of her class, North Carolina plantation mistress Catherine Edmondston concluded: "[A]s to the idea of a *faithful servant, it is all a fiction.*"[25] Cash cannot be blamed for writing in advance of the Federal Writers' Project interviews with ex-slaves, the volumes by the Freedmen and Southern Society Project, and that outpouring of brilliant interpretation that transformed our understanding of slave culture.[26] But Cash's ignorance of the institutions, the values, and the aspirations that slaves developed in the quarters crippled his interpretation of the South at war. When blacks moved to center stage as they did during Reconstruction, the blindness devastates his analysis.

To his credit, Cash does not reduce blacks to invisibility, but African Americans remain silly caricatures incapable of more than dressing up, showing off, and throwing sharp elbows in the ribs of whites.[27] We now recognize a very different people emerging from slavery. And we know that emancipation reached to the marrow of freedmen's lives.[28] Robert Fogel has deftly summarized why.

Slavery had permitted masters to exercise unrestrained personal domination over their slaves. Emancipation extended to blacks the modern democratic notion of personal freedom. Slavery meant a near-total denial of economic opportunity. Freedom offered the possibility of individual economic and social mobility, a critical aspect of which was geographical mobility. Slavery abrogated citizenship and thus utterly excluded slaves from civil and political rights. Free persons were legally entitled to protection against attacks on their person, violations of their family, and loss of their property. Slavery permitted an African-American culture and community to develop within the slave quarters. But only emancipation could provide blacks with the freedom free laborers possessed to develop their own culture and institutions.[29] As Armstead Robinson has said: "Being free did make a difference."[30]

Freedom brought an explosion of black churches, schools, self-help organizations, mutual aid associations, lodges and fraternal societies, and businesses. The search for autonomy also included the politicization of the freedmen. By enfranchising black men but not black women, politics differentiated the public sphere from the private sphere in ways unknown among blacks in the slave quarters. Self-determination also propelled ex-slaves to the South's cities, where black populations multiplied and a black middle class sank deep roots. Everywhere, ex-slaves took to the roads—desperately searching for family members, determinedly seeking better lives. Four million ex-slaves were joined in this new world by a quarter million ex-"free people of color," whose antebellum status altered just as surely as did that of the slaves. Though not without difficulty, the free and the freed gradually melded to form a single African-American community. Black assertion in pursuit of autonomy and self-determination led to confrontations in kitchens, fields, city streets, churches, party caucuses, state legislatures and in every other arena that brought whites and blacks together.[31]

No confrontation was more dramatic or indicative of the revolution unleashed by the war than the one that took place on plantations. Former masters and former slaves had very different notions of what free labor should mean, and the compromise of sharecropping satisfied neither. But it allowed landowners to resume production and freedmen to abandon the quarters for cabins on rented plots, where they, not their masters, decided who would work in the fields and how long, whether women would labor in the home, and whether children would go to school. Freedmen were not always successful in shielding family members from brutal field labor, but by 1870 the South's cotton fields were being worked by some 40 percent fewer blacks. Against all odds, moreover, some 200,000 blacks acquired land of their own in the half-century after emancipation. Violence against blacks continued and patterns of domination and subordination remained. Freedom was hard, but freedmen knew that they were no longer property that masters could buy, sell, trade, and move.[32] A mighty revolution had ended slavery, new relationships gradually and painfully emerged, and, as John Boles has observed, "one whole phase of southern history ended and another began."[33]

Although they tried, planters could not halt the transformation of the plantations. A decade after emancipation, planters had repudiated the proslavery ideology, accepted free black labor, denied paternalistic relationships, assumed no responsibilities beyond the strict letter of the contract, and reduced proximity to blacks.[34] In Gavin Wright's terms, antebellum "labor lords" had become postbellum "landlords."[35] Plantations filled with strangers, the consequences of black mobility, white tenancy, and absentee ownership. The new order bore so little resemblance to antebellum realities that we need new terms for "planter" and "plantation," for both words connote more continuity than is warranted. The metamorphosis of the plantation did not mean the breakup of large agricultural units, as Cash argues in what must be his lone underestimation of continuity. Plantations survived, and they also tended to remain in the hands of those families who owned them before the war, at least until 1870, when most studies stop.[36] But neither the persistence of large landholders nor large landholdings could stay what Michael Wayne has called the "transformation" of the plantation and antebellum planter class.[37] Emancipation stripped slaveholders of $3 billion in slave property, and while the destruction of slavery did not destroy planters' power, it alloyed and compromised it.

Emancipation undermined not only the old plantation but the basis of the entire antebellum political economy and social order. The postwar South witnessed the integration of yeomen into the cotton economy, the ascent of the merchants and industrialists, and the rapid growth of factories and towns. Between 1860 and 1900, the South's urban dwellers more than doubled—from 7.2 percent of the population to 15.2 percent.[38] According to Don Doyle's *New Men, New Cities, and New South*, the South's postwar cities and the business leaders who helped to make them were "central forces in the making of the modern South."[39] According to Cash, however, the old planter elite, with its traditional ideas firmly in place, nimbly stepped into the new roles of businessman and industrialist. In reality, planters did become businessmen— they added thick portfolios of investments in stores and gins, railroads and factories to their agricultural interests—but not without ceasing to be their Old South selves. Moreover, as David Carlton and others have shown, postwar planters were not the principal element in the new industrial elite that presided over the rise of mills and towns.[40] Made up of new men, this elite had not the slightest intention of enshrining the Old South in a textile mill. The industrialists' chief resemblance to the antebellum planter class lay in their willingness to squeeze labor until labor bled.

In the countryside, class and social relations among whites changed dramatically. So precipitous was the decline of the region's white yeomen that in certain respects the postbellum years brought almost as much change for them as for blacks. By the end of the century the number of white sharecroppers approached that of black sharecroppers, and it proved difficult to distinguish the treatment of white and black workers. Many whites abandoned agriculture entirely. Whole families entered the cotton mill proletariat. Accommodations between yeoman and planter had

soured during the war, and the yeoman's decline from independent farmer to dependent tenant, cropper, day laborer, and mill
hand did little to sweeten his disposition. Just as scores of thousands of Southern yeomen had entered the biracial Republican
party during Reconstruction, disgruntled white farmers in the
decades afterwards entertained radical, even bi-racial, solutions to
their problems. Planters and the rising merchant class managed a
mutually beneficial accommodation, but this hybrid class was
anything but the reincarnation of the antebellum ruling class. The
landlord-storekeeper elite, moreover, sat atop a radically transformed social and economic order.[41]

Racism continued to bind white men across class lines, of
course, but a new system of race relations emerged to replace
slavery. Slave labor dictated one set of social relationships between
the races, free labor (even "half free" labor) another. Since the
publication of C. Vann Woodward's *Strange Career in Jim Crow*
in 1955, a huge and impressive literature has debated how many
racial choices whites had before them after the war, how long it
took them to choose, and how we should evaluate the choice they
made. What is pertinent here, however, is the revolutionary nature of segregation. With emancipation, the South moved from
what Pierre van den Berghe calls a "paternalistic" to a "competi-
tive" model of race relations. Slavery, with its enormous social
distance and ascribed stations, allowed close contact, even inti-
macy, without threatening white status. Emancipation drastically
reduced the social distance between white and blacks, prompting
whites to reject intimate contact and to seek physical separation as
a buttress to their own status. Black assertion after the war had
already divided white and black societies, but whites adopted
segregation to punctuate their supremacy. It did that, with a
vengeance, but it did not restore the race relations of slavery to the
South's bi-racial society.[42]

But before landlords and storekeepers could affirm their power
and whites reaffirm their superiority, Reconstruction had to end.
Black participation in Southern political life after 1867, Eric Foner

argues, was the "most radical development of the Reconstruction years, a massive experiment in inter-racial democracy without precedent in the history of this or any other country that abolished slavery in the nineteenth century."[43] Political rights and black majorities among registered voters in several ex-Confederate states meant that freedmen had access, at least temporarily, to the power of the state to advance their interests. Their quest for economic autonomy did much to set Reconstruction's political agenda. Redemption ended the radical experiment, but it did not restore the South as a stronghold of two-party politics. Instead, it became a bastion of one-party rule.[44]

Redemption, moreover, could not annul the radical shift in power from South to North that followed Appomattox. Steven Hahn and others have emphasized the importance of the altered geography of power. Before the war, the South had exercised disproportionate influence in the national government. Defeat transferred power to Yankee Republicans (Cash's "tariff gang"), who controlled politics and economics for most of the next 70 years.[45] The South was hardly defenseless, for as David Potter demonstrated, it contrived to protect itself through the exercise of a kind of "concurrent majority."[46] But exercising a regional negative was a country mile from bending the national government to regional advantage. In a remarkable reversal of fortune, the South's planter class went from being one of the strongest agrarian classes in the West to being the weakest.

For continuity to have triumphed, as Cash claimed it did, for the Old South actually to have flowed unbroken into the New, the North would have had to allow the South to secede peacefully. Only then could the South have avoided war, defeat, emancipation, and the destruction of its slave-based society. Daydreamers in William Faulkner's Yoknapatawpha County entertain thoughts of the Old South triumphant. And after Appomattox real Southerners bent knees before the altar of the cult of the "Lost Cause," while "New South" propagandists groped for antebellum roots to their radical vision.[47] But nothing could change reality: the North had triumphed over the South, free labor had triumphed over slave labor, and industrial capitalism had triumphed over the political economy of slavery.

Watersheds, turning points, breaks in time—however much historians may exaggerate their occurrence—do occur.[48] Contemporary Southerners felt the ground shift. They were acutely aware of what Jefferson Davis called a "break in time." In December 1865 a Louisiana planter declared: "Society has been completely changed by the war. The [French] revolution of '89 did not produce a greater change in the 'Ancien Régime' than this has in our social life."[49] Two years later when Louis Manigault, the great patriarch of the South Carolina and Georgia low country, returned to his Savannah river plantations, he encountered a world turned upside down. "I almost imagined myself with Chinese, Malays or even the Indians in the interior of the Philippine Islands," he said.[50] Southern women, white and black, viewed the Civil War as a social cataclysm that changed their lives. Alabama plantation mistress, Octavia Otey, remarked in December 1867: "I am almost tempted to doubt my self sometimes and ask if this is really I, to doubt my own identity."[51] Aunt Sissy, an elderly Virginia slave, could only comprehend the changes in terms of religious conversion: "Isn't I a free woman now!" she declared. "De Lord can make Heaven out of Hell any time, I do believe."[52]

Revolutions can run backwards, and this one did. Forces of reaction wiped out much of the progress, but they could not negate the transformation. The compass of change did not always point in a progressive direction. The South's agriculture was not modernized and diversified. The blessings of industrialization did not descend. Economic backwardness, social reaction, and racial oppression persisted. But failure to achieve equality and justice is not equivalent to continuity. An "unfinished revolution" is still a revolution. The South did not return to 1860 or even 1865. Slavery was dead, and neither the white nor black community would ever be the same. The South did not cease to be distinctive because it had changed, but it did become distinctive in new ways.

Seventeen years after Appomattox, Mark Twain found that the Civil War remained at the center of the Southern "mind." The war was, he declared, "what A. D. is elsewhere; they date from it." And for good reason, he observed. The war had "uprooted institutions that were centuries old . . . transformed the social life of half the country, and wrought so profoundly upon the entire national character that the influence cannot be measured short of two or three generations."[53] Two generations later, Cash still had not learned what Twain knew—that the death of the Old South had not, after all, been vastly exaggerated.

Commentary / Lacy K. Ford, Jr.

It is a pity that Jack Cash did not live to see how popular and influential his book would become. For many cohorts of undergraduates, and others making their first attempt at understanding the South, *The Mind of the South* proved intoxicating stuff. Cash's passionate argument, carried by his flamboyant prose, convinced many readers that he had captured the timeless truths of the southern experience. Moreover, with a handful of exceptions, reviewers initially concurred with the reading public's appreciation of Cash.[1] To be sure, the conservative Agrarian Donald Davidson penned the expected negative review, and a young C. Vann Woodward filed some important caveats with his generally positive assessment in the *Journal of Southern History.*[2] But for the most part, Cash's *The Mind of the South* enjoyed both critical and popular acclaim from the time of its publication until 1969, when Woodward published a stunning new critique in the *New York Review of Books.*[3] This second Woodward review proved definitive and delimiting; it narrowed the perimeters and shallowed the channels of Cash's influence; it invited and encouraged other scholars to scrutinize Cash's work more closely. Some took up the challenge, and by the 1980s, only the tendentious few accepted Cash as authoritative on much of anything. After all, we now know,

Cash's so-called "great South" was really a more modest entity, the crescent-shaped Carolina Piedmont, the red clay hill-country where Cash was raised and spent virtually his entire life. Moreover, it is now a scholarly commonplace that Cash, as Woodward twice contended, greatly overstated both the continuity of southern history and the unity of southern white society.[4] In Cash's South, the more things changed the more they remained the same.

Most of the major complaints Woodward lodged against *The Mind of the South* in the influential 1969 essay were elaborations on objections noted in his earlier review. One major exception to this pattern, however, was Woodward's blunt assertation in his later essay that Cash had written "a book about the 'mind' . . . of the Southern Whites."[5] Woodward had not alluded to this deficiency in 1941, but by 1969, with the major legislative successes of the Civil Rights Movement still fresh in his mind, he saw it as crucial. Black southerners appear throughout Cash's book, Woodward noted, but only in passive roles. They were an "influence" on white thinking, "victims" of white racism, or a "threat" to the job security of white millworkers; they served as stage props but were seldom actors in their own right. While Cash recognized that the "black presence" shaped "a major component of the white mind," he ignored the possibility that the black mind might, in its own right, be a significant component of the southern mind.[6] Thus Woodward properly took *The Mind of the South* to task for its neglect of the black experience. Yet even Woodward's second review only implied a connection between Cash's one-dimensional treatment of southern blacks and his repeated insistence on the essential continuity of the southern experience.

Now James Roark has made that connection explicit. Focusing on Cash's treatment of Reconstruction, America's great but aborted social revolution, Roark explains how the Charlotte-based journalist could so readily discount the dramatic discontinuity in the South's history occasioned by the collapse of slavery. Viewing the tumultuous Reconstruction era almost solely from the white perspective, Cash saw Confederate defeat, emancipation, and a decade of "Black Republican" rule as little more than reenforcement for the prevailing "proto-Dorian" social ideals.[7] The psychology of defeat, and the practical necessity of restoring white supremacy and white rule in the region, served only to intensify the South's predominant "savage ideal." The "savage ideal," as Cash defined it, was that ideal "whereunder dissent and variety are completely suppressed and men become, in all their attitudes, professions, and actions, virtual replicas of one another."[8] The Reconstruction era's frontal assault on white supremacy, Cash maintained, etched "that old line between what was Southern and what was not" in stone and "defined in feeling down to the last detail" what "one must think and say and do." The maturation of the savage ideal "completed the South's old terrified truculence toward new ideas from the outside" and rendered "criticism, analysis, and detachment," the moral equivalent of "high and aggravated treason."[9] Looking at the era from the white perspective, Cash could only see that Reconstruction, "the Frontier the Yankee Made," had strengthened the savage ideal. What Cash could not see, but what a number of historians, including Professor Roark, have recently explained, was the extent to which war and emancipation were truly revolutionary experiences, and most revolutionary for the freedpeople. Their exercise of freedom and search for its full meaning prompted experiments with novel labor systems, shattered old patterns of racial etiquette, and sustained an indigenous southern Republican party that was openly committed, to one degree or another, to the principles of racial equality. The nation's eventual retreat from Reconstruction and the return of conservative whites to power in the South dashed many black hopes but could not reverse the fundamental change of the Reconstruction era, a change as radical as the difference between slavery and freedom.[10] Yet when Cash looked back on this era from his position in the segregated, one-party South of the 1930s, he could only see persistent white racism and growing cultural xenophobia. As always, the focus of Cash's "historical" analysis was on

how events, people, groups, classes and their interplay fostered an
atmosphere of cultural and intellectual repression in the South.
Put another way, Cash's primary focus was on how southern history, including the "black presence," effected white intellectuals
like himself. The analytical Cash grew at length narcissistic.[11]
    This is hardly an original observation. As many scholars have
pointed out, *The Mind of the South* was an intensely personal work.
Cash's presence suffuses every page, and, as Michael O'Brien has
observed, Cash's rage to explain the South was, at its core, not only
"a private passion" but also "a cry of pain" from a deeply unhappy
intellectual who believed himself rejected by his society.[12] An
intellectually-inclined youth growing up in the small-town South,
Cash suffered indignities, real and imagined, at the hands of
indifferent, and perhaps suspicious, townsfolk who valued "common sense" (which they believed they had) more than intellectual
achievement. The young Wilbur Cash was not handsome or athletic, or convivial, or rich. He preferred books, magazines, newspapers, and solitude to engines, guns, baseball, and church.
Easily tagged a "bookworm" by his school-mates, Cash was occasionally taunted by his peers. Wilbur Cash grew up "smart" in a
provincial world which did not appear to value "smarts" very
much, unless they were applied to making money or preaching
God's word. And Cash had neither the talent nor inclination for
either. Wounded as an adolescent, the vulnerable Cash carried his
emotional scars, and his concomitant sense of grievance against
the provincial establishment, both religious and secular, into
adulthood. In his first job as a school teacher, Cash quickly found
his pupils lacking motivation, and in his stint as editor of the
hometown *Cleveland Star,* he found little encouragement for
critical reporting. Publishers of small-town newspapers, dependent on advertising revenue from the local mercantile community,
seldom courted controversy. For Cash, the small towns of the
Piedmont were, indeed, repressive, though perhaps less self-
consciously so than the talented young wordsmith imagined.[13]
    Thus O'Brien is right to call *The Mind of the South* "a bitter

book," one "singularly devoid of heroes."[14] Yet, Cash's disdain for
heroes partially redeems his bitterness. Cash played no favorites.
He was even-handed with his ridicule. He spared no group his
scorn. His characterizations are as memorable as they are severe.
The Old South's planter elite was a sham aristocracy, a coarse
group of climbers who donned the trappings of a landed nobility
without fully understanding the responsibility that came with
their assumed status. Cash acknowledged that southern yeomen
were sturdy, but he also believed that these plain folk were easily
duped by their supposed "betters." Blacks, whether slave or free,
Cash considered sensuous, hedonistic, uncivilized and not disposed to accept civilizing. Beneath the pious and paternalistic
veneer of the New South's second generation cotton mill owners
Cash discerned avarice comparable with that of grasping Yankees.
Cash saw millworkers as vacant and docile, and he diagnosed the
affliction of the new middle classes of the South's inland towns as
Babbittry, that dreaded Yankee disease which transformed a keen
sense of personal honor into a fastidious concern for business
reputation.[15] W. J. Cash, the wounded youth turned bitter journalist, was an equal opportunity despiser.

   In *The Mind of the South,* Cash observed that the important
southern novelists of the 1930s, Faulkner, Caldwell, and Wolfe,
generally "hated the South a good deal less than they said and
thought."[16] The same might be said of Cash.[17] His seemingly
boundless supply of bitterness often failed him at crucial moments, betraying his capacity for empathy with those he often
ridiculed without ever fully revealing his own vulnerability. Cash
mustered the most empathy for those in southern society with
whom he most closely identified: the common and poor whites.
The yeomen of the Old South, Cash conceded, "took from aristocracy as much as, and no more than, could be made to fit their own
homespun qualities." The "result was a kindly courtesy, a level-
eyed pride, an easy quietness" that were among the region's finest
qualities. Even the poor whites, Cash allowed, assumed "a sort of
unkempt politeness and ease of port, which rendered them defi-

nitely superior . . . to their peers in the rest of the country."[18] Cash's depiction of southern textile workers laboring under the pressure of the "efficiency" movement of the 1920s revealed even more sympathy. To be deprived of "one's dignity as an individual and made into a sort of automaton," Cash pleaded, "to be stood over by a taskmaster with a stop-watch in his hand . . . to be everlastingly hazed on to greater exertion by curt commands and sneers, and to have to stand periodically and take a dressing down with a white face, just as though one were a nigger, under the ever present threat of being summarily dismissed—for this people so immensely proud . . . bred to the ancient Southern notion that each was a white man like any other, that each in some fundamental fashion was as good as any white man who walked the earth and entitled to be treated with respect and consideration" was "wellnigh or wholly intolerable."[19]

Cash at his best, when dropping the mask of bitterness ever so slightly, was quite good, and someone from whom we can still learn much if we heed the warnings of his now numerous critics. Cash's bitterness, however, was genuine, born of deep wounds and much personal torment. He was the South's scorned lover, his bitterness an outgrowth of unrequited affection for the region, a disguise for his romantic disappointment. Yet for Cash, writing *The Mind of the South* was more than a settling of old scores, more than a last-ditch therapy for his personal anguish. His effort had another, more practical, aim. Cash tried to fashion a convincing account of the southern experience so that he, and his journalistic peers, might better understand the evolution of the world they reported and commented on.[20] But Cash's "history" was decidedly present-minded, tending to assume that the characteristics of the Piedmont in the 1920s and 1930s were timeless southern traits. Particularly notable in this regard was his contention that Protestant Christianity, led by a censorious clergy, kept the region trapped in a kind of anti-intellectual thralldom. Cash held the South's fervent evangelicals and somber Calvinists responsible for all manner of the region's ills.[21] In fact, the southern church had been too often a champion of conformity in the region, but it had never held as tight a grip on the South as Cash believed. The white evangelical clergy learned early on the dangers of asking the laity to choose between racial and religious loyalty, and thereafter seldom challenged the racial status quo in the region.[22] Moreover, the sabbatarian, teetotaling Calvinists whom Cash held responsible for Prohibition, blue laws, and public prudery had actually seldom influenced major legislation prior to the 1920s, and the "local option" liquor laws which replaced prohibition catered to democratic expression rather than elitist dictation. The Charlotte from which Cash worked was indeed a Scotch-Irish Presbyterian stronghold, but however constricted its Calvinism became at times, the Presbyterian tradition, with its emphasis on a learned clergy, was intellectually rigorous in sorting the orthodox from the unorthodox. Orthodoxy always prevailed, but the intellectual exercise was considerable, as anyone who has tried to follow James Henley Thornwell's theological reasoning knows.[23] If anything, the Piedmont's cold Presbyterians were more often charged with excessive intellectualism, with trying to reduce faith to reason, with lacking the emotional fervor which made other, more aggressively evangelical, denominations so appealing to ordinary folk. The bootlegging and prostitution rings which flourished in Charlotte during Cash's time there marked not so much a corruption of the faith, as Cash thought, as they did the limits of its influence.

If Cash had lived a full three-score and ten, he would have survived to see the Piedmont of 1970, and he doubtless would have still seen much that smacked of continuity. Babbittry, Rotarianism, and the Duke Power Company had achieved even greater glory. Textile workers were still essentially unorganized. And Charlotte was still sometimes referred to as the buckle of the Bible-belt. But Cash would also have seen much to confound his earlier conclusions. The old planter elite was nowhere to be found, unless their grandsons the realtors count, and the yeomanry had pretty much disappeared as well, its sons off to college on the GI Bill or to jobs at the fast-arriving branch plants of the post World War II era. He would have seen the Charlotte elite, led at times by a "wet" Presbyterian mayor (John Belk) push hard for liberalized liquor laws over the vocal but largely ineffectual protest of rank-and-file Baptists. He would have seen the "blue laws" become the object of overwhelming popular ridicule. He would have seen one-party Democratic Charlotte turn into a Republican congressional stronghold well before the racial blacklash of the mid-1960s swept the region, and he would have seen the newspapers for which he had worked taken over by a national publisher with strong Republican leanings. Perhaps most surprisingly, Cash would have seen a fellow South Carolina native steeped in the Presbyterian tradition, James McBride Dabbs, argue eloquently that through "God's grace" a "despised minority" might teach the long-dominant majority the meaning of redemptive suffering.[24]

If Cash had achieved truly remarkable longevity, say something approaching that of Strom Thurmond (just three years Cash's junior), he would have seen even more striking changes in his native Piedmont. He would have seen Charlotte elect a black mayor. He would have seen a religious mini-empire employing nearly 2,000 people rise (and fall) on the Queen City's outskirts. But that empire was neither Baptist nor Presbyterian in origin. It did not even have an authentic southern pedigree. Its architects were a white Pentecostal couple from the upper Midwest. Cash would have seen sons of small town bankers build powerful national banks and employ internationally famous architects to construct skyscrapers so tall and impressive that even Jack Cash might have forgotten Jeb Stuart's cavalry when he saw them. And he could have shopped in specialty stores in sprawling suburban malls where barely more than one customer in two would speak with a recognizably southern accent. Charlotte, which once boasted of being home to proportionately more Presbyterians than any place this side of Edinburgh, now might boast of being home to proportionately more Yankee transplants than any place south of the Research Triangle and north of Hilton Head.

It would be unfair to expect Cash to have been a better prophet
than he was a historian, but it is worth noting that Cash not only
understated change in the southern past but also underestimated
the probability of change in the southern future. The intellectual
and cultural repression which Cash believed held the South hos-
tage to the status quo was never quite as potent or pervasive as he
imagined. And it was certainly overmatched by the broader social
and economic pressures for change which were emerging in the
South even as Cash wrote and which would envelop the region
shortly after his death. Cash not only read too much continuity into
southern history, he also despairingly projected too continuity for
the region's future. His historical model left his readers no reason
to expect and no power to understand the dramatic changes which
swept the South after 1940.

Thus *The Mind of the South*'s failings are legion. Cash confused
the Piedmont with the entire South. He ignored the black mind.
He exaggerated continuity. He caricatured the church. He read
the present into the past. Yet for all of these shortcomings, Cash
wrote a book of enormous and enduring emotional power. Many
talented southern journalists and writers working in the 1930s
wrote non-fiction books about the South and the southern experience, or a portion of it, at some point in their careers. A few wrote
more than one. The list of these writers who struggled to come to
grips with the southern experience is impressive indeed. A complete list would run well over two dozen names and include
Jonathan Daniels, Virginius Dabney, William A. Percy, John Temple Graves, Gerald Johnson, Ben Robertson, Hodding Carter,
Ralph McGill and others.[25] Some produced books more perfect
in small ways than Cash's, but no one rivaled his monumental
achievement, partly because no one was nearly as ambitious, but
largely because Cash understood something the other authors did
not. He understood the power of myth and the appeal of innocence
to the southern (and American) people. Other writers struggled to
understand the myth of the Lost Cause and its meaning for the
South, but Cash understood that it was not a single myth but a

pyramid constructed of many myths that shaped the southern white identity. If Cash intended to explode those myths, and as a journalist in the Mencken tradition he may have, then his charges of sham and hypocrisy surely failed every bit as fully as historians have failed to destroy myth with mere fact. Cash's success was in identifying the key myths behind the white southerner's self-conception and in explaining their lasting strength. Cash may himself have at times confused southern society with southern self-conception, but he understood, as many have not, that metahistory can overwhelm history.[26]

Cash also understood that the power of myth for the southern mind was closely related to the appeal of innocence. The only other southern writer of the 1930s to grapple with the theme of innocence in southern history as effectively as Cash was the novelist William Faulkner. In *Absalom, Absalom,* Faulkner's Thomas Sutpen saw his grand dynastic ambition thwarted by his innocence, his refusal to assume full responsibility for the consequences of his action.[27] Cash tacitly defined innocence pretty much as did Faulkner, as a refusal to learn, or to develop a keener moral sense, from the past. In recognizing the South's tenacious innocence, and thus the persistent power of its consensus ideal, Jack Cash, however flawed his history, came closer to understanding the way most white southerners understood their history and identity than anyone else. The wise and expert teachings of C. Vann Woodward not withstanding, most southerners have not, despite the burden of their history, distanced themselves that much from the prevailing myth of American innocence, the myth which Garry Wills has recently called that of "original sinlessness."[28] Americans believe that they are as good and noble as their prevailing myths declare, regardless of the "facts," and that they know "good" when they see it. It was perhaps appropriate that it was a South Carolinian, the late Lee Atwater, who most recently recognized the power of innocence and conformity in American life. Aware of southern history, and trained in the hard school of blacklash politics in the region, Atwater fashioned for George Bush in 1988 a campaign based on skillful manipulation of powerful consensus symbols. With the American flag, the pledge of allegiance, and Willie Horton, Atwater appealed to every atavistic, "proto-Dorian" spirit left in the southern (and American) psyche. And those spirits came from him when he called them. Three out of four white southerners voted for Bush. The appeal, of course, played nationally as well as in the South, suggesting that Cash's "not quite a nation within a nation" was more like the nation it is part of than not. Lee Atwater expected success. He had rehearsed his strategy in focus groups. Jack Cash, writing fifty years ago, deciphered as much "on the authority" of his own imagination.[29] Had Cash indeed enjoyed remarkable longevity and seen the 1988 campaign, he would surely not have been surprised that the old ideals he had written about had perduring appeal, and he would have been even less surprised that they were still savage after all these years.

W. J. Cash, the New South, and the Rhetoric of History

EDWARD L. AYERS

W. J. Cash began an early version of his manuscript, he claimed, by piling footnotes on almost every page, "writing a tome that was going to look like nothing so much as a doctor's thesis, and calculated to scare off all the cash customers—something I certainly hadn't planned. Wherefore, having gazed at the facts with the long reluctance of a lazy man, I at length heaved all I had done away and started all over again." Cash jettisoned most of the other conventions of academic history as well; the book has not lacked for cash customers, or doctoral studies, since. The question arises: are academic historians unable to write like Cash, encumbered with footnotes and all, or do we know too much to write like Cash? It is easy to imagine him watching over this affair, chuckling to himself in his sardonic way as we struggle with the book he struggled with for most of his life.[1]

Despite the attention devoted to the fiery early chapters of *The Mind of the South*, where Cash's language and audacity take us by surprise, the heart of the book lies in the New South. Cash wrote above all, I think, to explain why the white Southerners he knew—those in the cotton mill country of the Carolina Piedmont—behaved the way they did. Cash wanted to explain why there had not been more Gastonias or Elizabethtons when the hard times hit in the 1920s and 1930s, why mill workers stood with the mill owners when they had every reason to strike, why politicians vacillated between doing nothing and doing wrong, why the middle class remained inert, why religious intolerance and the Ku Klux Klan held the loyalty of so many white people. The years after Reconstruction consume two-thirds of Cash's book because those

113

are the years that troubled him, that posed the problems he felt most acutely.[2]

The chapters on the antebellum South, the Civil War, and Reconstruction purport to show how the average Southern white man became overwhelmed by a "blindness to his real interests." The "man at the center" had grown simple and hedonistic on the cotton frontier, awash in the violence, romance, and rhetoric of childish egos. He had descended into gyneolotry, conformity, intolerance. He had generated no class consciousness, he tolerated only limited government. Not only had he bought into the "paternalism" of the planters who became his captains during the war, he encouraged their noblesse oblige, their leadership against the carpetbaggers, scalawags, and blacks of Reconstruction.[3]

White solidarity threatened to dissolve, ironically, only after the native white triumph over Reconstruction. Class resentments began to build. Poorer white men, facing the decline of cotton prices, a shortage of money, and dependence on merchants and planters, slipped into a position not unlike that of black sharecroppers. Here we have to allow Cash to tell his story in his own language, for paraphrase fails. The common whites, Cash wrote, "may be said to have been groping in some dim, obscure, and less than conscious fashion toward perception of their position in the Southern world and have been gathering anger against it." Populism promised to bring class identity into the open, but it did not: "however mighty were the forces tending to project these common whites into class awareness and revolt, the forces tending to hold them back were mightier yet." These simple people "had no training in, and no power of, analysis, no notion of social forces as affecting their lives." The Democrats easily herded the farmers into line with token gestures of white supremacy. The farmers, guiltily listening in North Carolina in the 1890s as "black laughter rolled in flood through Tar Heel legislative halls once more," thought better of their rebellion and sidled back over to the Democrats.[4]

Chastened by the narrowly averted threat of poor white class consciousness and resentment, the planters—"the old Confederate captains in large part"—had a "dream. Let us, in this quandary, take a page from the book of Yankeedom. Let us meet the old enemy on his own ground. Let us, in short, turn to Progress. Let us introduce the factory in force. Let us, in particular, build cotton mills, here in the midst of the cotton fields." Poor white folk would be given a stake in the new order, provided a haven in the mill villages, brought into the bargain of Progress. "So far from representing a deliberate break with the past, the turn to Progress clearly flowed straight out of that past and constituted in a real sense an emanation from the will to maintain the South in its essential integrity," Cash insisted. "The New South meant and boasted of was mainly a South which would be new in this: that it would be so rich and powerful that it might rest serene in its ancient positions, forever impregnable."[5]

   It did not take long for Progress to have its effects. Resentment calmed even as the whites who came from the farms and hills to work in the mills soon bore the "physical stigmata" of their caste. "By 1900 the cotton-mill worker was a pretty distinct physical type in the South; a type in some respects perhaps inferior to even that of the old poor white, which in general had been his to begin with. A dead-white skin, a sunken chest, and stooping shoulders were the earmarks of the breed. Chinless faces, microcephalic foreheads, rabbit teeth, goggling dead-fish eyes, rickety limbs, and stunted bodies abounded—over and beyond the limit of their prevalence in the countryside. The women were characteristically stringy-haired and limp of breast at twenty, and shrunken hags at thirty or forty." The mill town became like a plantation: "the dependence which had been fastened upon the poor whites by post-bellum cotton-growing was being carried over into industry, and even extended if that were possible. Even more definitely than the tenant and the cropper, the cotton-mill worker of the South would be stripped of the ancient autonomy and placed in every department of his life under the control of his employer." The mill baron "knew these workmen familiarly as Bill and Sam and George and Dick, or as Lil and Sal and Jane and Lucy. More, he knew their pedigrees and their histories."[6]

   Those on the top were as simple as those on the bottom. The

nouveau riche mill owners sought the imprimatur of a distinguished past, even if they had to invent one. Cash told of the
mythical George Washington Groundling, whose father "had been
a drunken old farmer whose forty acres were perpetually under
mortgage and who bore upon his head the shame of having hid out
in the woods to avoid being drafted into the Confederate Army.
Still, George W. was president of the First National Bank, and
master of five cotton mills. George W. was said to be worth half a
million dollars, and indubitably had the making and breaking of
most of the families of the county—including, probably, your own.
And so, and though he was known secretly to vote the national
Republican ticket and the thing was bitter in your throat, what you
said in effect was: 'Oh, Mr. Groundling, we think it just too
wonderful that all by yourself you have got up to be one of us, and
won't you come to dinner Sunday and bring dear Mrs. Groundling?'" Mrs. Groundling and her daughters called in a genealogist
"who demonstrated that Groundling was only a corruption of the
Old French *Grauntligne,* and that a certain Viscount Fulk de
Grauntligne, who was questionless the ancestor of George W. and
the explanation of his masterful qualities, had certainly gone to
England with William in 1066."[7]

Some mill workers, faced with low wages, child labor, and their
employers' pretensions, allowed union organizers to rouse them
from their lethargy and go on strike. "The fact about the Southern
mill worker was plain," Cash argued. "He was willing enough to
join the union as a novelty, and to strike. It was a part of his simple
childlike psychology and curious romantic-hedonistic heritage, in
fact, that he was willing to join any new thing in sight, from a
passing circus or the Holy Rollers up—or down." The strikes
invariably collapsed, partly from violence and strikebreakers, but
mainly because of "the strikers' own minds. . . . Under the cold
and dangerous glance of their old captains, economic and political,
under the stern and accusing glance of their ministers, they wilted
much as the Populists had once wilted, turned shamefaced, shuf-
fled, and, as the first joy in battle and in expressing their will to

defiance died down, felt despairingly that they probably would be
read out of the Democratic party in this world and of paradise in
the next. So the strikes failed."[8]

Cash dutifully if somewhat reluctantly catalogued the changes
that came to the post-Reconstruction South. He named the cities,
counted the towns, enumerated the mills, nodded toward the
middle class, appreciated the schools, regretted the increasing
prominence of preachers, noticed the spread of a frank language of
acquisition and profit, recognized the rise of parvenus, denoted
the widespread "insecurity in rank," tallied the philanthropy,
detailed the reformers's efforts. Yet Cash insisted that all the
apparent change only strengthened the "Southern pattern," that
"simplicity and that pervasive unreality which has always been
associated with their simplicity." Cash found little cynicism among
these Southerners, no hypocrisy; rather, a "curious innocence."
Cash saw the New South, from the late nineteenth century on,
mired in cultural inertia, dysfunction, falsity, myopia. Strong stuff,
and for fifty years hundreds of thousands of readers have listened,
responding to the grain of truth in *The Mind of the South* and
admiring the rhetoric deployed with such skill and vehemence.[9]

It is tempting to hurl note cards and computer paper at Cash,
offering counter-examples, complicating his neat schemas. On a
subject-by-subject basis, in fact, I disagree with virtually everything Cash says. I would stress the diversity, change, and tension
that marked every facet of life in the New South: politics, work,
intellectual life, religious faith, popular culture, relations between
blacks and whites, gender, literature. Cash was right to emphasize
the centrifugal forces of the New South, the proliferation of social
distinctions among people of both races, the spread of commercial
motives, the rapid growth of industry, the anger and confusion of
the countryside. He was wrong to explain those away. He was
wrong to believe that Southerners of both races were so easily led
into complacency or resignation. Everywhere I have looked I have
found striving, struggle, resentment, self-awareness. The problems of the New South were not those of drift, but of obstacles and

constraints. It was not for lack of trying that the South did not flourish, that the Democrats were not overthrown, that race relations did not follow a different path. Cash wrote out too much of the history of the New South, explaining it away in his rush to get to the disappointing South of the 1930s.[10]

If we shove Cash to ground of our choosing, I am confident, we can overwhelm him by force of numbers if nothing else. It has been obvious from the first reviewers to the most recent analysts that Cash's is not a complete picture of the New South. Not only is his portrayal static and geographically narrow, but it is neglectful of politics, silent on the evolution of segregation and disfranchisement, shallow on the Populists. Subsequent scholarship has rendered large parts of Cash's argument inaccurate—worse, irrelevant. C. Vann Woodward's *Origins of the New South,* published in 1951, challenged Cash at every turn—and with footnotes on every page. Where Cash stressed continuity, Woodward stressed discontinuity; where Cash stressed community, Woodward stressed conflict; where Cash stressed gullibility, Woodward stressed pursuit of self-interest; where Cash stressed culture, Woodward stressed economics and politics. Woodward won. The most important books on Populism, economic development, and race relations have adopted Woodward's emphases, not Cash's.[11]

Within the last decade, moreover, scholars have focused on the very South in which Cash lived—the mill districts of the Carolina Piedmont—and all have found Cash's portrayal deficient. David Carlton revealed the depth of conflict between the mill people and the town people; Jacqueline Hall and her co-authors recaptured the full humanity of the mill people, dispensing with Cash's cruel caricature; I. A. Newby detailed mill workers' move off the farm, telling their story in their own words, reconstructing the complexity of their motives; Allen Tullos attacked any notion of mill-owner desire for white community, placing a stern Protestant spirit of moral and commercial domination at the heart of the New South.[12]

Despite fifty years of criticism, though, Cash's interpretation of the New South shows remarkable staying power. His argument for the continuity between the antebellum and postbellum eras has been echoed in recent books by Jonathan Wiener, Dwight Billings, Lawrence Shore, and Paul Escott, though these authors emphasize ruling class cohesion and advantage rather than lower-class obeisance. Cash is often called on to make cameo appearances, invoked at the beginning of books in acts of exorcism or at the end for homage. Cash turns up in Joel Williamson's exploration of race relations, in Ted Ownby's study of evangelicalism and male culture, in Jack Temple Kirby's account of the decline of rural life. Cash has become a prominent subject in his own right, winning attention in intellectual histories of the twentieth-century South by Richard King, Michael O'Brien, Fred Hobson, and Daniel Singal. He has been the subject of two biographies, including Bruce Clayton's fine new book.[13]

It is Cash's apparent disdain for the people of the New South, black and white, that poses the greatest difficulty in today's intellectual environment, that embarrasses even his defenders. His is a good-natured kind of criticism, a sort of smiling, head-shaking rumination over widely recognized intrafamilial weaknesses, thoroughly patronizing. Cash spoke condescendingly of black Southerners without apparent shame or hesitation. Unlike many white writers of the late nineteenth and early twentieth centuries, Cash, to his credit, did not claim to know the mind of the black South. He did not put words into the mouths of black Southerners. But Cash's reticence was not so much an act of humility as it was a simple narrowness of concern with black people. The presence of black Southerners shaped the private actions and public culture of the white South, Cash recognized, but Cash's blacks exerted their influence from a distance. Cash saw black people important as a problem to whites, as a mass, not as individuals. Cash glanced through a few windows in black neighborhoods, heard the echo of laughter and screams, noted sullen stares and furtive glances. Readers of his book never met black people face to face, never heard what they had to say.[14]

Cash ignored women of every description. Black women appear

only as objects of white men's sexual convenience; white women appear only as objects of white men's sexual displacement and veneration. White women are bystanders, pale and ghostly. The interesting relationships in *The Mind of the South* all turn around white men moonstruck over other white men—their bosses, their captains, their preachers, their politicians. White women, like black Southerners of both genders, are important only as referents by which white men steer, as the people against whom white men define themselves.

But Cash did not write to celebrate white men. He patronized them most of all. He had no hesitation about putting words in the mouths of farmers and mill hands, in telling us of their deepest fears and wishes. According to Cash, they felt only dog-like loyalty, a dull throb of longing, inarticulate resentment. Perhaps Cash felt entitled to this kind of mind-reading, this useful ventriloquism. He had, after all, put in hours in steamy cotton mills during his college summers; he had watched his parents suffer in the depression; he had worn cardboard in his shoes; he had written his book in a freezing room lit by a single light bulb while neighborhood boys tossed gravel at the window, mocking this strange man who sponged off his parents well into his thirties. Maybe his words grew out of pain and empathy.[15]

The problem is that his words don't sound like it. Cash did not voice the sympathy for the oppressed that has marked, in varying degrees, virtually every book of New South history published since World War II. Fortunately for Cash's reputation today, he was also contemptuous of the South's planters, businessmen, and politicians, fair game throughout the intervening half century and into the foreseeable future. Yet, by today's standards, Cash would have to be considered racist, sexist, and elitist.

Perversely enough, in the light of all I have just said, I would like to spend the rest of my time suggesting that Cash's book still has things to teach us about the New South. *The Mind of the South*, as a pioneering effort at social history, calls our attention to strategies of understanding and narrative that have fallen into unpopularity and disuse. Cash dealt with facets of experience for which we do not currently have a language. By taking Cash seriously despite his sins, we can see some of the boundaries of our own ideas. I say "we" and "our," for what follows is a critique of my own ideas as much as anyone else's. The notions I discuss are shared to a disconcerting degree across political and methodological lines; they are not so much arguments of any given school as they are widely held assumptions, articles of faith. Let me be clear: I do not argue that we return to the prejudices of Cash. But I do believe that we should recognize our entrenched predilections for what they are, that we think about the limits imposed by our own rhetoric, our own poetics. We need a language that captures some of the power and range of Cash's.

In most ways, writing on the New South has followed the general contours of European and American historiography over the last fifty years. New South historiography has seen a typical succession of interests and trends: quantification, case studies, comparative perspectives, interest in work and labor, the dominance of social history. There has been a turn toward anthropology, recent experimentation with narrative. The field has been heavily politicized, especially over the role of the capitalist market and the meaning of race. Some of the most exciting new work concerns itself with gender. In all these ways, New South history reflects recent historical practice. Cash stands as an affront to most of them.

First of all, Cash turned to psychology to show why poorer whites followed the leaders of the South even when there was no good reason for them to do so—which was almost always. The common white man, Cash wrote, "identified his ego with the thing called the South as to become, so to say, a perambulating South in little." It felt good, Cash thought, for the common man, poor and defeated, to meld his identity with those of his superiors. Cash built from this individual consciousness out, filling the South with the projection of what he imagined to be the psychological traits of the man at the center. As a result, Cash's South was drenched with violence, fantasy, escapism, irrationality. Cash's South has a dreamlike, nightmarish quality to it; the sense of proportion and time are those of sleep, not of sociology. Cash's mind of the South was a gland, secreting uncontrollable substances. His leading men were as lost as his followers.[16]

Current historians have no taste for such irrationality. We look back on the myth and symbol school of the fifties with satisfaction in our subsequent intellectual growth; we shake our heads over Richard Hofstadter's misguided and condescending portrayal of the befuddled Populists; we note the short and conflicted life of psycho-history. The lesson seems clear: social behavior has a social explanation whose logic can be discovered. Everything from disease to ideas of sexuality appear to us as socially based, ideologically driven, culturally determined. We are just as certain of this as Cash was certain that the id played a key role. For Cash, everything was personalized; in history today, nothing is personalized. Only Joel Williamson has been willing to venture into such territory in the New South, and even he distances himself from Cash. Most social historians today seem uncomfortable discussing individual psychology at all.[17]

We stress the rationality of the oppressed and the oppressors. Notice how few poor people in our books of today act against their own interests. Their interests are often thwarted by the powerful, of course, or done in by circumstance, but the failures seldom grow out of mistaken motives or sheer lack of knowledge among impoverished protagonists. The Populists, for decades an embarrassment to liberal and leftist historians, now appear perfectly rational, in fact superrational. Charles Macune, cerebral inventor of the subtreasury plan, has replaced the raving, one-eyed demagogue Ben Tillman as the Populist prototype. Some historians even labor to show that lynching had social correlates, that feuding was economically motivated, that segregation grew naturally out of modern institutions, that disfranchisement was a shrewd move by white Democrats to forestall white rebellion under the guise of killing the black vote. You see the pattern. Cash might well have been skeptical.[18]

The closest historians of today come to irrationality is in the notion of "hegemony." Hegemony seeks to explain the same thing Cash sought to explain: why conflicts that should have broken into the open did not. In a hegemonic argument, people act out of motives of class, filtered, camouflaged, yet logical beneath it all. Eugene Genovese and like-minded historians find hegemony at work in the antebellum South, mediating relations among whites and between slaves and masters. Yet few historians have spoken of hegemony as such in the New South. Historians see white supremacy and Democratic loyalty feeding into class hegemony in the New South, but the post-Reconstruction era seems too filled with conflict and brute force to grant forces of ideological cohesion much power. Paul Gaston, in one of the most innovative books on the New South, did explore the construction of myths that explained away failure and shortcomings. Yet Gaston, too, mentions Cash only to criticize him for his continuity thesis. Charles Reagan Wilson and Gaines Foster, imaginative students of the Lost Cause and its powerful obfuscating effects, also refuse to enlist Cash as an ally. These historians, discussing distinctly Cashian themes—illusion, deflection of criticism, the building of cultural bonds among whites—are unwilling to be tarred with the Cashian brush.[19]

No one can blame them. To be seen as an ally of Cash is an embarrassment. Cash, after all, sought to explain the coherence and cohesion across class lines. We, on the other hand, intently search for the cracks, visible and otherwise, in the Solid South. We look for potential conflicts, hidden resentments, manifestations of suppressed class anger. We celebrate the rebels and ignore those who went along. Cash explained away conflict; we explain away compromise, agreement. Cash ridiculed Populism, but today we lionize the rebels. Few historians today ask why more farmers did not vote for the Populists when they had every rational reason to do so. We assume Democratic fraud or inadequate education by the

Farmers' Alliance, not farmers' party loyalty and veneration of the heroes of the Civil War and Reconstruction.[20]

There is an irony in this, for Southern social historians, like other social historians, idealize "community." We look for the egalitarian bonds of mutuality, shared ideals, and common interests that unite people. Outside lurk merchants, planters, and politicians, driven by interests that would destroy community, replace it with anomie and alienation. Our stories about the New South tend to be stories of community betrayed. Cash's merchants and planters, on the other hand, face their customers and tenants face-to-face; they build bridges of loyalty and obligation. His politicians win power through flattery and cajoling, through barbecues and swigs on the same bottle, not through fraud and intimidation. His poor, unlike ours, seem to pay little attention to one another, their gaze, in Cash's portrayal, is fixed on the mill owner, the charismatic demagogue, the planter with their future in his hands. His portrayal is an affront to our vision of a more communal, democratic past that holds out hope for a better future. Cash was less sanguine.[21]

We might ask ourselves, then, whether some of Cash's questions no longer need to be asked. Given the wrenching social change and poverty of the post-Reconstruction South, why was there not more rebellion? Given the pathological racial violence and distrust of that time and place, should we not make more room for psychological explanations? Given the enduring popularity of the Confederacy among whites, should we not talk more about social solidarity, about shared memory and identity across class lines? Given the bonds of patronage, kin, and religion, should we not grant cultural bonds a greater role than structural conflict? Even the questions make me uncomfortable.

Current historians have not distanced themselves from Cash in every regard. Certain commonalities remind us of shared, if unspoken, assumptions, remind us that historians are still children of Cash's first modernist age. Although Freud has declined in stature, we still assume that reality is somehow hidden beneath the obvious manifestations of everyday life. Although the Monkey Trial has long since passed, most modern historians of the New South grant no more autonomy for religion than Cash granted. Although we have articulated more complicated ideas of culture, we portray its operation in many of the same ways as Cash.

Despite their differences, Cash and C. Vann Woodward shared several assumptions and have passed them down to us. Both Cash and Woodward came of age in the interwar era in which "realism" of one sort or another was the goal. Both H. L. Mencken, Cash's inspiration, and Charles Beard, Woodward's inspiration, professed to see through history to its essence underneath. For Mencken, that essence was often the common man's gullibility; for Beard, that essence was economic. Menckenism tended to glorify the man in the know, whether he was an aristocrat, the educated person conversant with Darwin or Freud, or the author and readers of *The Mind of the South*. Menckenism exaggerated that man's wisdom and caricatured the average American's perceptions. Woodward's Beardianism, on the other hand, had a more democratic bent. For Woodward, all men had economic interests that encouraged them to behave rationally. The common man, black as well as white, knew what he needed and wanted (women were not mentioned), though powerful people had their hands on the machinery of power. The hidden aspect of Woodward's argument came in the political realm, where corrupt bargains and smoky-room deals tended to count more than public campaigns. Both Cash and Woodward assumed that reality lay beneath appearances.[22]

Southern historians adopted this realist perspective immediately and then pursued it with new means in the 1970s and 1980s. Quantification offered the possibility of cutting beneath the rhetoric and stereotypes of the Southern past to the reality underneath. We could find out how the slaves really fared, what the yeomen really felt about secession, who really supported the Populists, who really pushed disfranchisement. Marxian analysis and anthropology, too, detect powerful submerged currents running through history. Both frames of reference portray forces that people at the time could not fully see or describe, even if contemporaries could feel the power of mercantile capitalism and an archaic honorific culture. Those of us who use those categories thereby assume ourselves able to perceive what our subjects could not. It comes across in our language, distanced, knowing, and judgmental.

Cash's realism and Woodward's realism had something else in common: neither had a good word to say about religious faith. Woodward, in fact, had barely a word of any kind to say about religion. *Origins of the New South* maintained a sort of embarrassed silence on the subject; Woodward admitted that churches grew rapidly in the post-Reconstruction era, but he did not dwell on the meaning of that growth. Cash, on the other hand, had plenty to say about religion, all of it bad. Woodward and Cash, both from religious families, had come of age in the shadow of the events in Dayton, Tennessee. The church, it appears, seemed to both men an impediment to a realistic understanding of the common man's true position. Religion seemed a hall of mirrors, otherworldly compensation for hard times that could better be confronted in the here and now. That is pretty much the attitude of everyone else who has written on religion in the New South. We turn out one book after another on the failed Populist crusade yet ignore the simultaneous development of Holiness and Pentecostal denominations that today claim millions of adherents. Surely that is inadequate.[23]

The realism we have inherited from Cash and Woodward tends to define Southern history by what failed to happen. Our questions are not why, but why not. Why did the common whites not balk at the power of the planters, especially at the time of secession? Why did they not desert the Confederacy in greater numbers? Why did they not turn against their captains after defeat? Why did they not strike class alliances in Reconstruction? Why did they not push aside the Democrats in the agrarian crusade? Why did they not fight harder against the capitalists who increasingly ran their lives? Implicit in all these questions is a vision of what should have happened had people acted rationally. A different kind of realism, one that stresses things over which no one had control—poor land, world economic trends, population growth—is less common; only Gavin Wright has put such issues at the heart of Southern history. Most historians have tended to look for the cause for poverty in the ideas and acts of Southerners, in the greed of the rich and the lack of will or the inability of the white poor to fight for and win what they needed. This makes for stirring history, but it does not fully reckon the odds.[24]

Despite many superb studies, in other words, New South historiography has not moved very far from ideas staked out several generations ago. We keep turning the same problems over and over, worrying them smooth and familiar with so much handling. We adopt new techniques and perspectives to answer the same questions that bedeviled Cash, that bothered Woodward. By this time, virtually everything has been debunked. There is scarcely a popular myth to demolish about the post-Reconstruction South; for most Americans, whatever their race, only the South's poverty, injustice, and ignorance seem worth noting. Youngsters raised on *Mississippi Burning* and *Deliverance* are scarcely shocked by anything we tell them in our history books about the South between 1870 and 1970. First-time readers of *The Mind of the South* can scarcely feel the sense of risk and danger that surrounded that book in its early years. In fact, the challenge now, I would argue, is to bring the people of the New South back to life by portraying the complexity of their motives, the difficulty and multiplicity of the choices they faced, the variety and contradictions of their actions. How can we expect readers and students to care about a society where every endeavor could only fail, where the oppressed saw every meaningful option closed? The rhetoric of social history, and of New South social history in particular, has become impoverished, foreclosing important questions, condescending to the past in a way different from Cash but condescending to it nevertheless.

Whatever else we might say about Cash's book, the pain he felt for the South came through in every word. *The Mind of the South* was a book of passion. As such, it was one of many written between 1929 and 1941. In those bleak years, after decades of segregation and disfranchisement, after the ravages of the Great Depression, sensitive writers could feel the change in the Southern air. Some wrote to hasten the change, others to slow it, others to salvage what they could of the old. The Nashville Agrarians espoused the glories of the South's rural civilization (ironically, Frank Owsley and his wife Harriet pioneered in quantitative social history to help prove the Agrarian case). William Alexander Percy wrote an elegant conservative apologia for the life of a Delta planter. Douglas Southall Freeman won enormous national success by composing tributes to Robert E. Lee. Margaret Mitchell's triumph revealed that Cash's acerbic view was very much a minority view of the white South even in the North and abroad. The 1930s marked, too, a golden age for sociologists and anthropologists studying the South, led not only by Howard Odum but also by Liston Pope, Charles S. Johnson, John Dollard, and Hortense Powdermaker. W. E. B. DuBois and Carter G. Woodson challenged many of the ideas about black Southerners that Cash unblinkingly perpetuated. Jean Toomer, Zora Neale Hurston, Thomas Wolfe, and William Faulkner created complex visions of a complex South.[25]

In the year of *The Mind of the South* and Cash's death, James Agee brought post-modern anguish to the act of writing about people such as poor Southerners. "It seems to me curious, not to say obscene and thoroughly terrifying," Agee admitted at the beginning of his book on Alabama sharecroppers, *Let Us Now Praise Famous Men*, "to pry intimately into the lives of an undefended and appallingly damaged group of human beings, an ignorant and helpless rural family, for the purpose of parading the nakedness, disadvantage and humiliation of these lives before another group of human beings, in the name of science, of 'honest journalism' (whatever that paradox may mean), of humanity, of social fearlessness, for money, and for a reputation for crusading and unbias which, when skillfully enough qualified, is exchangeable at any bank for money." Agee's prose twisted and contorted under the pressure of his doubt. Cash's prose surged and swayed, doubled back on itself, questioned its own sweeping assertions. Ours, by contrast, is placid, cool, clinical.[26]

To compare our own work with that of Cash and his contemporaries is to notice how we have narrowed our questions and constricted our answers. The South's past is no less tortured today than it was fifty years ago. We have no more mastered the Southern past than Cash did. But where is the range of voices that wrote in 1941? Where is the diversity, the anguish? Regardless of politics, the history books of today speak with a common tone, a tone of authority, a judgmental bent. Our ideal is understatement, concision; we live under a self-imposed tyranny of Strunk and White. We distrust people who write in idiosyncratic ways; the profession rewards the well-placed rejoinder more than it does a singular vision. It is considered bad taste for a Southern historian of the South to reveal any emotional identification with the region; we are supposed to be distanced from the South, to cultivate—or feign—a professional interest uncolored by parochial loyalties.[27]

Humor in various guises—sarcasm, parody, satire, mimicry—gave Cash's book much of its power, drive much of its analysis. Cash, reading our books about the South, might wonder whether the American Historical Association had passed a by-law against the use of humor in the writing of history. Southern historians today seem no more likely to commit humor than they are to insist on the literary merit of Thomas Nelson Page. It simply isn't done. We go about our work with a mien of solemnity, deploying appropriately lugubrious language. I cannot help but think that the subjects of Southern history—men and women, black and white, rich and poor—would smile in amusement at our straight-faced and straight-laced accounts of their lives. They recognized the tragedies of the South's, their own, histories, but it was the most oppressed people of both races who created the most rebelliously joyous music, the most joyous faith, in the face of that tragedy. We might follow their example, and Cash's. We have forgotten laughter's power to resist indignity, to deflate pretension.

Maybe some will say that the course of Southern history since

1941 has necessarily led us to write in the way that we do, that we cannot, in this prosaic day and age, be expected to maintain the fire of the Southern Renaissance. Maybe Southern historians of today are writing on borrowed time. The glorious movement against segregation and disfranchisement has come and gone, after all, leaving ambiguity and unfocused frustation along with a heroic standard succeeding generations despair of matching. The forces of progress and the forces of evil are not as clearly marked as they once were. Histories written in an era such as ours are not likely to hold the kind of passion Cash and his contemporaries possessed.

But perhaps our position is not without its compensations. Maybe there is something to be gained if a passionate empathy should replace a passionate indignation. A lot about the South still needs to be explained to ourselves and to our children, in our own voice. Because softly, behind the roar of the interstate and the chatter of the satellite dish, do you not hear the clank of chains, the sounds of a revival, the rustle of crinoline, and maybe even the chuckle of Jack Cash, all tempting us to explore, one more time, with feeling, the minds of the South?

Commentary / Linda Reed

Comments for any session do not usually come with a title, but on my first reading and rereadings of Ayers's paper, I thought my comments should dwell on the "New South McDonaldsized: We've Come a Long Way." This would be appropriate because Ayers has summarized in brief form some of what southern history meant in 1941 and the development of the field through present times. Because Ayers has changed slightly his last page, it is necessary to give the context of his use of "McDonaldsization." In the last paragraph of the original paper, he states:

> Maybe some will say that the course of Southern history since 1941 has necessarily led us to write in the way that we do, that we cannot, in this prosaic day and age, be expected to maintain the

fire of the Southern Renaissasnce. Maybe Southern historians of today are writing on borrowed time. Maybe the McDonaldsization of the South has eroded not only our material but the sense of difference and anguish that drove Cash into writing his book. Or softly, do we not hear, behind the roar of the interstate and the chatter of the satellite dish, the clank of chains, the sounds of a revival, the rustle of crinoline, and maybe even the chuckle of Jack Cash, all tempting us to explore, one more time, with feeling, the minds of the South?

Fortunately, southern history has grown to be more inclusive or representative of the people who populate the South. Especially in the last decade, as Ayers points out, we have seen a proliferation of studies that address questions of class, gender, and race. Finally, the historical profession has begun to appreciate diversity, diversity in the sense of illustrating positive differences to show that we as individuals from the varying backgrounds of class, gender, and race have impacted each other in one form or the other. Influences flow in both directions, and we must conclude that diversity inevitably is a term of inclusiveness and not exclusiveness. Therefore, unlike Ayers, I do see the passion in our historical writing. Even if the writing itself is not "passionately" written (that there is an effort at objectivity), the mere fact of the choice expresses a passion for the subject. We choose our subjects for research, in other words, according to things for which we have the greatest interest. For example, when I was considering a dissertation topic, I knew I wanted to write about the South. Furthermore, I wanted particularly to address questions of gender and race. The project I settled on (the history of the Southern Conference for Human Welfare and the Southern Conference Educational Fund) fulfilled my objective. I am presently working on a topic that more directly fulfills my interest in class, gender, and race: a biographical study on Fannie Lou Hamer (black woman sharecropper and political activist from Mississippi). My contention, then, is that the South has been McDonaldsized in the sense that McDonald's fast food establishments have become a major industrial entity within the South, indeed the world, but our material on southern history has not become so weak that we do not express anger or excitement about the region.

As historians we have been trained to piece together the past according to the available evidence. We do this through information from diaries, correspondence, telegrams, telephone logs (especially in the most recent past), church records, oral history interviews, and many other sources. We have been encouraged to draw conclusions carefully and sensitively. Indeed, we have been discouraged from making interpretations that border on editorializing, not to make broad sweeping generalizations. Yet, we come together to commemorate W. J. Cash and *The Mind of the South*, who editorialized extensively and drew conclusions, with which almost all we totally disagree.

I want to emphasize that I fully appreciate the New South context within which Ayers places Cash's work. But I am puzzled by a question he raises toward the beginning of the essay: "are academic historians unable to write like Cash, encumbered with footnotes and all, or do we know too much to write like Cash?" My sense of the matter is that our footnotes give us more leverage and help us to feel freer as we write. This gets me to the point of dwelling on the fact that we have come a long way since 1941. Ayers, however, recognizes the value of his question because he even states later, "We look back on the myth and symbol school of the fifties with satisfaction in our subsequent intellectual growth." Cash and Ayers help us to see that we are a product of our generation and that any era can produce a W. J. Cash at the same time that it can produce a C. Vann Woodward.

The same South that produced Cash and Woodward had more white southerners who agreed with Cash than with Woodward, at least most of the evidence tells us so. As late as 1938 white southerners, who largely and unjustifiably blamed blacks for the South's economic backwardness, did not readily embrace discussions about the region that included input from blacks. In 1938 President Franklin Delano Roosevelt, motivated by a possible political purging of the conservative Democrats from the presently held offices, set up the National Emergency Council (NEC) to investigate the southern economic situation. The NEC reported that the South was the nation's number one economic problem, and many southerners responded to the report by becoming a part of the Southern Conference for Human Welfare (SCHW) which was founded in Birmingham in 1938. The uniqueness of SCHW rested in its willingness to invite black southerners, for the first time, to discussions about the South's ills. The entire development of the Southern Conference Movement, so called because SCHW in 1946 established the Southern Conference Educational Fund (SCEF) and the same individuals essentially struggled to democratize the South from the 1930s through the 1970s, illustrates the majority of white southerners' allegiance to Cash's South. Neither SCHW's nor SCEF's membership, inclusive of blacks, ever numbered more than 10,000. The Southern Conference Movement did not get its fullest support until the 1960s, and even then that support came largely from the black community, especially those who believed in mass demonstrations.[1]

In a way Ayers's point that "for fifty years hundreds of thousands of readers have listened, responding to the grain of truth in *The Mind of the South* and admiring the rhetoric deployed with such skill and vehemence," brings cause for alarm. I am reminded of the saying that the more things change, the more things stay the same. Understanding Cash is to recognize that southerners have accepted change very slowly. Although tragic, we are not to be amazed that the Civil Rights Movement had to take on the violent reaction it did in the 1950s and 1960s; literally, change in the South became a matter of life and death. My hope is that our present-day homage to Cash is not an embracement of his hope or passion for the South of his times. Ayers goes on record that this is not his mission.

One of the other things that Ayers mentioned was the lack of humor in our current historical writing. Mind you, the South has presented so many tragic moments and so much irrationality that it does become almost impossible to find lighter moments as we look over so many disappointments in the way people behaved. But I found a light moment in the 1940s when the SCHW was campaigning heavily against the poll tax and the poll-tax legislators. The SCHW made Senator Theodore "The Man" Bilbo a major target for political defeat. Bilbo likewise targeted SCHW as "the South's No. One Enemy," borrowing from the NEC 1938 report which referred to the South as the nation's number one economic problem. As SCHW set out to rid the South and nation of the "Bilbo crowd" tensions mounted. I share with you my writing of the situation:

> Although all the southern demagogues equally disliked the Conference and expressed themselves just as forcefully, Bilbo became the epitome of their opposition toward SCHW. Many Conference leaders began to refer to Bilbo and his lot as "the Bilbonic plaque." The Conference was good at making the best of a bad situation, and it led a campaign to raise SCHW funds "with Sen. Bilbo's help." It mailed out a postcard appeal at Christmas 1945 over Bilbo's signature with the message: Please send a Christmas contribution to Bilbo's Enemy Number One—Now." By May 1946 this appeal had brought in $1,000 as "public enemies of Sen. Bilbo responded."

SCHW's efforts turned out to be unsuccessful on both the fight against the poll tax and Senator Bilbo. But when I interviewed white SCHW-SCEF member Virginia Foster Durr and the subject of Bilbo came up, she said of the man who had repeatedly disparaged blacks and particularly black World War I and II soldiers or any of the Southern Conference Movement ideals, she said that he appropriately died suffering with cancer of the mouth.[2]

In conclusion, Ayers is to be commended for his courageous efforts at placing Cash in a South that Cash would not have recognized or appreciated. Ayers carefully pointed out important works by blacks—Charles S. Johnson, W. E. B. Du Bois, Carter G. Woodson, Jean Toomer, Zora Neale Hurston, and others. We must remember that by 1941 the Harlem Renaissance still flourished and that New York City was not all inclusive of the richness that blacks contributed to American society. To his credit, Ayers does not overlook "the most rebelliously joyous music" of an oppressed people. In terms of cultural significance, blacks played a key role for the South, indeed all of America: black Americans presented the United States with its original music form (jazz, some argue even blues). I especially believe that we have come a long way when this development cannot be left out of any discussion about the American South.

The Mind of the South and Southern Distinctiveness

JOHN SHELTON REED

"I am not at all trying to lay out a thesis, far less to substantiate or to solve." This quotation is obviously not from *The Mind of the South*. It comes instead from *Let Us Now Praise Famous Men*, another powerful book written a half-century ago by a Southern observer of the South, James Agee. W. J. Cash put a thesis on the table in a way that Agee did not—and in a way that I don't plan to, either. All I intend is to offer a few observations based on a dozen readings of the book since 1960 or so, a good deal of thought about it, and a few attempts to teach from it over the years.

Let me summarize that thesis of Cash's once more.[1] He argued that "the South" (leave aside for now the question of whom *that* included) had exhibited a "fairly definite mental pattern," continuous throughout its history. This collective "mind" was characterized by romanticism and hedonism, on the one hand, and by individualism, on the other. It had been produced by the frontier and sustained after that by frontier-like conditions that Cash claimed to find in the plantation, in Reconstruction, and in the world of the textile industry.

Cash discussed such "complicating influences" as regional conflict and the presence of an aristocratic tradition embodied in what he called "the Virginians." Nevertheless, he insisted that the South was *different*, and (despite its diversity) *solid*, set apart from the rest of the nation by its attitudes, values, and assumptions.

The Mind of the South does not explicitly state hypotheses and test them. That is, it is not a scientific treatise. In fact, it does not much resemble scholarship of any sort. As Bertram Wyatt-Brown has pointed out, Cash employed a lawyerly sort of exposition:

giving examples, telling stories, appealing to his readers' experience and common sense; constantly making concessions, but never a fatal one; acknowledging exceptions and limitations, but always reverting to the main line of the argument.[2] In other words, he wrote as an advocate, and his rhetoric is subtle, not to say slippery.

Nevertheless, *The Mind of the South* is packed with propositions that could be subjected to empirical test, generalizations that are by their nature at least mostly true or mostly false. Whatever James Agee was doing—ethnography, premature New Journalism, or (as he said) a special sort of burglary or espionage—whatever it was, his book has not been held to the same empirical standards as Cash's treatise. In some ways Cash was bolder than Agee, and he has paid a price for his forthrightness, in the form of closer critical attention to what he was up to.

Much of that attention has been biographical in nature, and rightly so: Cash's circumstances unquestionably shaped and limited his view of the South. As C. Vann Woodward pointed out twenty-odd years ago, for instance, Cash wrote as virtually a life-long resident of the Carolina piedmont, and that distorted his view.[3] We should recognize that he also wrote as someone who aspired to be both a great writer and a member of the New South's smart set, and those aspirations affected both his prose and his opinions, not always for the better. Finally, let us concede that Cash wrote as a Southern white man of the lower middle class—particularly unfortunate origins right now. Everyone has to come from somewhere, of course, but viewed through the currently fashionable prism of race, class, and gender, both Cash and his analysis come up short.

Incidentally, some historians have made this last point at length, and I must say that it is passing strange to find them, of all people, trading in anachronistic criticism.[4] Even a sociologist can recognize that times change, and that (as Michael O'Brien put it) "Cash himself was a liberal in racial matters by the standards of his time, that is, he had adjusted his views to deprecate the enemies of blacks, but not yet altered his opinions to sympathize with black culture and personality."[5] Fair enough—and so?

As for Cash's other limitations, I could point out that, when he wrote, the Carolina piedmont and similar parts of other states were coming into their own, contesting the old plantation belt's economic, demographic, and even symbolic dominance of the South. I could also observe that, when Cash wrote, Southern white men of his class had attained a cultural and political hegemony that they had never had before, and have lost since.[6]

What Cash had to say may or may not have been true for Southern women, or for black Southerners—I will come back to this—but even if it was not, it is worth knowing about the mind of the white male piedmont South. One could say that if we have to choose a race, class, and gender, Cash's combination is the most important one to hear from. One could say that, although I will not.

No, let us take all of those criticisms at full strength, and subtract from Cash's achievement the maximum allowance for all of his biographical limitations. The residue is still impressive.

This is a good book. For a lower-middle class Southern white man from the Carolina piedmont writing in the 1930s (if you insist), it is a *great* book. Besides, so far as I know, nobody from any other race, class, gender, or subregion has even tried what Cash tried. Give him credit for that.

What, exactly, did he do? We can evaluate his book in at least three ways: as a literary work, as an intellectual event, and, finally, as an empirical account and analysis of Southern history and culture.

Vann Woodward has written that "social scientists, especially sociologists, seem to have a special affinity" for *The Mind of the South*.[7] Maybe so. I do, anyway. Once I even went so far as to suggest in Cash's defense that it almost does not matter whether he was "right" or "wrong." "His South may not correspond perfectly or even very well to the real one," I wrote, "but it's certainly a fascinating place. . . . [A]s a work of the imagination, *The Mind of the South* is a remarkable achievement—far better, as [Bruce] Clayton suggests, than any novel Cash was ever likely to write."[8]

It is not so much his distinctive prose, although I admire that, too. Michael O'Brien has written that Cash's style, "like that of Thomas Wolfe, [is] best relished in youth," but I have learned by requiring students to read it that it is not to the taste of many readers of the MTV generation.[9] Maybe those great rolling periods should be read aloud, so the snappy colloquialisms can punctuate them appropriately, but who has *time* for that, these days?

Anyway, Cash's real artistry lies in his daring conceptualization. Woodward observed that Cash himself "was merely illustrating once more that ancient Southern trait that he summed up in the word 'extravagant'"—and that is exactly what some of us like about the book: not just the sound of its words, but the sweep and dash of its history, the boldness and the flamboyance and the very exaggeration of its characterizations.[10] ("Softly; do you not hear behind that the gallop of Jeb Stuart's cavalrymen?"[11])

Notice, though, that this tack tries to do for Cash what Louis Rubin did some time ago for the Vanderbilt Agrarians, Cash's contemporaries who wrote *I'll Take My Stand*.[12] You say the description is inaccurate, the analysis all wet? Well, this is not history, or sociology. The "South" is an imaginative construction here, a trope.

But, you know, both the Agrarians and Cash really were trying to engage in social analysis, and it is more than a little patronizing to tell them that they were not, never mind that you go on to say that they were doing something finer. Both books deserve to be taken seriously as what their authors intended them to be, even if that means savaging them. In any case, a good many readers have insisted on seeing them as something other than works of art.

Many, indeed, have taken *The Mind of the South* as gospel, which means that, right or wrong, it is undeniably important as an event in the South's intellectual and cultural history, as Vernon Burton has pointed out. I suspect this symposium exists because reading Cash's book was a formative experience for today's sym-

posium-going class of Southerners. For decades, it was the one
book to read if you were only reading one. (In some circles, it still
is. A while back I came across the Penguin edition in a Buck-
inghamshire bookshop, almost surely the only book about the
American South in that little English village.) Some of Cash's great
organizing concepts—"the man at the center," "the savage ideal,"
"the proto-Dorian bond," the "rape complex," and so forth—still
shape our thought about the South, whether we like it or not.

Indeed, whether we *know* it or not. For better or for worse,
many of Cash's broad-brush characterizations of Southern life and
culture, stripped of their catchy labels, have become almost conventional wisdom among literate Southerners. The Trinidadian-
Indian writer V. S. Naipaul, for instance, unwittingly paraphrases
Cash again and again in his recent book, *A Turn in the South*, as he
quotes various Southerners' "observations."[13] In fact, Naipaul's
informants were probably repeating things that they had read or
heard in college. Some of these ideas were not original with Cash,
true, but he gave them popular currency. If we want to know
where our ideas have come from, Cash's book is still required
reading.

But it really does matter whether those ideas are right or wrong.
Cash did ask to be judged, not as an artist or a walking intellectual event, but as a social analyst. As I have said, I think he was a
pretty good one—although, Cash-like, we must allow the necessary qualifications and limitations. A while ago, when *Southern
Living* held an editorial conference at Ole Miss with the theme,
"Where have we come from? Where are we going?", a curmedg-
eonly friend grumbled that he was more interested in the question, "Now that we're here, where the hell are we?" Well, all three
questions are worth asking, and Cash addressed them all, with
varying degrees of success.

Historians differ, obviously, about how good an answer Cash
gave to the question of where we have come from. Maybe they
always will differ. It is what they do. But at least Cash did some
useful myth-busting. In particular, unlike his patron and fellow-

iconoclast H. L. Mencken, he was not captivated by the prevailing Southern view of life Before the War. I once saw a can of paint-remover with a magnolia-blossom logo, the brand-name "Old South," and the notice, "Danger: Harmful or Fatal If Swallowed." Cash refused to swallow it: his insistence that the Southern colonies housed a "rough young society" where "the test of a gentleman" was "the possession of sufficient property" was a useful corrective to the sort of misconception that led a student to tell me once in a paper about the aristocratic descent of white Southerners that "the gynecology of the Southern stock was very truly royal-like."[14] Cash's account of "the Irishman" can be read alongside the sagas of the Sutpens and the O'Haras, and it may hold up pretty well as a social history of the settling of the Southern interior.[15]

In other respects, of course, his history is less satisfactory. The problem, however, usually seems to be that his account is partial, and how much that matters (except perhaps on Reconstruction), how misleading it is, often seems to be an open question.

The question of where the South was going Cash tried to duck. On his last page, he stated explicitly, "Of the future I shall venture no definite prophecies."[16] But if we refuse to let him off the hook that easily, if we insist that his thesis implies continuity whether he likes it or not—well, whatever kind of historian he was, he made a lousy prophet. As Lacy Ford has pointed out, the changes of the last fifty years surely put the lie to his implicit predictions. In particular, he certainly saw little likelihood of dramatic racial change, much less of its coming about by black initiative. It is pointless to speculate about whether he would have adjusted happily to the postwar South, like some white Southern liberals, or been bewildered by it, like others, but there is no question that he would have found it surprising. Today's South is not one he could have imagined in 1940, much less predicted.

On the question of what the South looked like in his own time, though, I think he was a far better guide. The "mental pattern" he identified did characterize a great many Southerners, and some aspects of it—by no means all, not even most, but some—still do. Let us take a look at what he had to say about those two allegedly major aspects of the Southern mind, romanticism and individualism.

His treatment of romanticism is the less persuasive. Frankly, I would like more evidence than Cash provides that the South's farmers and businessmen were any more romantic then farmers and businessmen anywhere else. Of course, many Southern *writers* have been romantic, and certainly Cash himself was. The assertion that the tough customers who built and ran the South were romantic came, after all, from a young man who burst into tears at Chartres cathedral.

There is a larger point here than simply the speculation that Jack Cash may have been projecting his own characteristics onto his fellow Southerners. As I said earlier, in sociological terms—race, class, gender, time, place—Cash represented an important population. In those respects, he was enough like other Southern white men to understand a great deal about them. But psychologically he was anything but representative. Consider the portrait of the artist that emerges from Bruce Clayton's biography.[17] Here is "Sleepy" Cash, 36 years old, unable to hold a job for long, living with his parents. His recurrent attacks of "neurasthenia" and "melancholia" are notorious; he also suffers from goiter and (secretly) from fears of impotence. He seems to spend his days riding his bicycle, chopping wood, and dozing in the sun in front of the courthouse. He stays up nights talking with an unemployed Baptist preacher. He drinks too much, smokes too much, and probably doesn't eat his vegetables. In short, he is a mess. And hardly typical.

Bertram Wyatt-Brown writes with authority about the psychodynamics of literary creation, but let me simply add the sociological commonplace that marginality can produce the heightened consciousness required for social analysis.[18] If Cash's atypicality may sometimes have led him astray, it may have led him to write his book in the first place—and when he got it right it may have been because he was far enough removed from the mainstream of white Southern life to see it whole.

When it came to *black* culture and personality, of course, Cash's understanding was obviously unsatisfactory. We should, however, acknowledge his remarks on the black influence on white Southerners. "Negro entered into white man as profoundly as white man entered into Negro," he wrote, "subtly influencing every gesture, every word, every emotion and idea, every attitude."[19] Today, that is almost a cliche, and certainly that understanding is simply taken for granted in much recent scholarship on the South. We need to recall, though, that in 1940 it was neither an obvious observation nor a popular one.[20]

Since Cash's few references to religion also come under the head of romanticism and hedonism, this may be the place to remark on another empathetic failure. It seems to me that his treatment of Southern religion is almost willfully blinkered.[21] Much of what he says about Southern religion is true, but so is much that he does not say. Another North Carolina journalist, Gerald Johnson, wrote once that "the man who will deny that religious admonition is the most powerful influence for public decency in the South simply does not know the South."[22] But you will learn no more about that from *The Mind of the South* than from—well, than from the writings of H. L. Mencken.

If Cash was perversely obtuse when it came to Southern religion, though, I think he was right on the money in his discussion of civic pride, a Southern trait that shows few signs of abating.[23] One recent study has shown that, controlling for city size, wealth, and other factors, the South now has *more* than its share of museums, symphony orchestras, and other cultural institutions.[24] Surely this burgeoning jungle of the *beaux arts* reflects less devotion to high culture for its own sake than the touching eagerness of our new urban elites to make their cities "world-class." What Cash wrote of skyscrapers in Charlotte could as well be said of World Fairs in Knoxville and New Orleans, or the Olympics in Atlanta—that these towns have little more use for them than a hog has for a morning coat.[25] How else to account for these undertakings, then, than as quests for civic glory, shaped by a taste for the grand gesture and the defensive desire to *"force [some] recognition of* our worth and dignity of character"? (That is Cash, quoting the Raleigh *News and Observer* from 1880.[26])

You know, maybe our business leaders really *are* more romantic. Anyway, the other aspect of the Southern mind—what Cash called "individualism" and we might as well, too—is both better documented than romanticism in the first place, and more clearly characteristic of Southern culture fifty years after Cash. Listen to Cash on the mind of the Old South: its "dominant trait," he said, "was an intense individualism—in its way, perhaps the most intense individualism the world has seen since the Italian Renaissance."[27] This trait was found, "mutatis mutandis," he said, at all levels of white society, from the planter, "wholly content with his autonomy and jealously guardful that nothing should encroach upon it," to "the farmers and the crackers [who] were in their own way self-suffcient, too—as fiercely careful of their prerogatives of ownership, as jealous of their sway over their puny domains, as the grandest lord."[28]

Like other aspects of the Southern mind, Cash argued, this was originally a frontier trait, but it was preserved by the South's subsequent pseudo-frontiers, or frontier-equivalents. "Southerners in 1900," Cash wrote, "would see the world in much the same terms in which their fathers had seen it in 1830; as, in its last aspect, a simple solution, an aggregation of self-contained and self-sufficient monads, each of whom was ultimately and completely responsible for himself."[29] (As Hank Williams, Jr., puts it, a country boy can survive.) According to Cash, the "ruling element" in this tradition was "an intense distrust of, and, indeed, downright aversion to, any actual exercise of authority beyond the barest minimum essential to the existence of the social organism."[30] In short, Cash believed that Southerners love politics but hate government.[31]

There might seem to be a paradox here. How do you square individualism with the "savage ideal" of communitarian conformity? What is this—regimented anarchy? Cash offered no answer; indeed, he did not seem to recognize that there is a problem.

Could this be because, in the South, there is none? Richard Weaver—University of Chicago philosopher, Cash's fellow-Tar Heel, and the Agrarians' fellow-traveler—suggested as much in an essay in which he distinguished between two *types* of individualism.[32]

One type, which Weaver found exemplified by a New Englander, Thoreau, reflects the absence or rejection of cultural prescriptions. This is the modern individualism against which Alasdair MacIntyre contends in his book *After Virtue*, a form of social organization (if we can call it that) in which "I am what I myself choose to be."[33] The other sort of individualism Weaver described is different: it is itself culturally prescribed. One is individualistic because one is supposed to be.[34] Weaver took as an exemplar of this sort of individualism a Virginian, John Randolph of Roanoke, and I think this Southern, communitarian ethic is what Cash was observing. When he said individualism, he did not mean free-thinking nonconformity. He was talking about a norm of self-reliance, an anti-institutional orientation that says: you should be responsible for the welfare of you and yours. You should not be dependent on the government, the church, the labor union, the law-court—on "society."[35]

A sociologist is inevitably reminded of Emile Durkheim's observation that some people kill themselves because they are adrift, without personal ties, but others, like Japanese kamikaze pilots, give their lives because they are too well integrated for their own good.[36] Like suicide, individualism may be what is expected from well-socialized, well-integrated members of a community. "Anti-institutional," that is, does not necessarily mean anti-social.

Notice Cash's male pronouns, by the way: each monad "responsible for himself." This is not just grammatical convention. When Cash spoke of "Southerners" he did mean white men, people very much like (but for the grace of God) himself.

Consider this sentence: "No man felt or acknowledged any primary dependence on his fellows, save perhaps in the matter of human sympathy and entertainment."[37] Cash surely did not mean that no black person or white woman felt or acknowledged dependence. Indeed, that was the role that the dominant social ideologies envisioned for them and, with considerable success, imposed upon them.

Or take this passage, about the individualism of the plantation world: "[It] was full of the chip-on-the-shoulder swagger and brag of a boy—one, in brief, of which the essence was the boast, voiced or not, on the part of every Southerner, that he would knock hell out of whoever dared to cross him."[38] Plainly, Cash did not mean "every Southerner" to include Southern blacks and Southern women. For a woman to reveal that attitude would have been unladylike; for a black to display it could have been fatal.

But to say that Cash was not writing about white women and blacks does not mean that what he said did not apply to them— "mutatis mutandis," of course. To say that they were supposed to be dependent does not mean that they always internalized that role, always saw themselves that way—and one readily available alternative has been to appropriate the self-reliant, chip-on-the-shoulder ideal of white men for themselves.

It is significant that, among themselves, many black Southerners have admired a long line of heroic "bad niggers," from Stagolee and That Bully of the Town down to Superfly and Shaft in our own time.[39] These are men who could teach W. J. Cash a thing or two about prickly individualism and autonomy. Black women, too, have had their pride and independence: think only of the story of Frankie and Johnny.

As for white women—well, Scarlet O'Hara has shaped the self-image of a good many Southern women, if we can believe their testimonials. This is the same Scarlett who was once described as "J.E.B. Stuart in drag." Once upon a time, about the only woman celebrated in country music was the long-suffering dependent "angel," but these days Nashville offers a number of alternatives, from the good-timing, hell-raising good old girl to the supercompetent, autonomous "good woman," who treats her man as no better than an equal.[40] Even when it comes to violence—Thelma and Louise may be something new in the movies, but they have been hanging around country music for some time now.

If we take as our index of Southern-mindedness knocking hell out of people who cross us, both survey and crime data show that Southern women, although less touchy than Southern men, are more dangerous than Northern women—and blacks are the most Southern of us all.

Southern individualism is still with us. Just after Jimmy Carter was elected, Roy Reed described it for the worried readers of the *New York Times:*

> For all the American encroachments, the South is inhabited and given [its] dominant tone by men—and women who acquiesce in this matter—who carry in their hearts or genes or livers or lights an ancient, God-credited belief that a man has a right to do as he pleases. A right to be let alone in whatever plain of triumph he has staked out and won for his own. A right to go to hell or climb to the stars or sit still and do nothing, just as he damn well pleases, without restraint from anybody else and most assuredly without interference from any government anywhere.

Reed believed that the fight for this orientation was lost "about the time [a man] lost the irretrievable right to take a leak off his own front porch." Still, he wrote, "they have not yet taken [Southerners'] right to curse and defy."[41]

Maybe this is Cashian overstatement, but certainly we can find anti-institutionalism in many aspects of Southern life. It is stated frankly, for example, in scores of country songs, by singers like Hank Williams, Jr., Charlie Daniels, Bobby Bare, Merle Haggard, and David Allan Coe. It can also be found in Southerners' inclination to redress grievances privately, without recourse to third-party mediation. This means (as Cash recognized) that disputes are often settled violently—and that is what a lot of those country songs are about.

Anti-institutionalism may also be reflected in Southern localism and familism, a preference for the known, tried, and true, as

opposed to the distant and formal. It also marks and is probably
reinforced by the Evangelical Protestantism to which most Southerners subscribe, a strikingly individualistic form of religion in
which, as singer Tom T. Hall sums it up, "Me and Jesus got our own
thing goin'. / Don't need anybody to tell us what it's all about."
And, finally, individualism underlies the economic libertarianism
of many Southerners, a self-help orientation that seems, if anything, increasingly common among Southern whites, and perhaps
among Southern blacks, too.

All of these attributes are more widespread in the South than
elsewhere in the United States. You can deplore them—Cash
did—but it is hard to deny that they exist. They show up as
regional differences in everything from political attitudes to homi-
cide rates, gun ownership to union membership. Some of these
traits are more common among educated Southerners than unedu-
cated ones, or among urban Southerners than rural ones. Laissez-
faire economic views are even more common among migrants to
the South than among natives, so Yankee immigration will not
reduce *that* difference. In most of these respects, the South is not
becoming more like the rest of the country: some of these differences are even larger now than when Cash wrote, and in other
ways the rest of the country is becoming "Southernized."

A belief that says you are ultimately responsible for your own
welfare fits poorly with the realities of a class-ridden society, but of
course Cash argued that the "yoke" of class "weighed but lightly" in
the South.[42] He did not deny that there were class distinctions in
the South—indeed, he emphasized them, as an aspiring intellectual of the 1930s should. But he insisted that there had been an
"almost complete disappearance of economic and social focus on
the part of the masses."

More overstatement, perhaps, but can we agree with Cash and
Professor Ayers that there was nowhere near as much class consciousness as there *should* have been? Cash made a valuable point
when he observed that in the South, for whatever reason, "one
simply did not have to get on in this world in order to achieve

security, independence, or value in one's own estimation and in that of one's fellows."[43] In explanation, he mentioned kinship ties, geographical and social mobility, and the presence of a black underclass.[44] If not for that blind spot when it came to religion, he could have mentioned that, too, as a factor contributing to security and self-esteem.

It is also in this context that we first encounter what becomes a recurring theme: the importance of Southern manners. Barely forty pages into the book, Cash argued that the "kindliness and easiness" of Southern backcountry life became the "essential kernel" of "the famous Southern manner," and he observed that manners governing relations between the classes have served as "a balance wheel in the Southern social world and . . . a barrier against the development of bitterness"—or, you could as easily say, against the development of class consciousness.[45] Again and again, Cash insisted that the Southern etiquette of class has deemphasized distinctions between rich and poor, just as the etiquette of race continually emphasized the gulf of caste. He argued, for instance, that in the Old South the yeoman seldom encountered "naked hauteur." The gentleman "patronize[d] him in such fashion that . . . he seemed not to be patronized at all but actually deferred to." In a characteristic vignette, quoted by Professor Jones, Cash showed how that might have worked, and he concluded that the "working code of the Old South" was "in its peculiar way, simply an embodiment of . . . the old basic democracy of feeling."[46]

In Cash's view, the Civil War did nothing to alter this "working code." Indeed, the experience of war meant that "the captains knew [even] better how to handle the commoner, to steer expertly about his recalcitrance, to manipulate him without ever arousing his jealous independence."[47] And the rise of the mills meant merely that "the old personal easy relations" of the countryside were brought indoors. Professor Ayers has given us the pertinent passage: "The baron knew these workmen familiarly as Bill and Sam and George and Dick, or as Lil and Sal and Jane and Lucy"—

and so forth. [48] The description does go on, and on, and it is easy to make fun of it. But surely we can allow Cash some license in describing the human face of paternalism, since he was unsparing in his treatment of its defects. In any case, Cash's description was not just a flight of romanticism, grotesquely applied to the textile mill. He was on to something important.

I will not soon forget what a friend said one time, when he stopped off to see us in North Carolina on his way back home to Mississippi from a sociological convention in the Northeast. He had noticed something interesting about how some sociologists dealt with the staff of the convention hotel. "Damn Marxists," he said, "go on and on about the *workers*—and they treat the help like dirt." He was right, although I think he should have said "Yankee Marxists," because this is really a regional matter. From a Southern point of view, many New Yorkers—Marxists or not— treat *everyone* like dirt, and if you are working for one, those manners rub your face in the fact of your subordination. Southern- ers, as Cash recognized, usually treat each other as equals, what- ever their private opinions (that is, unless they *want* to insult someone). [49]

This regional difference can cause problems. Not long ago, my hometown was buzzing with the story of the Yankee newcomer who took a work crew to task for some fault with their work. The workers simply packed up their tools and left him sputtering in mid-criticism. "Sonofabitch wants to boss you around like he owns you" was thought to be sufficient explanation.

That is a significant phrase, isn't it? "Like he *owns* you." As Cash's discussion of the "proto-Dorian bond" implies, the legatees of a slave society—whether one's ancestors were on the top, bottom, or side—may have a special understanding of the impor- tance of independence, dignity, and pride. It makes sense that the fictive equality among white men should have been embodied in manners that did not bring into question the other's worth or self- respect.

Those manners seem to be outlasting the conditions that gave rise to them. Indeed, most white Southerners now extend them to Southern blacks, most of whom seem willing to return the favor. But they are threatened, and not just by Northern newcomers. In fact, they were already threatened in 1940, as Cash recognized. He acknowledged that the rise of the middle class and the emergence of the second generation of mill owners meant that even then the "gulf was growing" between Southern workers and their bosses.[50] Many sons and successors of the early industrialists "had been trained in the tradition of the old close personal relationship between man and master and . . . often sought to continue it," but they were so caught up in speculation and the country club that "the feeling which had lain at the heart of the old notion of paternalistic duty was fast dwindling, leaving only the shell—at the same time that the notion of paternalistic *privilege* was remaining as strongly entrenched as ever, and even perhaps being expanded."[51]

Cash was deadly on the imported "Yankee cult of the Great Executive," a way of thinking that often "cut straight across the tradition":

> Seducing the vanity especially of the young men who had been educated in the Northern business schools, and their imitators, it led them to surround themselves with flunkies and mahogany and frosted glass, with the result that the worker who had been accustomed to walking into the Old Man's office without ceremony could no longer get to them save at the cost of an effort and a servility which were foreign to his temper and tradition.[52]

Well, we have our own business schools now, but there are still Southern enterprises run on the old principles, and those principles still shape the expectations of many Southern workers. A while back I took a class on a field trip to one of the few remaining family-owned textile mills in North Carolina. The trip had been arranged far in advance, but we arrived to find the place virtually shut down. The entire managerial staff and all but a skeleton crew of workers had gone to the funeral of a retired weave-room worker. That mill will not be unionized any time soon.

Just up the road, however, in Winston-Salem, we witnessed an instructive cultural conflict not long ago, when Reynolds Tobacco merged with Nabisco and acquired a new management team. A recent bestseller, *Barbarians at the Gate*, tells the story of Ross Johnson, the Canadian CEO who came to Winston-Salem from Nabisco. Compared to the junk-bond sharks who eventually stripped him of his company and his job, I must say that Johnson comes off as a rather amiable buccaneer, just a guy out of the sales division who liked to fly around the country in private jets and hang out with professional athletes. But his Great Executive style was inconsistent with the old-fashioned Southern corporate culture of RJR. Mr. R. J. Reynolds and his heirs had not exactly led lives of asceticism and self-denial, but they had been managers of the sort Cash described: walking the factory floor, greeting workers by name, inquiring after their families. It was understood that Reynolds executives drove nothing bigger than a Buick. When David Rockefeller came to Winston-Salem for a speech and asked for a limousine, there was none to be found in the entire city. In the 1950s, one worker recalled, "I remember some mornings pulling up beside Mr. Whitaker [the president] in his little brown Studebaker. He'd give me a wave and I'd give him a wave back. We were going in to work together. We were all after the same thing."[53]

Well, Ross Johnson came to work by helicopter. Do you wonder why Winston-Salem never took to him? Folks were especially cruel to his trophy wife, Laurie, a California Girl widely known as "Cupcake." (After she and her husband were given honorary degrees by a needy Florida college, she was known as "Dr. Cupcake.") Johnson got even by moving his corporate headquarters to Atlanta, observing as he left that Winston-Salem was too "bucolic." All over town cars sprouted bumper stickers with the legend "Honk If You're Bucolic."[54] Sure, there is deference in the South to men of high standing, but it should not be taken for granted, and it depends on a measure of self-deprecation. Cash had that exactly right.

Can anti-institutionalism of the sort Cash described survive in a complex, hierarchical, urban, industrial society like today's South? It is still with us, yes, but is just that it has not been long enough since the passing of the frontier and its various surrogates? Will individualism soon be found only among fans of Hank Williams, Jr., up the hollers? Perhaps, but let me suggest another line of thought. What was it about the frontier, after all, that encouraged individualism?

In part, it was the openness of the white Southern class structure, the fact that many Southerners had risen in it, apparently by their own efforts, and that even those who had not risen knew and were kin to some who had. Well, consider the fact that the South's class structure has never been more fluid than in the fifty years since Cash wrote. In 1940 roughly one Southern worker in six was in a white-collar, professional, or managerial job; half were farmers, the rest industrial workers. Now more than half of Southern workers do their work in offices. The South's per capita income has gone from a level roughly that of Venezuela's today, a level about half of that elsewhere in the U.S., to near-parity with the rest of the country. Those statistics mean that it is difficult—not impossible, but very difficult—to find adult Southerners who are worse off economically than their grandparents were. Can this explain the increase in economic libertarianism among Southerners? The message of self-help is better received in societies where many people actually *have* improved their circumstances.

Consider a related change: The South has gone from a rural society, where only a third of the population lived in towns (and most of those towns did not amount to much), to a society where more than two-thirds now live in cities, suburbs, and towns; several of the South's cities are among the nation's largest and fastest growing; and much of the countryside has been effectively urbanized. This *must* mean that many Southerners are rural-to-urban migrants or the children of such migrants. Is it fanciful to suggest that the Southern city is the latest frontier, with these uprooted rural Southerners as the new pioneers? Mightn't a frontier ethic of self-reliance serve such migrants well, in a new environment that is strange and in some ways threatening? Might this latest phase of Southern history be teaching some of the same lessons that Cash thought Southern history has always taught?

Finally, consider what many saw as the failure of major American institutions in the 1960s and 1970s. Could Viet Nam, Watergate, Iran, assassinations, urban riots, economic stagnation, double-digit inflation, rising crime rates, urban decay—could these and a host of other distressing, frustrating, alienating developments have reinforced Southerners' distrust of large, distant, formal organizations? Some survey evidence suggests that they may have done so (and they may even have led some other Americans to share that distrust).[55]

But that is another book. Too bad Jack Cash isn't here to write it.

The book Cash did write was enough for one short life, though. I quoted Gerald Johnson earlier; let me quote him again, to close. Johnson wrote in Howard Odum's journal *Social Forces* that

the South must develop its own critics. They can criticize most effectively, in the first place because they have the Southern viewpoint and can be understood, and in the second place because they have the most reliable information, and therefore can most frequently spot the joints in Southern armour. [But] they must be critics, not press-agents. Too much has been said of the South's need for "sympathetic" criticism. This demand has resulted in some so-called criticism that is sympathetic, not with the South, but with the South's least admirable traits, with bigotry, intolerance, superstition and prejudice. What the South needs is criticism that is ruthless toward those things— bitter towards them, furiously against them—and sympathetic only with its idealism, with its loyalty, with its courage and its inflexible determination.[56]

That is a pretty fair description of the job W. J. Cash undertook in *The Mind of the South*. Like Eugene Gant, Cash hated a lot about the South. Occasionally he was imagining things, sometimes he was just being fashionable, but often hate was exactly the right response. Like Gant, he hated what was hateful in the South because he obviously loved the place, too, in his way. What started out as a smart-aleck essay for H. L. Mencken's magazine wound up as a book that any reader should recognize as a cry from the heart.

Gerald Johnson was right about what the South needed. He was right, too, when he said that the sort of criticism he wanted might not be popular, but would be "respected and in the end admired." This symposium speaks to that.

Commentary / Bertram Wyatt-Brown

John Shelton Reed has been so perceptive about W. J. Cash that I find much too little about which to complain. His presentation offers a number of rich insights into *The Mind of the South*, particularly regarding an attention to the gendered character of Cash's language, the ambivalence with which Cash addressed so many issues, the persistence of paternalism which has a positive as well as negative aspect, and also Cash's failure to recognize the salience of Southern religion. Wisely, too, Professor Reed reminds us that Cash was a poor boy from the hills who wrote a classic. He was no William Gilmore Simms, William Faulkner, or Will Percy whose forbears had ruled the districts in which these writers were raised.

Yet, given the adversarial nature of the task in historical circles, the commentator can always find something about which to argue. In this case, the issue is methodology. Reed approaches his subject largely without reference to Cash's life or psychology. That is certainly a long-honored approach to an academic subject. Yet in light of Cash's longstanding and increasingly virulent depression, his difficulty in producing this one book, and his tragic death by suicide, much can be learned about the nature of *The Mind of the South* with reference to his biography. Two accounts of his life now exist, the second by Bruce Clayton, being by far the more illuminating.[1] The point, then, is to suggest that a look at the life can help us better to understand both Cash's strengths and weaknesses. This design will be helpful in dealing with three topics

which Reed has explored: first, the issue of Cash's attitudes toward gender; second, his meaning of individualism; and third, the
question of Cash's standing as either a social analyst or an historian.

With regard to the first issue—Cash's alleged anti-feminism—I
am harsher on the writer than our speaker has been. Reed defends
Cash on the grounds that he was product of his day and also that,
given the prevailing mores of that time, Cash wisely sought to
reach primarily the white male constituency who had the power to
change things. That is satisfactory so far as it goes. More, however,
must be said. Cash's views on women do represent a defect in his
otherwise remarkable level of social criticism.[2] The same can be
said regarding African Americans, though time does not permit
exploration here.

Given his alienation from Southern life generally and his success
in other realms of social criticism, for consistency's sake, Cash
might have risen to the challenge in this sector. He did not. The
source of his bias was rooted in the culture he was describing and
by which he was imprisoned. As a result, there are no flesh-and-
blood women in the book, no penetrating insights into their
outlook. Instead, we see the women only through the prism of
Southern white males. The representations that do appear com-
bine familiarity and oddness—the gothic-sentimental mode of
romanticism, ideals which Cash denounced but also to which he
clung.

The Mind of the South provides the familiar stereotype of the
woman on the pedestal—passive, ethereal, and anything but
down-to-earth. He calls the Woman of Southern imagination the
"lily-pure Maid of Astolat," from Tennyson's *Idylls of the King*. She
was the virgin princess Elaine Le Blanc who loves Lancelot in vain
and dies at the end of Tennyson's poem. Cash himself believed
in the myth of Southern feminine purity. He was no "hell-of-a-
fellow," but the very opposite. Rather than describing how Southern women really reacted, Cash elaborated further in classical and
Christian terms. He likened the Southern female icon to "the

shield-bearing Athena," "the hunting goddess of the Boetian hill," Diana, and Mary, "the pitiful Mother of God."[3] These images were not merely a reflection of Old Southern culture but also a personal defense that Cash raised up because of his own mixed feelings regarding sexuality. The women he had described through the mythical imagery were largely dangerous or sexless creatures. Either they were manly women like Diana and Athena, who could unnerve even a warrior or at least a pubescent boy, or else they were like the very unthreatening maiden Elaine Le Blanc. According to Tennyson's poem, "the lily-maid of Astolat" was so timid that, despite Lancelot's many entreaties to know what was on her mind, it took days for her to explain her desire never to be separated from him.

In Virginia Woolf's sardonic view, the late Victorian woman of the kind Cash liked to idolize was an "Angel in the House." The English novelist borrowed the phrase from a poem by Coventry Patmore. Such a creature's main attribute was, of course, an infinite capacity for purity—the stainlessness of the mother of God, as Cash put it.[4] In portraying the isolation of the Old South plantation, Cash recapitulated the prevailing myth: "there grew up an unusually intense affection and respect for . . . the wife and mother upon whose activities the comfort and well-being of everybody greatly depended." Perhaps he had in mind his own mother whom he so greatly adored.[5] This paragon, in any event, was "the angel" in the plantation household, as it were.

Cash knew perfectly well that these archetypes of Southern belle and formidable matron were not real. Only once in *The Mind of the South* did he puncture the old image, though not to illustrate a question of gender but one of class. You may recall the passage. When Cash's famous parvenu planter dies his widow, a pipe-smoking illiterate, outlives him by ten years. Her portrait was noted, Cash fancied, for two things: the loveliness of her hands, "knotted and twisted just enough to give them character, and a finely transparent skin through which the blue veins showed most aristocratically."[6] Striking as the depiction is, that is the last we hear of the sex for quite a number of pages. Nor does he ever give us a single example of internal dialogue from a woman in the manner that brings alive the Southern bigot, the landlord, the proud but easily misled small farmer, textile-mill boss and other voices in the account.

Although Cash strove hard to deal with the plight of Southern poor white males, he could not retrieve the thoughts of their women. He portrays them as "stringy-haired and limp of breast at twenty, shrunken hags at thirty or forty."[7] The comment is poignant, but again class-related and designed to make palpable the general plight of the Southern poor. His characterization did not indicate a recognition of the poor women's dignity.

Katherine Rogers, one of his closest friends, thought that *The Mind of the South* would have been a better book if he had only talked with some of his fellow journalists at the Charlotte *News* who "knew and appreciated the ordinary, decent Tar Heels" and their "folk ballads,—mountain ballads, especially—'sing downs' at country churches, play parties,'" and so on.[8] Such information might have led him toward a greater understanding of women's roles in such functions as well as a larger grasp of folk culture which he virtually ignored, as Professor Reed observes.

Cash's handling of the "rape complex" is one of the more outstanding insights into the Southern male mind but, once again, has little to do with what women themselves might have thought.[9] In handling black women he is far off the mark. They are mentioned for "their easy compliance for commercial reasons."[10] Rape and less severe sexual coercions in the slave quarters or isolated freedman's cabin does not concern him. Still more revealing, he fails to notice the moral strength that so many black women manifested in raising their children under the grimmest of conditions.

His attitude toward black women reflected the darker side of the Victorian and the Southern mind—the woman as harlot, the source of danger as well as forbidden pleasure. A word or two about Cash's sexual difficulties are in order because that was the source of his inability to deal well with the Southern woman as she

was in all her humanity. All his life the young journalist was very
prone to tears. During his European tour in the early twenties, he
went to Chartres and was so overcome, he said, "I found myself
crying. I didn't believe a God-damned word of the notions that
inspired such a masterpiece, but I kept on weeping." More tell-
ingly in 1932 or so he burst into sobs describing to his friend
Katherine Rogers a visit to New York he had just completed. He
had been with Peggy Ann, from Georgetown College, Kentucky,
where he had once briefly taught. She had become an actress and
lived well, whereas he was poor, lonely, and careerless. In this
confessional to Katherine Rogers he said that economic differences
did not separate him from Peggy Ann so much as his initial failure
as a lover years before in Georgetown. He had "'thoroughly titil-
lated' her and had her 'panting' for the final act," but had been
unable to carry through. After telling Katherine Rogers about the
episode, Cash "bust into tears."[11]

His companion had some common sense. She reported, "For a
few moments I sat silent, confident he would turn on himself later
for making this confession, and on me for having been a listener."
So she got up and pulled out a picture of Michelangelo's "Pietà."
She forced him to gaze at it, and then gave him a thorough verbal
pasting. "You come out here acting the crucified Christ and treat-
ing me as an all-understanding Madonna. Well, you ain't and I
aint. You are awash in self-pity." She accused him of hiding behind
the "misogyny" of H. L. Mencken, the "Virgin worship" of Henry
Adams, and the courtly love traditions of the South that novelist
James Branch Cabell celebrated.[12] "Strip away the rhythmical and
high falutin' prose," Katherine Rogers told him, and he would
discover that "subconsciously" he was "just another sentimental
Victorian male, strictly dividing females into just two classes—the
all-good and the all-bad and considering only the first class as that
from which a self-respecting male could choose a wife." His "crip-
pling" ideas of "honor," she continued, would not allow him to
"'violate the purity'" of his beloved.

Cash's chastiser was actually rather kind in not suggesting that his lofty code was really a mask for a deep-seated anger against and fear of women, arising from his own self-despising. But, not having had his essential feelings questioned, he was able to smile and protest, "Don't you go trying out amateur psychoanalysis on me." She persisted, however, along the same lines: "There's better proof available than words. In five minutes flat, I could prove you're as virile as any callow, over-hasty kid of 17. But by God, I won't. When you leave here you can just hunt up the Countess of Albermarle again." She was referring to a local prostitute whom the Charlotte *News* reporters had dignified with a Tennysonian nickname. Of course, she was right about his virility. Cash's marriage, brief though it was, was happy in that respect. But such a seasonable outcome came *after* the publication of *The Mind of the South* and, sadly, not long before he was struck down by psychotic depression and suicide.

Years of residence at home, oedipal resentment of his unintellectual, unappreciative father, over-dependence on his mother, prolonged virginity, and late marriage had drastically narrowed the range of his encounters with women. According to Katherine Rogers, he wrote a novella in the early thirties that illustrated that state of affairs. A romantic fantasy, it concerned a white woman who became a goddess to a primitive tribe. The pot-boiler was intended for a romance magazine but "in the theme and manner of telling this story," Katherine Rogers said, "Jack revealed his true temperament—the temperament of a romanticist such as Coleridge—that his warring, analytical mind was never able to conquer."[13] Parenthetically, it is noteworthy that even Katherine Rogers, perceptive as she was, failed to mention his neglect of women in *The Mind of the South*.

This recitation is not meant to belittle Cash's achievement by any means. Before, during and after his time, most male novelists, historians, and journalists have seldom given the female component of their subjects much genuine understanding. Cash's failure in this regard is by no means his alone, but the defect of vision cannot be ignored.

A second issue concerns Cash as the interpreter of Southern individualism, which, I shall argue, is very closely connected with the first problem of gender. Reed asks the salient question regarding this matter: "How do you square individualism with what Cash insisted was the South's 'Savage Ideal' of community conformity?" Reed points to two different forms of individualism. The first is one in which nonconformity and antinominian self-definition are asserted—in the manner of Henry David Thoreau. The other style, is one that is "culturally prescribed," as the speaker aptly puts it. He says that Richard Weaver—another South-Watcher—once offered John Randolph of Bizarre as an example of the second type. I would more or less agree. Yet Randolph, because of his own ambiguous sexual orientation, does not make the most unclouded model of Southern individualism. Essentially Cash and others of that era had in mind no gender-free, race-free concept of individualism. Instead, it referred exclusively to adult white men acting as men were supposed to act. That is, their honor was a function of their liberty to achieve the highest ideals of *masculine* independence within that given order and never to stray from it for a moment. This prized independence, however, was always subject to compromise, usually unacknowledged. Only the wealthiest— and probably not even they—required no patron with wide influence, no source of external credit, no intermediary in disputes.

To assert one's so-called "individualism" was almost invariably a defensive simulation—to "prove" that one was *not* a dependent upon another, in a word, not a shameful slave or emasculated creature of some sort. Hence much of the personal violence of the South was derived from imputations of lost manhood, lost freedom, lost reputation—charges that had to be answered by weapons or fists. Not to do so would mean submission to public ridicule and indignation.[14] Women and blacks, of course, were supposed to be dependent, and therefore Cash never refers to their sense of "individualism." The writer would have been better served to use a more accurate term, perhaps of his own coining, to describe the phenomenon. To be sure he was essentially right—

just unaware how gender- and race-connected his designation might seem to readers fifty years later.

Finally, Reed speaks of Jack Cash as a "social analyst" and not a historian. Thus, as a sociologist himself, Reed does not make the error that I think too many in the history profession do. They assume that because an author deals with past events, he is therefore a historian and must be judged by its procedures. This demand flies in the face of Cash's intentions, methods, and framework as we can adduce from what Professor Reed says of him. Too often historians assume that their methods are the only ones applicable for the treatment of the past. Others have quoted Michael O'Brien's criticism of Cash based on the premise that he was a historian. There is no need to repeat O'Brien's points here.[15] By such a yardstick, *The Mind of the South* was bad history. It has no footnotes, no balanced chronology, little recitation of facts. Nor did Cash check the poetic and literary impulse as historians must if they wish to achieve a posture of cool "objectivity." Rather than quote from letters and documents he has various anonymous voices reveal how Southern white men think. Most unhistorical. But should criteria of scholarship apply to a work of this kind?

Our colleagues in English literature teach us to pay attention to a reader's response. Most lay readers of the book are not looking for a sketch of Southern history but rather a greater understanding of their contemporary surroundings: as Yankee newcomers, curious why Southerners love capital punishment and hate gun controls; as white Civil Rights reformers wondering why sheriffs are so unfriendly; or native-born Southerners seeking enlightenment about who they are themselves. These motives for reading Cash are not those of the traditional historian. Should they be set aside for that reason?

Nowadays, we historians should be careful about who we exclude from our midst. Peter Novick in *That Noble Dream* has thrown a skeptical light on our assumptions of objectivity. Simon Schama and others experiment with the historical form and uses of evidence. Even such scholars using traditional methods as Wil-

liam Freehling seek verisimilitude by creating half-fictional mono-
logues.[16] These efforts may or may not be successful, but in light of
them, Cash's internalized voices and his narrator's periodic entries
into the text seem less unhistorical than his critics have intimated.
Moreover, it strikes me as perverse that some Southern intellectual historians consider *The Mind of the South* outside the pale of
intellectual history when the book has actually generated more
academic ferment than any of the dry-as-dust proslavery authors,
theologians, and university presidents that they usually study.[17]

The fact is, *The Mind of the South* is about the past but only as a
means to an end—the illumination of the current Southern *mentalité*, as the French Annalists call it. That task required retrospec-
tion but not detailed history-writing. As Reed reminds us, it
explored a cast of mind and set of behavioral guidelines that Cash
both loved and hated in the way that has become a Quentin
Compsonian cliché, as it were. To attack Cash's rendering of
Southern history is like complaining that Hamlet is based on myth
and does not adequately reflect the economic and political realities
of medieval Denmark.

Cash never called himself a historian. In describing his plans
early in the book's germination, he reported to Alfred Knopf, his
publisher, that "ultimately the book is one man's view—a sort of
personal report—which must rest in large part on the authority of
my imagination and understanding at play upon patterns into
which I was born and which I have lived, most of my life." Clearly
he considered himself a writer with literary more than historical
ambitions. That self-definition was also evident in his choices of
subject. He once planned a literary life of Lafcadio Hearn, a
novelist. His Guggenheim project before he died in Mexico City
was a novel based upon the experiences of his own family through
several generations. This design flowed naturally from the one
book he did publish. His purpose in *The Mind of the South* was to
arouse white Southern males to the dangers of living too much in
the past, the perils of myth-making and myth-believing.[18] If Cash
had wished to be academic as his critics would like him to have

been, he could not have achieved that essential purpose. Nobody—at least no ordinary layman—would have read it. Thus, by learning what Cash hoped to accomplish and by recognizing the personal factors in the kind of work he wrote, we can appreciate more fully his achievement. We are grateful that despite all the miseries of his life—poverty, mental depression, sexual dysfunction—he wrote a superb study that partially withdraws the veil surrounding the Southern enigma.

Notes

Notes to INTRODUCTION

1. C. Vann Woodward, "The Elusive Mind of the South," in *American Counterpoint: Slavery and Racism in the North-South Dialogue* (Boston: Little, Brown, 1971), 263.
2. George Brown Tindall, *The Emergence of the New South, 1913–1945* (Baton Rouge: Louisiana State University Press, 1967), 591; Fred Hobson, *Tell About the South: The Southern Rage to Explain* (Baton Rouge: Louisiana State University Press, 1983), 247; Richard H. King, *A Southern Renaissance: The Cultural Awakening of the American South, 1930–1955* (New York: Oxford University Press, 1980), 146; Daniel Joseph Singal, *The War Within: From Victorian to Modernist Thought in the South, 1919–1945* (Chapel Hill: University of North Carolina Press, 1982), 373.
3. Woodward, "The Elusive Mind of the South," 275; Joel Williamson, *The Crucible of Race: Black-White Relations in the American South Since Emancipation* (New York: Oxford University Press, 1984), 3; Michael O'Brien, "A Private Passion: W. J. Cash," in *Rethinking the South: Essays in Intellectual History* (Baltimore: Johns Hopkins University Press, 1988), 127, 179, 180.
4. Carl Abbott, "Tracing the Trends in U. S. Regional History," *Perspectives*, February 1990, 8; O'Brien, "A Private Passion: W. J. Cash," 179, 180.

Notes to NO ORDINARY HISTORY: W. J. CASH'S *THE MIND OF THE SOUTH*
by Bruce Clayton

1. W. J. Cash to Alfred A. Knopf, May 17, 1936, in Joseph L. Morrison Papers, Southern Historical Collection, University of North Carolina, Chapel Hill. For a fuller discussion of Cash's response to Knopf see Bruce Clayton, *W. J. Cash: A Life* (Baton Rouge: Louisiana State University Press, 1991), 107–111. For an overview of Cash's life see also Joseph L. Morrison, *W. J. Cash: Southern Prophet: A Biography and Reader* (New York: Alfred A. Knopf, 1967). Edwin Mims, *The Advancing South* (New York: Doubleday, Page and Co., 1926). For an analysis of Mims and the New South generation see Bruce Clayton, *The Savage Ideal: Intolerance and Intellectual Leadership in the South, 1890–1914* (Baltimore: Johns Hopkins University Press, 1972)
2. *Ibid.*, 6–14; Clayton, *Cash*, 3–20.
3. W. J. Cash to Alfred A. Knopf, author's form, April 8, 1940; Charlotte *News*, February 9, 1936; Morrison, *Cash*, 15–24.
4. Clayton, *Cash*, 25–40; Suzanne Cameron Linder, *William Louis Poteat* (Chapel Hill: University of North Carolina Press, 1966), 35, 92, 100–101; Fred Hobson, ed., *South-Watching: Selected Essays by Gerald W. Johnson* (Chapel Hill: University of North Carolina Press, 1983), x.

5. Morrison, *Cash*, 36–47; Clayton, *Cash*, 41–78; W. J. Cash, "Editorial Notes," *American Mercury*, XXIV (1931), xxxii; Application for a John Simon Guggenheim Memorial Fellowship, October, 1936, Morrison Papers; Charlotte *News*, October 23, 1937.

6. Fred C. Hobson, Jr., *Serpent in Eden: H. L. Mencken and the South* (1974; Chapel Hill, rep. Baton Rouge: Louisiana State University Press, 1978), 80–120, 223–31.

7. W. J. Cash, "The Mind of the South," *American Mercury*, XVII (1929), 185–92; for an overview and analysis of Cash's writings for Mencken see Hobson, *Serpent in Eden*, 111–120 and Clayton, *Cash*, 79–106.

8. Application for a John Simon Guggenheim Memorial Fellowship, October, 1936; W. J. Cash to Alfred A. Knopf, November 27, 1935, both in Morrison Papers.

9. W. J. Cash to Alfred A. Knopf, May 17, 1936, Morrison Papers.

10. Mary Cash Maury, "The Suicide of W. L. Cash," MS in Morrison Papers. For an account of the reception of Cash's book and his last months see Clayton, *Cash*, 163–191.

11. William James, *Pragmatism: A New Name for Some Old Ways of Thinking* (1907; New York, rep. Cambridge: Harvard University Press, 1977), 27–44, 95–114; Michael Polanyi, *Personal Knowledge: Towards a Post-Critical Philosophy* (Chicago: University of Chicago Press, 1958).

12. W. J. Cash, *The Mind of the South* (1941; New York, rep. 1969), 117, 125, 126, 310; Walter White, *Rope & Faggott: A Biography of Judge Lynch* (New York: Alfred A. Knopf, 1929); Arthur F. Raper, *The Tragedy of Lynching* (Chapel Hill: University of North Carolina Press, 1933); J. D. Chadbourn, *Lynching and the Law* (Chapel Hill: University of North Carolina Press, 1933).

13. Cash, *Mind of the South*, 384–89; Bruce Clayton, "W. J. Cash and the Creative Impulse," *Southern Review* XXIV (Autumn 1988), 777–790; Richard H. King, *A Southern Renaissance: The Cultural Awakening of the American South, 1930–1955* (New York: Oxford University Press, 1980), 20–38.

14. Cash, *Mind of the South*, 15 383.

15. For Cash's reviews of each of these books see Charlotte *News*, December 8, 1935, June 13, 1937.

16. Cash, *Mind of the South*, 13–14, 18–19, 20–21, 64, 65, 69, 73–74, 110.

17. G. W. Dyer, *Democracy in the Old South Before the Civil War* (1905; New York, rep. New York: Arno Press, 1973), 7, 30–33, 81–82. Cash, *Mind of the South*, 3, 39.

18. Dyer, *Democracy in the South*, 81; Cash, *Mind of the South*, 40, 69–70, 115. Bruce Clayton, "The Proto-Dorian Convention: W. J. Cash and the Race Question," in *Race, Class and Politics in Southern History*, ed. Jeffrey J. Crow, Paul D. Escott, and Charles L. Flynn, Jr. (Baton Rouge: Louisiana State University Press, 1989), 282–288.

19. William E. Dodd, *The Cotton Kingdom: A Chronicle of the Old South* (New Haven: Yale University Press, 1921), 24, 32, 69–70.

20. *Ibid.*, 111–115; Dyer, *Democracy in the South*, 66; Cash, *Mind of the South*, 94–97; see also William E. Dodd, *Statesmen of the Old South* (New York: Macmillan Company, 1929), 66–67.

21. For an incisive analysis of the thought of Odum and the Chapel Hill sociologists see Daniel Joseph Singal, *The War Within: From Victorian to Modernist Thought in the South, 1919–1945* (Chapel Hill: University of North Carolina Press, 1982), 115–152, 302–338. Howard W. Odum, *An American Epoch: Southern Portraiture in the National Picture* (New York: Henry Holt and Company, 1930),

30–42, 48–51. King, *Southern Renaissance*, has written that "From Vance and Odum, Cash undoubtedly took the importance of the frontier and the elevation of the yeoman over the planter as the key figure in Southern history," a suggestive contention, certainly, but one that cannot be proven [153].

22. Cash, *Mind of the South*, 19, 62–64; Clayton, *Cash*, 198.

23. U. B. Phillips, *American Negro Slavery* (1918; New York, rep. Baton Rouge: Louisiana State University Press, 1969), 291–308, 454–458 88, 514; U. B. Phillips, "Conservatism and Progress in the Cotton Belt," *South Atlantic Quarterly*, III, (January 1904), 3; U. B. Phillips, *Life and Labor in the Old South* (1929; Boston, rep. Boston: Little, Brown, and Co., 1957), 208–217, 354–61, 366; Singal, *War Within*, 52–57.

24. Cash, *Mind of the South*, 85–86.

25. *Ibid.*, 329–330; Vernon L. Wharton, "Reconstruction," in *Writing Southern History: Essays in Historiography in Honor of Fletcher M. Green*, ed. Arthur S. Link and Rembert M. Patrick (Baton Rouge: Louisiana State University Press, 1965), 297, 300.

26. Cash, *Mind of the South*, 108, 117–18, 125.

27. *Ibid.*, 116–17.

28. *Ibid.*, 180–81; Gerald W. Johnson, "Service in the Cotton Mills," *American Mercury*, V (June 1925), 219–23; C. Vann Woodward, *Origins of the New South, 1877–1913* (Baton Rouge: Louisiana State University Press, 1951), 222–26.

29. Cash, *Mind of the South*, 203–4, 218, 229.

30. *Ibid.*, 162–65; Francis Butler Simkins, *The Tillman Movement in South Carolina* (Durham: Duke University Press, 1926).

31. C. Vann Woodward, "The Elusive Mind of the South," in *American Counterpoint: Slavery and Racism in the North-South Dialogue* (New York: Little, Brown, 1971), 261–83.

32. U. B. Phillips, "The Central Theme in Southern History," *American Historical Review*, XXXIV (October 1928), 30–43.

33. Cash, *Mind of the South*, 326–27.

34. Singal, *War Within*, 296–301.

Notes to THE CASH NEXUS
by Anne Goodwyn Jones

1. Resisting readers they may have been, but they were also good ones. My thanks for their ideas, which helped to inspire and now permeate this essay unacknowledged. My thanks as well to the friends and colleagues at the University of Florida who took their time to listen to me go on about Cash and Gramsci, to give me leads, and in some cases to give critical readings to this essay: among them are Dan Cottom, Robert D'Amico, David Leverenz, Maureen Turim, and Bertram Wyatt-Brown.

2. One might say that they are separable because, though all fiction presumably lays claims to art, all art is not necessarily fiction, even in the broad sense of the latter term. Thus history can be "art" without being "fiction." Perhaps "craft" more accurately represents the sense in which some historians seem to mean "art," since it can suggest (though probably misleadingly) a deliberate process of shaping, but not wholesale invention. See Peter Novick, *That Noble Dream: The "Objectivity Question" and the American Historical Profession*, [Cambridge: Cambridge University Press, 1988], 600, 386. Unlike Novick's approach, this paper does not

attempt a historical or contextual understanding of Cash's quarrel with objectivity (and the related issues of history vs. fiction, etc.). But that would be a worthy project, for Cash composed *The Mind of the South* during the 1930s, a period Novick characterizes (in particular for the profession of history) as "Objectivity Besieged"; it was published at the end of that period, and its own interpretive history has been shaped by the postwar "reconstruction" of objectivity. Of course Cash was not a professional historian; nevertheless, he was well aware of the issues, for as Novick shows, they permeated modernist discourse.

3. C. Vann Woodward, review of *The Mind of the South, Journal of Southern History*, VIII (1941), 400–402, quotation on 400; and Louis D. Rubin, Jr., "The Mind of the South," *Sewanee Review*, LXII (1954), 683–95, quotation on 687.

4. Michael O'Brien, *Rethinking the South: Essays in Intellectual History* (Baltimore: Johns Hopkins University Press, 1988), 179–80.

5. Particularly in its earlier form as "W. J. Cash, Hegel, and the South," *The Journal of Southern History*, XLIV (August, 1978), 379–398. For example, "Hegelianism . . . permits on to make the complicated interconnections that seem to exist between [consciousness and reality]," 395.

6. Rubin, "The Mind of the South," 685.

7. Richard King, *A Southern Renaissance: The Cultural Awakening of the American South, 1930–1955* (Oxford: Oxford University Press, 1980), 147–9.

8. Michael Dean, "W. J. Cash's *The Mind of the South*: Southern History, Southern Style," *Southern Studies*, XX (1981).

9. Bertram Wyatt-Brown, "Introduction: The Mind of W. J. Cash," *The Mind of the South* (New York: Knopf, 1991).

10. Dean, "W. J. Cash," 297; Hobson, *Tell About the South: The Southern Rage to Explain* (Baton Rouge: Louisiana State University Press, 1983) 273.

11. Novick, *That Noble Dream*, 279.

12. Rubin, "The Mind of the South," 689; Bruce Clayton, *W. J. Cash: A Life* (Baton Rouge: Louisiana State University Press, 1991), 198.

13. Drew Gilpin Faust, *The Ideology of Slavery: Proslavery Thought in the Antebellum South, 1830–1860* (Baton Rouge: Louisiana State University, 1982), 4.

14. Quoted from Louis Althusser, *For Marx*, 235–6, in James Kavanagh, "Ideology," in Frank Lentricchia, ed., *Critical Terms for Literary Study* (Chicago: University of Chicago Press, 1990), 313.

15. Wilbur J. Cash, *The Mind of the South* (New York: Knopf, 1941), viii.

16. Cash, *Mind of the South*, 43.

17. This method of analysis can be found throughout the book. See, e.g., pages 8, 14, 63–7, 50, 68, 98, 162, 166, 172, 189, 214, 250, 258, 364, 379, 422, 428.

18. Terry Eagleton, *Ideology: An Introduction* (London: Verso, 1991), 115.

19. Cash, *Mind of the South*, 37.

20. Eagleton, *Ideology*, xiii; Cash, *Mind of the South*, 115, 80.

21. Edmund Jacobitti, "The Religious Vision of Antonio Gramsci or the Italian Origins of Hegemony," *Italian Quarterly* XXV, 97–98 (Summer-Fall, 1984), 103.

22. Cash, *Mind of the South*, 22.

23. On Gramsci's difficulties working out the relation between coercion and consent, see Perry Anderson, "The Antinomies of Antonio Gramsci," *New Left Review* 100 (November 1976–January 1977), 5–81.

24. Cash, *Mind of the South*, 276, 161–2, 206.

25. Jacobitti, "The Religious Vision," 103.

26. Cash, *Mind of the South*, 366, 429; Jacobitti, "The Religious Vision," 115.

27. As a theorist of ideology, Cash can be located on the boundary between Gramsci and Althusser: like Gramsci in his understanding of hegemony as consent

backed by coercion and of the organic intellectual as a possible agent for change, and yet more soberly abandoning such optimism as he moved closer to Althusser's Lacanian understanding of the illusory claims and actual powerlessness of the individual, even the collective, ego.

28. On Gramsci's *Prison Notebooks* as coded and non-linear text, see Joseph Buttigieg, *Boundary 2*, 1990, and Forgacs, 10–11. On all of these issues for Cash, see Clayton, *W. J. Cash*. David Forgacs, *Gramsci Reader: Selected Writings, 1916–1935* (New York: Schocken, 1988).

29. See Gramsci, "Some Aspects of the Southern Question," in Forgacs, *Gramsci Reader*, 171–185, quotations on 173, 179, and 183.

30. Cash, *Mind of the South*, vii–xi; quotations on viii and x.

31. *Ibid.*

32. *Ibid.*, 199 and 224.

33. This may be an anachronistic reference to Frederick Taylor's *Principles of Scientific Management* (1911), a work that interested Gramsci (Forgacs, *Gramsci Reader*, 289–296); Cash says that "nobody in the world at the time, save only a handful of advanced investigators who were commonly set down for crackbrains, had any clear notion that [laws of the machine] existed" (*Mind of the South*, 185).

34. Cash, *Mind of the South*, 185, 327, 334–335.

35. Cash, "The Mind of the South" [1929], in Joseph L. Morrison, *W. J. Cash, Southern Prophet: A Biography and Reader* (New York: Knopf, 1967), 193.

36. Forgacs, *Gramsci Reader*, 183.

37. Cash fluctuates in this insight, particularly when he reads black women's "complaisant" sexuality in one moment as "taught" and in another as "natural." The sames goes for the southern lady's "Kindness" and "grace." Gramsci fluctuates in similar ways. See Forgacs, *An Antonio Gramsci Reader*, 280–282.

38. Thus same gene pool, as Cash tells the story, can produce a kinship system that connects poor white and plantation master, mill worker and owner. This kinship system works then on the side of consent to reproduce hegemony.

39. Cash, *Mind of the South*, 15 and 29.

40. Cash, *Mind of the South*, 39; David Leverenz, *Manhood and the American Renaissance* (Ithaca: Cornell University Press, 1989), 72.

41. See Anne Goodwyn Jones, "Rethinking Agrarianism: The Work of Gender in Katherine Anne Porter's 'Holiday,'" paper delivered at the Southern Intellectual History Circle conference, Gainesville, Florida, February, 1991.

42. See, for instance, my own assaults on Cash in *Tomorrow Is Another Day: The Woman Writer in the South, 1859–1936* (Baton Rouge: Louisiana State University Press, 1981), buried in a footnote on 364.

43. But see, for instance, page 33, where he describes the family as a scene in which even the common man's "individual will would stand as imperial law" and the planter, even more, would "wax continually in lordly self-certainty." Here patriarchal dominance seems under scrutiny.

44. Cash, *Mind of the South*, 183, 185, 29.

45. Teresa De Lauretis, "Gramsci Notwithstanding, or, the Left Hand of History," in *Technologies of Gender: Essays on Theory, Film, and Fiction* (Bloomington: Indiana University Press, 1987), 93.

46. Gramsci continues: "My own feeling is that we should experience a catharsis, as the Greeks used to say, by virtue of which sentiments are recreated 'artistically' as beauty, and are no longer felt as passion which is still at work in use, and in which we participate. . . ." Turi Prison, 8 August 1933. Hamish Henderson, ed., *Gramsci's Prison Letters* (London: Zwan, 1988), 262.

47. See Teresa De Lauretis, "Gramsci Notwithstanding."

Notes to COMMENTARY
by Michael O'Brien

1. John M. Cammett, *Antonio Gramsci and the Origins of Italian Communism* (Stanford: Stanford University Press, 1967), 11.
2. "Some Aspects of the Southern Question," [1926] in David Forgacs, ed., *An Antonio Gramsci Reader: Selected Writings, 1916–1935* (New York: Schocken, 1988), 178, 181.
3. Ibid., 184.
4. Piero Gobetti, *Scritti Politici* (Turin, 1960), 1003, quoted in James Joll, *Antonio Gramsci* (New York: Penguin, 1978), 89.
5. In fact, I suspect the South/Mezzogiorno matter is inessential to Jones' argument, which centers more on techniques of representation than on the social conditions that might have formed the ideology of Cash and Gramsci.
6. "Mr. Cash and the Porto-Dorian South," [1941] in Donald Davidson, *Still Rebels, Still Yankees and Other Essays* (Baton Rouge: Louisiana State University Press, 1957), 191–212.
7. George M. Curtis III and James J. Thompson, Jr., eds., *The Southern Essays of Richard M. Weaver* (Indianapolis: Liberty Press, 1987), 229.
8. At least, not in *The Mind of the South*. His collected journalism might tell a different story.
9. Bruce Clayton, *W. J. Cash: A Life* (Baton Rouge: Louisiana State University Press, 1991), 192–222.

Notes to THE BURDEN OF SOUTHERN HISTORIOGRAPHY:
W. J. CASH AND THE OLD SOUTH
by Orville Vernon Burton

1. Michael O'Brien, "A Private Passion: W. J. Cash," *Rethinking the South: Essays in Intellectual History* (Baltimore: Johns Hopkins University Press, 1988), 179–80. See also his "W. J. Cash, Hegel and the South," *Journal of Southern History* XLIV (August 1978), 379–398.
2. Daniel Joseph Singal, *The War Within: From Victorian to Modernist Thought in the South, 1919–1945* (Chapel Hill: University of North Carolina Press, 1982), 373.
3. Richard King, "The Mind of the Southerner: Narcissus Grown Analytical" *New South* 27 (Winter 1972), 15.
4. C. Vann Woodward, "W. J. Cash Reconsidered," *New York Review of Books*, 4 December 1969, reprinted and revised as "The Elusive Mind of the South," *American Counterpoint: Slavery and Racism in North South Dialogue* (New York: Oxford University Press, 1971), 261–283; Eugene Genovese, *The World the Slaveholders Made: Two Essays in Interpretation* (New York: Pantheon, 1970), 137–50. One cannot help but wonder what the opinion of Cash would have been if instead of Woodward having published his devastating critique, David Donald, who was also a commentator at the session had published his paper which was a critique of Woodward and which according to the report of the 1969 meeting written by Richard Maxwell Brown, "David Donald of Johns Hopkins University praised Cash, incisively denied Woodward's conclusions, and maintained that 'In basic matters the South, is and always has been, unchanging.'" Richard Maxwell Brown, "The Thirty-Fifth Annual Meeting," *The Journal of Southern History*, XXXVI (Feb. 1970), 63–64.

5. O'Brien, "A Private Passion," 179–80.

6. C. Vann Woodward, "The Elusive Mind of the South," 282.

7. For example, Kenneth Stampp, *The Peculiar Institution: Slavery in the Antebellum South* (New York: Knopf, 1956) on U.B. Phillips, *American Negro Slavery: A Survey of the Supply, Employment and Control of Negro Labor as Determined by the Plantation Regime* [orig. 1918] (Baton Rouge: Louisiana State University Press, 1966); James Oakes on Eugene Genovese (books cited completely elsewhere in this essay); Jonathan M. Weiner, *Social Origins of the New South: Alabama, 1860–1885* (Baton Rouge: Louisiana State University Press, 1978) on C. Vann Woodward, *Origins of the New South, 1877–1913* (Baton Rouge: Louisiana State University Press, 1951).

8. A large historiography has developed on Cash and these have helped shape the ideas in this essay. See the bibliography at the end of this volume. Other helpful sources include Michael O'Brien, "The Nineteenth-Century American South," *Historical Journal* 24 (Sept. 1981): 751–63, *Rethinking the South: Essays in Intellectual History* (Baltimore: Johns Hopkins University Press, 1988), 179–80, *The Idea of the American South, 1920–1941* (Baltimore: John Hopkins University Press, 1979), 213–25, and "The Lineaments of Antebellum Southern Romanticism," *Journal of American Studies* 20 2, (1986) 165–88, and "The Nineteenth-Century American South" A Review Essay, *Historical Journal* 24 (Sept. 1981), 751–63; Robert J. Brugger, "The Mind of the Old South: New Views," *The Virginia Quarterly Review* 56 (Spring 1980), 277–295; Donald Davidson, "Mr. Cash and the Proto-Dorian South," *Southern Review*, VII (Summer 1941), 1–20, reprinted in Davidson's *Still Rebels, Still Yankees and other Essays* (Baton Rouge: Louisiana State University Press, 1972), pp. 191–212; Ray Mathis, "Mythology and the Mind of the New South," *Georgia Historical Quarterly* 60 (Fall 1976): 228–238; Lewis Rubin, *The Edge of the Swamp: A Study in the Literature and Society of the Old South* (Baton Rouge: Louisiana State University Press, 1989); George C. Rable, "Bourbonism, Reconstruction, and the Persistence of Southern Distinctiveness," *Civil War History* 29:2 (June, 1983): 135–53.

9. Letter to author from Hardy Jackson. See Harvey H. Jackson, "Time, Frontier, and the Alabama Black Belt: Searching for W. J. Cash's Planter," *Alabama Review* 44 (October 1991), esp. pp. 241–2. The Wake Forest symposium, "The Minds of the South," occurred 8–10 February 1991. See Eric Bates, "Of Different Minds," *Southern Exposure* 19 (Spring, 1991), 47–51.

10. Quoted in Bruce Clayton, *W. J. Cash: A Life* (Baton Rouge: Louisiana State University Press, 1981), 93.

11. W. J. Cash, *The Mind of the South* (New York: Alfred A. Knopf, Inc., 1941), x. All citations are to the Vintage Book paperback edition.

12. W. E. B. Du Bois, *Souls of Black Folks* (Chicago: A. M. McClurg, 1903); C. Vann Woodward, *Tom Watson: Agrarian Rebel* (New York: Macmillan, 1938); Richard King, *A Southern Renaissance*, p. 164, described Du Bois's book as "the black counterpart" of *Mind of the South*.

13. Cash, *Mind of the South*, 51.

14. *Ibid.*

15. Bertram Wyatt-Brown, "W. J. Cash and Southern Culture," in Walter J. Fraser, Jr. and Winfred B. Moore, Jr., *From the Old South to the New: Essays on the Traditional South* (Westport, CT: Greenwood Press, 1981), 195–214, or with slight editorial changes in *Yankee Saints and Southern Sinners* (Baton Rouge: Louisiana State University Press, 1985), 131–154.

16. Carl Degler, "Racism in the United States: An Essay Review," *Journal of*

Southern History 38 (Feb. 1972), 102 and *Place Over Time: The Continuity of Southern Distinctiveness* (Baton Rouge: Louisiana State University Press, 1977). See also my discussion in Burton, "'The Black Squint of the Law': Racism in South Carolina," 161–185 in *The Meaning of South Carolina History: Essays in Honor of George C. Rogers, Jr.* Eds. David R. Chesnutt and Clyde N. Wilson (Columbia: University of South Carolina Press, 1991).

17. Jackson, "Time, Frontier, and the Alabama Black Belt," 241–266.

18. Daniel Joseph Singal, *The War Within: From Victorian to Modernist Thought in the South, 1919–1945* (Chapel Hill: The University of North Carolina Press, 1982): 373. Although David Hackett Fischer accepted Cash's description of the Carolina piedmont, he accused him of what quantitative historians term the ecological fallacy, what Fischer called the fallacy of composition, that is conclusions about an individual are based on the group. Although Fischer did not agree with Cash, he stated that "Cash took the plantation legend and turned it upside down." David Hackett Fischer, *Historians' Fallacies: Toward a Logic of Historical Thought* (New York: Harper & Row, 1970), 219–221, quotation on p. 221.

19. Bertram Wyatt-Brown, "W. J. Cash and Southern Culture," *Yankee Saints and Southern Sinners* (Baton Rouge: Louisiana State University Press, 1985), 131–154 (quotation is p. 133). Earlier version of same essay is found in pp. 195–214 in Walter J. Fraser, Jr. and Winfred B. Moore, Jr., *From the Old South to the New: Essays on the Traditional South* (Westport, CT: Greenwood, 1981): see p. 196 for slightly different wording in quotation.

20. Joel Williamson, *The Crucible of Race: Black-White Relations in the American South Since Emancipation* (New York: Oxford University Press, 1984), 3.

21. John Herbert Roper, *C. Vann Woodward, Southerner* (Athens: University of Georgia Press, 1987), 253.

22. See Clayton, *W. J. Cash*, 227–8; Francis Butler Simkins, *The South Old and New: A History, 1820–1947* (1947) revised as *A History of the South* (1956) and with Charles Pierce Roland (New York: Knopf, 1972); William R. Taylor, *Cavalier and Yankee: The Old South and American National Character* (New York: George Braziller, 1961).

23. The best review of Cash and the literature is Clayton, *W. J. Cash*, 192–222.

24. Arthur S. Link and Rembert W. Patrick, eds., *Writing Southern History: Essays in Historiography in Honor of Fletcher M. Green* (Baton Rouge: Louisiana State University Press, 1965); John B. Boles and Evelyn Thomas Nolen, *Interpreting Southern History: Historographical Essays in Honor of Sanford W. Higginbotham* (Baton Rouge: Louisiana State University, 1987).

25. Malcolm C. McMillan, "Jeffersonian Democracy and the Origins of Sectionalism," in *Writing Southern History*, 94–5, note 14, p. 95.

26. James C. Bonner, "Plantation and Farm: The Agricultural South," in *Writing Southern History*, 150.

27. Herbert J. Doherty, Jr., "The Mind of the Antebellum Souther," in *Writing Southern History*, 202.

28. Drew Gilpin Faust, "The Peculiar South Revisited: White Society, Culture, and Politics in the Antebellum Period, 1800–1860," in *Interpreting Southern History*, 102–3, n. 38.

29. Randolph B. Campbell, "Planters and Plain Folks: The Social Structure of the Antebellum South," in *Interpreting Southern History*, 52–3, n. 8.

30. Burton and Robert C. McMath, Jr., eds., *Class, Conflict, and Consensus: Antebellum Southern Community Studies* (Westport, CT: Greenwood, 1982), see esp. pp. xx–xxii. See also, Burton, *In My Father's House Are Many Mansions:*

Family and Community in Edgefield, South Carolina (Chapel Hill: University of North Carolina Press, 1985), 7–9.

31. Genovese later jettisoned "prebourgeois" and also asserts that he never "regarded the Old South as feudal, seigneurial, or medieval." Eugene Genovese, *The Political Economy of Slavery: Studies in the Economy and Society of the Slave South* 2nd ed. (orig. pubd. 1965) (Middletown CT: Wesleyan University Press, 1989), xii.

32. Genovese, *The Political Economy of Slavery; Roll Jordan Roll: The World the Slaves Made* (New York: Pantheon, 1974); *From Rebellion to Revolution: Afro-American Slave Revolts in the Making of the Modern World* (Baton Rouge: Louisiana State University Press, 1979); *In Red and Black: Marxian Explorations in Southern and Afro-American History* (NY: Pantheon, 1971); with Elizabeth Fox-Genovese, *Fruits of Merchant Capitalism* (New York: Oxford University Press, 1983); Elizabeth Fox-Genovese, *Within the Plantation Household: Black and White Women of the Old South* (Chapel Hill: University of North Carolina Press, 1988), and "The Fettered Mind: Time, Place, and the Literary Imagination of the Old South," A Review Essay of *The Edge of the Swamp: A Study in the Literature and Society of the Old South* (Baton Rouge: Louisiana State University Press, 1989) *Georgia Historical Quarterly* 74 (Winter 1990), 622–50; Steven Hahn, *The Roots of Southern Populism: Yeomen Farmers and the Transformation of the Georgia Upcountry, 1850–1890* (New York: Oxford University Press, 1983).

33. I have had a number of students write papers on Cash and Genovese. The most brilliant is a paper by a graduate student, Adam Stephanides, whose arguments I have relied heavily on here.

34. Genovese, *Roll, Jordan, Roll,* 3–7, 25–49.

35. Cash, *Mind of the South,* 63.

36. Cash, *Mind of the South,* 96–97.

37. Genovese, *The World the Slaveholders Made,* 244.

38. Eugene D. Genovese and Elizabeth Fox-Genovese, "The Religious Ideals of Southern Slave Society," *Georgia Historical Quarterly* LXX (Spring 1986), 1–16, and "The Divine Sanction of Social Order: Religious Foundations of the Southern Slaveholders' World View," *Journal of the American Academy of Religion* LV (Summer 1987), 211–34.

39. Cash, *Mind of the South,* 63. Adam Stephanides argued in a paper for my class that Cash never said Southerners felt guilty over slavery. He believes Cash's position is that the planters felt a moral ambivalence and the desire to protect themselves from Northern attacks. A wonderfully suggestive essay is Gaines M. Foster, "Guilt Over Slavery: A Historiographical Analysis," *The Journal of Southern History* LVI (Nov. 1990), 665–694.

40. James Oakes, *The Ruling Race: A History of American Slaveholders* (New York: Oxford University Press, 1983). An interesting twist to planter capitalism is the "slaveholding capitalism" interpretation presented in Laurence Shore, *Southern Capitalists: The Ideological Leadership of an Elite, 1832–1885* (Chapel Hill: University of North Carolina Press, 1986).

41. Stephanides follows Wyatt-Brown, "W. J. Cash and Southern Culture," in *Yankee Saints and Southern Sinners,* p. 148, in thinking that Cash and Genovese agree that the South was not capitalistic. Much depends on the definition of capitalism, but I place Cash in the planter capitalism school.

42. Cash, *Mind of the South,* 4–5, 70–81.

43. Oakes, *Ruling Race,* ix–xiii, 69–95, 123–150, 176–177, 192–224, see esp. pp. 197–198. Frank Valadez was an undergraduate student of Oakes and wrote a paper

comparing Cash, Oakes, and Genovese, and focused on Oakes, *Slavery and Freedom: An Interpretation of the Old South* (New York: Knopf, 1990). Claus Meyer wrote a paper on paternalism and comments here were influenced by both those papers.

44. Edward L. Ayers, "The World the Liberal Capitalists Made," a review of James Oakes, *Slavery and Freedom: An Interpretation of the Old South* in *Reviews in American History* 19 (June 1991), 194–199, quotation on p. 197.

45. The classic statement is Frank L. Owsley, *Plain Folk of the Old South* (Baton Rouge: Louisiana State University Press, 1950).

46. Forrest McDonald and Grady McWhiney, "The Antebellum Southern Herdsmen: A Reinterpretation," *Journal of Southern History* 41 (May 1975), 147–66 and "The South from Self-Sufficiency to Peonage: An Interpretation," *American Historical Review* 85 (Dec. 1980), 1095–1118; and McWhiney, *Cracker Culture: Celtic Ways in the Old South* (Tuscaloosa: University of Alabama Press, 1988).

47. See especially Jane Turner Censer, *North Carolina Planters and Their Children, 1800–1860* (Baton Rouge: Louisiana State University Press, 1984); Robert C. Kenzer, *Kinship and Neighborhood in a Southern Community: Orange County, North Carolina, 1849–1881* (Knoxville: University of Tennessee Press, 1987); Burton, *In My Father's House Are Many Mansions.*

48. In so many different ways one cannot lump these "republican" theory scholars together. Although both Hahn, *The Roots of Southern Populism* and J. Mills Thornton, III, *Politics and Power in a Slave Society: Alabama, 1800–1860* (Baton Rouge: Louisiana State University Press, 1978), agree on republicanism among whites, how their yeomen use republicanism differs. See also J. Williams Harris, *Plain Folk and Gentry in a Slave Society: White Liberty and Black Slavery in Augusta's Hinterlands* (Middletown, CT: Wesleyan University Press, 1985). The latest prize-winning book to make use of republicanism concludes with a delightful vignette of southern aristocrats playing homage to a muddied barefoot well-digger described by diarist Mary Boykin Chesnut's diary. The scene could have come right out of *The Mind of the South.* See Lacy K. Ford, Jr. *Origins of Southern Radicalism: The South Carolina Upcountry, 1800–1860* (New York: Oxford University Press, 1988), 372–73. See also Allan Kulikoff, "The Transition to Capitalism in Rural America," *The William and Mary Quarterly* 3d Series, XLVI (Jan. 1989), 120–144.

49. Burton, "'Black Squint'," 164; Lawanda Cox, "From Emancipation to Segregation," 237–38, n. 62 in *Interpreting Southern History.*

50. First quotation from David M. Potter, "The Enigma of the South," *Yale Review* 51 (Autumn 1961), 142–51, second from *The Impending Crisis, 1848–1861* (New York: Harper & Row, 1976), 458–59.

51. Bertram Wyatt-Brown, "The Ideal Typology and Antebellum Southern History: A Testing of A New Approach," *Societas* 5 (Winter 1975), 1–29, quotations on pp. 4, 3, 28, and *Southern Honor: Ethics and Behavior in the Old South* (New York: Oxford University Press, 1982).

52. Currently intellectual history of the American South is thriving. Historians of southern ideas have recently even begun holding annual meetings. Recently, scholars who are studying ideas in the United States refer to the American exception, the South, in a favorable light as Dorothy Ross who recently analyzed the development of the social sciences in the U.S. concluded "Southern social science, for all its ingenuity, went down to defeat with the Confederacy." See Dorothy Ross, *The Origins of American Social Science* (Cambridge: Cambridge University Press, 1991), 33; James C. Britton, "The Decline and Fall of Nations in Antebellum

Southern Thought: A Study of Southern Historical Consciousness, 1846–1861 (Ph.D. diss., University of North Carolina, 1988). On Southern intellectual history, see Michael O'Brien and David Moltke-Hansen, eds., *Intellectual Life in Antebellum Charleston* (Knoxville: University of Tennessee Press, 1986); Drew Gilpin Faust, *A Sacred Circle: The Dilemma of the Intellectual in the Old South, 1840–1860* (Baltimore: Johns Hopkins University Press, 1977); and the works of Lewis P. Simpson, especially, *The Dispossessed Garden: Pastoral and History in Southern Literature* (Athens: University of Georgia Press, 1975).

53. Waldo E. Martin, *The Mind of Frederick Douglass*, Chapel Hill: University of North Carolina Press, 1985).

54. Joseph Dorfman, *The Economic Mind in American Civilization*, 5 vols. (New York: Viking Press, 1946–59); Norman Pollack's *Populist Mind*, (Indianapolis: Bobbs-Merrill, 1967), Perry Miller, *The New England Mind: The Seventeenth Century* (New York: MacMillan, 1939); Henry Steele Commanger, *The American Mind: An Interpretation of American Thought and Character Since the 1880's* (New Haven: Yale University Press, 1950); Arthur K. Moore, *The Frontier Mind: A Cultural Analysis of the Kentucky Frontiersman* (Lexington: University of Kentucky Press, 1957); Rush Welter, *The Mind of America, 1820–1860* (New York: Columbia University Press, 1975).

55. Lewis P. Simpson, *Mind and The Civil War: A Meditation on Lost Causes* (Baton Rouge: Louisiana State University Press, 1989); Clement Eaton, *Mind of the Old South* (Baton Rouge: Louisiana State University Press, 1967).

56. Woodward, *American Counterpoint*, 265. See also the observations of Bertram Wyatt-Brown, "W. J. Cash and Southern Culture," in Walter J. Fraser, Jr. and Winfred B. Moore, Jr., *From the Old South to the New: Essays on the Traditional South* (Westport, CT: Greenwood, 1981): 195–214, and in *Yankee Saints and Southern Sinners* (Baton Rouge: Louisiana State University Press, 1985), esp. p. 138; O'Brien, "Private Passion," 180, 183; Dewey W. Grantham, Jr., "Mr. Cash Writes a Book," 41; Richard King, *A Southern Renaissance*, 158 and "The Mind of the Southerner," 17.

57. David Roller and R. Twyman, eds., *The Encyclopedia of Southern History* (Baton Rouge: Louisiana State University Press, 1979); Charles Reagan Wilson and William Ferris, eds., *Encyclopedia of Southern Culture* (Chapel Hill: University of North Carolina Press, 1989).

58. E. Le Roy Ladurie, *Montaillou: Cathars and Catholics in a French Village, 1294–1324*, trans., Barbara Bray (London: Scolar, 1978). When I first made this argument, I had not noticed that Wyatt-Brown had actually used the words, "the southern ethic or *mentalite*" (*Yankee Saints and Southern Sinners*, 147), "Southern ethic of mentalite" (in earlier version in *From the Old South to the New*, 202). The earlier version mentions the Annales school.

59. Donald Davidson, "Mr. Cash and the Proto-Dorian South," 1–20.

60. John Shelton Reed, "New South or No South? Regional Culture in 2036," in *The South Moves into the Future: Studies in the Analysis and Prediction of Social Change* edited by Joseph S. Himes (Tuscaloosa: University of Alabama Press, 1991), 226.

61. Ray Mathis, "Mythology and the Mind of the New South," 228–238. One of my graduate students, Frank Freemon, an M.D. who is also doing a Ph.D. in History, wrote a paper entitled "A Synthesis Created by the Right Cerebral Hemisphere." He argued from a neurological tradition that divides the brain into two cerebral hemispheres that Cash wrote from the right side with intuition while most scholars use the left half for historical analysis.

62. See for example Ted Ownby, *Subduing Satan: Religion, Recreation, and*

Manhood in the Rural South, 1865–1920 (Chapel Hill: University of North Carolina Press, 1990).

63. Perhaps I can illustrate Cash and his "sociological ideas" through a story of some friends of mine back home in Ninety Six. One afternoon I was visiting with our neighbor on his front porch. J. Hilton Lewis is still a bear of a man even though he is in his mid-eighties. Years of sawmilling as a youngster made him strong, still strong today even, and according to him, he single-handedly won World War II. While I sat listening to his tales, Pee Wee Ellison and Bubba Smith, two men with children my age, drove up. They asked Hilton if he had heard the news about a recent murder. Hilton replied that he had not, at which time Bubba, who used to work in the cotton mill with me before he became game warden, launched into an explanation: "Well, on Wednesday, no it might have been Tuesday night, or was it Thursday morning? at any rate, this here fellow done shot, or did he stab him, maybe he clubbed the other fellow to death out in the country near Edgefield, or was it McCormick, or Saluda?" At that point, Hilton interrupted Bubba and said, "Oh, yeah, I had heard about it, I just didn't get the details until now."

64. J. Russell Smith and M. Ogden Phillips, *North America: Its People and the Resources, Development, and Prospects of the Continent as an Agricultural, Industrial and Commercial Area* (New York: Harcourt, Brace and Co., [orig. publd. 1925], 1942), 358.

65. David Hackett Fischer, *Albion's Seed: Four British Folkways in America* (New York: Oxford University Press, 1989). By the way, the book includes on page 636 a truly great map with two prominent places in South Carolina, one of which is Ninety Six, my home town.

66. Terry G. Jordan and Matti Kaups, *The American Backwoods Frontier: An Ethnic and Ecological Interpretation* (Baltimore: Johns Hopkins University Press, 1989). See the devastating review by James Lemon, *American Historical Review* 95 (Dec. 1990), 1617–1618. See especially the two articles, one by Peter H. Wood and the other by Gregory A. Waselkov, in *Southern Exposure* XVI (Summer 1988), 23–37, and the special issue, "We are Here Forever: Indians of the South," *Southern Exposure* XIII (Nov./Dec. 1985); and the work of Theda Perdue, *Slavery and the Evolution of Cherokee Society, 1540–1866* (Knoxville: University of Tennessee Press, 1979) and *Nations Remembered: An Oral History of the Five Civilized Tribes, 1865–1907* (Westport, CT: Greenwood 1980). Joan E. Cashin, *A Family Venture: Men and Women on the Southern Frontier* (New York: Oxford University Press, 1991), discusses the effect of geography on women on the frontier.

67. See for example, Daniel C. Littlefield, "'Abundance of Negroes of that Nation': The Significance of African Ethnicity in Colonial South Carolina'" in *The Meaning of South Carolina History*, 19–38.

68. Quotation from Barbara J. Fields, "Ideology and Race in American History," in J. Morgan Kousser and James M. McPherson, eds., *Region, Race, and Reconstruction: Essays in Honor of C. Vann Woodward* (New York: Oxford University Press, 1982), 144; see also her "Racism in America," *New Left Review* 181 (May/June, 1990), 95–118. See my Burton, "'Black Squint of the Law'."

69. An excellent example of applying careful economic theory and insights to society is the important book by Peter A. Coclanis, *The Shadow of a Dream: Economic Life and Death in the South Carolina Low Country 1670–1920* (New York: Oxford University Press, 1989).

70. Wyatt-Brown, *Southern Honor* and Edward L. Ayers, *Vengeance and Justice: Crime and Punishment in the 19th-Century American South* (New York: Oxford University Press, 1984).

71. Michael Hindus, *Prison and Plantation: Crime, Justice, and Authority in Massachusetts and South Carolina, 1767–1878* (Chapel Hill: University of North Carolina Press, 1980); Rachel N. Klein, *Unification of a Slave State: The Rise of the Planter Class in the South Carolina Backcountry, 1760–1808* (Chapel Hill: University of North Carolina Press, 1990), looks at the Regulator Movement as class conflict and is able to use the passage of laws to support her case. The debate on fence laws between Steven Hahn, *Roots of Southern Populism*, and J. Morgan Kousser promises to deepen our understanding of both the laws, class, and society. See Shawn E. Kantor and J. Morgan Kousser, "Common Sense or Commonwealth? The Fence Law and Institutional Change in the Postbellum South," Social Science Working Paper # 703 (July 1989), Division of the Humanities and Social Sciences, California Institute of Technology.

72. I have long thought that especially on religion, Cash was seeking revenge on the small town mentality that had tormented him as a youth. David Carlton has confirmed my own suspicions that Cash was writing out of that American genre in general. The best introduction to the literature on religion and the South is John B. Boles, "The Discovery of Southern Religious History," in Boles and Nolen, eds., *Interpreting Southern History*, 510–548.

73. George C. Rable, *Civil Wars: Women and the Crisis of Southern Nationalism* (Urbana: University of Illinois Press, 1989), 288. See also my "On the Confederate Homefront: The Transformation of Values From Community to Nation in Edgefield, South Carolina," unpublished paper presented at the Woodrow Wilson International Center for Scholars, 19 July 1989. Richard H. Sewell, *A House Divided: Sectionalism and the Civil War, 1848–1965* (Baltimore: Johns Hopkins Press, 1988) in the bibliography for his chapter on "Wartime Reconstruction" notes, "Also insightful, though sometimes wrong-headed, is W. J. Cash's classic, *The Mind of the South* (1941)."

74. To test that the South makes a difference, the scholar must look at phenomena in other regions as well as in the South. Social science argues in one form that without variance, there is no analysis. See for example, Jane H. Pease and William Henry Pease, *The Web of Progress: Private Values and Public Styles in Boston and Charleston, 1828–1843* (New York: Oxford University Press, 1985); Hindus, *Plantation and Prison;* Daniel Scott Smith, "'All in Some Degree Related to Each Other': A Demographic and Comparative Resolution of the Anomaly of New England Kinship," *American Historical Review* 94 (Feb. 1989), 44–79. I am indebted to Smith for emphasis on the social science and comparative perspective.

75. This was the theme of perhaps the best paper I have received on W. J. Cash and *The Mind of the South*. Bruce Tap insightfully explored the literature on the racism of the antebellum North. Another student, Henry Kammerling, rebutted Tap and argued that there are quantitative and qualitative differences in southern and northern racism. Both of these essays influenced my thoughts on Cash, the South, and America. See Leon F. Litwack, *North of Slavery: The Negro in the Free States, 1790–1860* (Chicago: University of Chicago Press, 1961); Michael Feldberg, *The Turbulent Era: Riot and Disorder in Jacksonian America* (New York: Oxford University Press, 1980); Eugene H. Berwanger, *The Frontier Against Slavery: Western Anti-Negro Prejudice and the Slavery Extension Controversy* (Urbana: University of Illinois Press, 1967; V. Jacque Voegeli, *Free but Not Equal: The Midwest and the Negro During the Civil War* (Chicago: University of Chicago Press, 1967); Phillip S. Paludan, *A Covenant with Death: The Constitution, Law, and Equality in the Civil War Era* (Urbana: University of Illinois Press, 1975); Allan Nevins, *Ordeal of The Union: Fruits of Manifest Destiny* (New York: Charles

Scribner's Sons, 1947), 511–524; Leonard Curry, *The Free Black in Urban America, 1800–1850: The Shadow of a Dream* (Chicago: University of Chicago Press, 1981); Ira Berlin, *Slaves without Masters: The Free Negro in the Antebellum South* (New York: Pantheon, 1975).
  76. *Daily Illini*, Feb. 28, 1991, quote p. 8, story pp. 3, 8.
  77. Woodward, *American Counterpoint*, 282.

Note to COMMENTARY
by Don H. Doyle

  1. I was explaining to an Italian friend what Cash's book was about and compared it to Luigi Barzini's *The Italians*, written by an Italian journalist in 1964. The soul, the essence of Barzini's Italians are revealed through a collection of essays on Italian history and biography which, like Cash, employ the same acerbic, knowing tone of a native son trying to explain his culture to foreigners and fellow countrymen. As my Italian colleagues often warned me, Barzini was a glib journalist, not a scholar and historian; he should be read with caution if not disbelief. But when pressed for a better introduction to Italy, none could offer a better substitute.

Notes to "SO MUCH FOR THE CIVIL WAR": CASH AND CONTINUITY IN SOUTHERN HISTORY
by James L. Roark

  1. W. J. Cash, *The Mind of the South* (New York: Knopf, 1941), p. x. Cash is equally insistent, of course, about Southern unity. Continuity and unity, as C. Vann Woodward observes, are the "warp and woof" of Cash's book. Woodward, "The Elusive Mind of the South," in *American Counterpoint: Slavery and Racism in the North-South Dialogue* (Boston: Little, Brown, 1971), 271. Woodward's essay is a revised version of the piece that initiated the reevaluation of Cash: "W. J. Cash Reconsidered," *New York Review of Books* (December 4, 1969). It is not easy to keep one's eyes on the threads that run lengthwise in a fabric and ignore those that cross at right angles, but following my assignment I'll focus on the warp of continuity rather than the woof of unity.
  2. Dan T. Carter, "From the Old South to the New: Another Look at the Theme of Change and Continuity," in Walter J. Fraser, Jr., and Winfred B. Moore, Jr., *From the Old South to the New: Essays in the Transitional South* (Westport, Conn.: Greenwood Press, 1981), p. 30.
  3. C. Vann Woodward, *Origins of the New South, 1877–1913* (Baton Rouge: Louisiana State University Press, 1951), p. 22.
  4. John Herbert Roper, *C. Vann Woodward, Southerner* (Athens: University of Georgia Press, 1987); C. Vann Woodward, *Thinking Back: The Perils of Writing History* (Baton Rouge: Louisiana State University Press, 1986); James M. McPherson, *Battle Cry of Freedom: The Civil War Era* (New York: Oxford University Press, 1988); Eric Foner, *Reconstruction: America's Unfinished Revolution, 1863–1877* (New York: Harper & Row, 1988).
  5. Cash, *The Mind of the South*, p. 112.
  6. Cash, *The Mind of the South*, pp. 104–7.
  7. Cash, *The Mind of the South*, pp. 123, 125, 132, 155, 219.
  8. Cash, *The Mind of the South*, pp. 107, 111, 127–30.

9. Cash, *The Mind of the South*, pp. 158, 168, 175.

10. Cash, *The Mind of the South*, pp. 175, 183, 369–77.

11. Cash, *The Mind of the South*, pp. 111, 136, 141, 184.

12. Woodward, "The Elusive Mind of the South," p. 280.

13. Vernon L. Wharton, "Reconstruction," in Arthur S. Link and Rembert W. Patrick, eds., *Writing Southern History: Essays in Historiography in Honor of Fletcher M. Green* (Baton Rouge: Louisiana State University Press, 1965), 295–315; Bernard A. Weisberger, "The Dark and Bloody Ground of Reconstruction Historiography," *Journal of Southern History* 25 (November 1959), 427–47; Foner, *Reconstruction*, xix–xxvii.

14. Bruce Clayton, *W. J. Cash, A Life* (Baton Rouge: Louisiana State University Press, 1991), pp. 192–222; Joseph L. Morrison, *W. J. Cash: Southern Prophet* (New York: Knopf, 1967), pp. 3–106; Michael O'Brien, "W. J. Cash, Hegel and the South," *Journal of Southern History* 44 (August 1978), pp. 379–98; Michael O'Brien, *The Idea of the American South, 1920–1941* (Baltimore: Johns Hopkins University Press, 1979); Bertram Wyatt-Brown, "W. J. Cash and Southern Culture," in *Yankee Saints and Southern Sinners* (Baton Rouge: Louisiana State University Press, 1985), 134–36; Fred Hobson, *Tell About the South: The Southern Rage to Explain* (Baton Rouge: Louisiana State University Press, 1983), pp. 244–73; Richard H. King, *A Southerner Renaissance: The Cultural Awakening of the American South* (New York: Oxford University Press, 1980), pp. 146–72.

15. Woodward, "The Elusive Mind of the South," pp. 276–77; Woodward, *Thinking Back*, pp. 22–23; Joel Williamson, *Crucible of Race: Black-White Relations in the American South Since Emancipation* (New York: Oxford University Press, 1984), 459.

16. Cash, *The Mind of the South*, p. x.

17. Henry Adams, *The Education of Henry Adams: An Autobiography* (Boston: Houghton Mifflin, 1918); T. J. Jackson Lears, *No Place of Grace: Antimodernism and the Transformation of American Culture, 1880–1920* (New York: Pantheon Books, 1981), pp. 262–97; Alfred Kazin, *An American Procession: The Major American Writers from 1830–1930—The Crucial Century* (New York: Vintage Books, 1984), 277–309.

18. For recent historiographical surveys of these decades, see Michael Perman, *Emancipation and Reconstruction, 1862–1869* (Arlington Heights, Ill.: Harlan Davidson, 1987), and Howard N. Rabinowitz, *The First New South, 1865–1920* (Arlington Heights, Ill.: Harlan Davidson, 1992).

19. For example, see James M. McPherson, *Abraham Lincoln and the Second American Revolution* (New York: Oxford University Press, 1990).

20. Cash, *The Mind of the South*, p. 103.

21. Charles Royster, *The Destructive War: William Tecumseh Sherman, Stonewall Jackson, and the Americans* (New York: Knopf, 1991); Maris A. Vinovskis, "Have Social Historians Lost the Civil War? Some Preliminary Demographic Speculations," in Vinovskis, ed., *Toward a Social History of the American Civil War: Exploratory Essays* (Cambridge: Cambridge University Press, 1990), pp. 1–30.

22. Paul D. Escott, *Many Excellent People: Power and Privilege in North Carolina, 1850–1900* (Chapel Hill: University of North Carolina Press, 1985); Wayne K. Durrill, *War of Another Kind: A Southern Community in the Great Rebellion* (New York: Oxford University Press, 1990); Stephen V. Ash, *Middle Tennessee Society Transformed, 1860–1870: War and Peace in the Upper South* (Baton Rouge:

Louisiana State University Press, 1988); Phillip S. Paludan, *Victims: A True Story of the Civil War* (Knoxville: University of Tennessee Press, 1981).

23. Lawrence N. Powell and Michael S. Wayne, "Self-Interest and the Decline of Confederate Nationalism," in Harry P. Owens and James J. Cooke, eds., *The Old South in the Crucible of War* (Jackson: University Press of Mississippi, 1983), pp. 29–46; James L. Roark, *Masters Without Slaves: Southern Planters in the Civil War and Reconstruction* (New York: W. W. Norton, 1977), pp. 35–110.

24. Roger L. Ransom, *Conflict and Compromise: The Political Economy of Slavery, Emancipation, and the American Civil War* (Cambridge: Cambridge University Press, 1989).

25. Mrs. Catherine Ann Edmondston Diaries, September 9, 1862, North Carolina State Department of Archives and History, Raleigh.

26. Still, Cash could have returned to W. E. B. Dubois's *Black Reconstruction in America: An Essay Toward a History of the Part Which Black Folk Played in the Attempt to Reconstruct Democracy in America, 1860–1880* (New York: Harcourt, Brace, 1935), but, evidently, he did not.

27. Cash recognizes, however, that blacks were victims and not perpetrators of violence, *The Mind of the South*, pp. 113–20.

28. Ira Berlin, Joseph P. Reidy, and Leslie S. Rowland, eds., *Freedom: A Documentary History of Emancipation, 1861–1867* (Cambridge: Cambridge University Press, 1982–1900), ser. 1, vol. 1: *The Destruction of Slavery*; ser. 2: *The Black Military Experience*; ser. 1, vol. 3: *The Wartime Genesis of Free Labor: The Lower South*.

29. Robert W. Fogel, *Without Consent or Contract: The Rise and Fall of American Slavery* (New York: W. W. Norton, 1989), pp. 393–400.

30. Armstead Robinson, "The Difference Freedom Made: The Emancipation of Afro-Americans," in Darlene Clark Hine, ed., *The State of Afro-American History: Past, Present, and Future* (Baton Rouge: Louisiana State University Press, 1986), pp. 51–74.

31. The literature is immense. As examples, see Foner, *Reconstruction*; Joel Williamson, *After Slavery: The Negro in South Carolina during Reconstruction, 1861–1877* (Chapel Hill: University of North Carolina Press, 1965); Leon F. Litwack, *Been in the Storm So Long: The Aftermath of Slavery* (New York: Vintage, 1979); Orville Vernon Burton, *In My Father's House Are Many Mansions: Family and Community in Edgefield, South Carolina* (Chapel Hill: University of North Carolina Press, 1985); Jacqueline Jones, *Labor of Love, Labor of Sorrow: Black Women, Work, and the Family from Slavery to the Present* (New York: Basic Books, 1985); Barbara Jeanne Fields, *Slavery and Freedom on the Middle Ground: Maryland During the Nineteenth Century* (New Haven: Yale University Press, 1985); Clarence E. Walker, *A Rock in a Weary Land: The African Methodist Episcopal Church During the Civil War and Reconstruction* (Baton Rouge: Louisiana State University Press, 1985); Clarence C. Mohr, *On the Threshold of Freedom: Masters of Slaves in Civil War Georgia* (Athens: University of Georgia Press, 1986); Peter Rachleff, *Black Labor in Richmond, 1865–1890* (Philadelphia: Temple University Press, 1985); William Cohen, *At Freedom's Edge: Black Mobility and the Southern White Quest for Racial Control, 1861–1915* (Baton Rouge: Louisiana State University Press, 1991).

32. Roger L. Ransom and Richard Sutch, *One Kind of Freedom: The Economic Consequences of Emancipation* (Cambridge: Cambridge University Press, 1977); Pete Daniel, *Breaking the Land: The Transformation of Cotton, Tobacco, and Rice Cultures since 1880* (Urbana, University of Illinois Press, 1985); Harold Woodman,

"Sequel to Slavery: The New History Views the Postbellum South," *Journal of Southern History* 43 (November 1977), pp. 523–54; Thavolia Glymph and John J. Kushma, eds., *Essays on the Postbellum Southern Economy* (College Station, Tex.: Texas A & M University Press, 1985); Eric Foner, *Nothing But Freedom: Emancipation and Its Legacy* (Baton Rouge: Louisiana State University Press, 1983); Loren Schweninger, *Black Property Owners in the South, 1790–1915* (Urbana: University of Illinois Press, 1990).

33. John B. Boles, *Black Southerners, 1619–1869* (Lexington: University Press of Kentucky, 1983), p. 182.

34. Ransom and Sutch, *One Kind of Freedom*, pp. 55–105; Wayne, *The Reshaping of Plantation Society*, pp. 110–49; Roark, *Masters Without Slaves*, pp. 111–209.

35. Gavin Wright, *The Political Economy of the Cotton South: Households, Markets and Wealth in the Nineteenth Century* (New York: W. W. Norton, 1978); Gavin Wright, *Old South, New South: Revolutions in the Southern Economy since the Civil War* (New York: Basic Books, 1986).

36. Jonathan M. Wiener, *Social Origins of the New South: Alabama, 1860–1885* (Baton Rouge: Louisiana State University Press, 1978); Randolph B. Campbell, *A Southern Community in Crisis: Harrison County, Texas, 1850–1880* (Austin: Texas State Historical Association, 1983).

37. Wayne, *The Reshaping of Plantation Society*; Jack P. Maddox, *The Reconstruction of Edward A. Pollard: A Rebel's Conversion to Postbellum Unionism* (Chapel Hill: University of North Carolina Press, 1974).

38. David R. Goldfield, *Cotton Fields and Skyscrapers: Southern City and Region, 1607–1980* (Baton Rouge: Louisiana State University Press, 1982); Howard N. Rabinowitz, "Continuity and Change: Southern Urban Development, 1860–1900," in Blaine A. Brownell and David R. Goldfield, eds., *The City in Southern History: The Growth of Urban Civilization in the South* (Port Washington, New York: Kennikat Press, 1977), pp. 92–122.

39. Don H. Doyle, *New Men, New Cities, New South: Atlanta, Nashville, Charleston, Mobile, 1860–1910* (Chapel Hill: University of North Carolina Press, 1990), p. xi.

40. David L. Carlton, *Mill and Town in South Carolina, 1880–1920* (Baton Rouge: Louisiana State University Press, 1982); James C. Cobb, "Beyond Planters and Industrialists: A New Perspective on the New South," *Journal of Southern History* (February 1988), pp. 45–68; James C. Cobb, *Industrialization and Southern Society, 1877–1984* (Lexington: University Press of Kentucky, 1984).

41. Steven Hahn, *The Roots of Southern Populism: Yeoman Farmers and the Transformation of the Georgia Upcountry, 1850–1890* (New York: Oxford University Press, 1983); Wayne Flint, *Poor But Proud: Alabama's Poor Whites* (Tuscaloosa: University of Alabama Press, 1989); I. A. Newby, *Plain Folk in the New South: Social Change and Cultural Persistence, 1880–1915* (Baton Rouge: Louisiana State University Press, 1989); Jacquelyn Dowd Hall et al., *Like A Family: The Making of a Southern Cotton Mill world* (Chapel Hill: University of North Carolina Press, 1987); Allen Tullos, *Habits of Industry: White Culture and the Transformation of the Carolina Piedmont* (Chapel Hill: University of North Carolina Press, 1989); Lacy Ford, "Rednecks and Merchants: Economic Development and Social Tensions in the South Carolina Upcountry, 1865–1900," *Journal of American History* 71 (September 1984) pp. 294–318; David F. Weiman, "The Economic Emancipation of the Non-Slaveholding Class: Upcountry Farmers in the Georgia Cotton Economy," *Journal of Economic History* 45 (March 1985), pp. 71–93.

42. C. Vann Woodward, *The Strange Career of Jim Crow* (New York: Oxford

University Press, 1955); C. Vann Woodward, "*Strange Career* Critics: Long May They Persevere," *Journal of American History* 75 (December 1988), pp. 857–68; Howard N. Rabinowitz, *Race Relations in the Urban South, 1865–1890* (New York: Oxford University Press, 1978); George M. Fredrickson, *The Black Image in the White Mind: The Debate on Afro-American Character and Destiny* (New York: Harper & Row, 1971); Joel Williamson, *The Crucible of Race: Black-White Relations in the American South Since Emancipation* (New York: Oxford University Press, 1984); Neil R. McMillen, *Dark Journey: Black Mississippians in the Age of Jim Crow* (Urbana: University of Illinois Press, 1989); John W. Cell, *The Highest State of White Supremacy: The Origins of Segregation in South Africa and the American South* (Cambridge: Cambridge University Press, 1982).

43. Foner, *Reconstruction*, p. xxv.

44. Thomas Holt, *Black Over White: Negro Political Leadership in South Carolina during Reconstruction* (Urbana: University of Illinois Press, 1977); Michael W. Fitzgerald, *The Union League Movement in the Deep South: Politics and Agricultural Change During Reconstruction* (Baton Rouge: Louisiana State University Press, 1989).

45. Steven Hahn, "Class and State in Postemancipation Societies: Southern Planters in Comparative Perspective," *American Historical Review* 95 (February 1990), pp. 75–98.

46. David M. Potter, *The South and the Concurrent Majority.* Edited by Don E. Fehrenbacher and Carl N. Degler (Baton Rouge: Louisiana State University Press, 1972).

47. Gaines M. Foster, *Ghosts of the Confederacy: Defeat, the Lost Cause, and the Emergence of the New South* (New York: Oxford University Press, 1987); Charles Reagan Wilson, *Baptized in Blood: The Religion of the Lost Cause, 1865–1920* (Athens: University of Georgia Press, 1980); Paul M. Gaston, *The New South Creed: A Study in Southern Mythmaking* (New York: Knopf, 1970).

48. Marcus Cunliffe, "American Watersheds," *American Quarterly* 13 (Winter 1961), pp. 480–94.

49. McPherson, *Battle Cry of Freedom*, p. 861.

50. "Visit to 'Gowrie' and 'East Hermitage' Plantations, Savannah River, 22d March, 1867," Charles and Louis Manigault Records, Georgia Historical Society, Savannah.

51. Octavia Otey Diary, April 2, 1867, Wyche and Otey Family Papers, Southern Historical Collection, University of North Carolina, Chapel Hill.

52. Litwack, *Been in the Storm So Long*, p. 218.

53. McPherson, *Battle Cry of Freedom*, p. viii.

Notes to COMMENTARY
by Lacy K. Ford, Jr.

1. Bruce L. Clayton, *W. J. Cash: A Life* (Baton Rouge: Louisiana State University Press, 1991), 163–222.

2. Donald Davidson, "Mr. Cash and The Proto-Dorian South," *The Southern Review* 7 (1941–42), 1–20; C. Vann Woodward, "Review of *The Mind of the South*," *Journal of Southern History* 7 (August, 1941), 400–401.

3. C. Vann Woodward, "W. J. Cash Remembered," *The New York Review of Books* 13 (December 4, 1969), 28–34. A slightly different version of Woodward's essay was later published as "The Elusive Mind of the South," in his *American*

Counterpoint: Slavery and Racism in the North-South Dialogue (Boston: Little, Brown and Co., 1971), 261–283.

4. The single best assessment of Cash's standing in recent historiography is Michael O'Brien, "Private Passion: W. J. Cash," in his *Rethinking The South: Essays in Intellectual History* (Baltimore: Johns Hopkins University Press, 1988), 179–189.

5. Woodward, "The Elusive Mind of the South," p. 267.

6. *Ibid.*, 267–268.

7. W. J. Cash, *The Mind of the South* (New York: Alfred A. Knopf, 1941), 105–147.

8. *Ibid.*, 93–94.

9. *Ibid.*, 138–139.

10. See Leon F. Litwack, *Back in the Storm So Long: The Aftermath of Slavery* (New York: Alfred A. Knopf, 1979); Eric Foner, *Reconstruction: America's Unfinished Revolution, 1863–1877* (New York: Harper and Row, 1988); and James L. Roark, *Masters Without Slaves: Southern Planters in the Civil War and Reconstruction* (New York: W. W. Norton, 1977).

11. Richard H. King, "Narcissus Grown Analytical: Cash's Southern Mind," in his *A Southern Renaissance: The Cultural Awakening of the American South, 1930–1955* (New York: Oxford University Press, 1980), 146–172.

12. O'Brien, "A Private Passion," 184, 188.

13. On Cash's personal life I have relied on Clayton, *W. J. Cash*, especially pp. 3–78, and Joseph L. Morrison, *W. J. Cash: Southern Prophet* (New York: Alfred A. Knopf, 1967), 3–74.

14. O'Brien, "A Private Passion," 184.

15. Cash, *The Mind of the South*, 58–81, 85–89, 194–197, 224–243.

16. *Ibid.*, 386.

17. Fred Hobson, *Tell About the South: The Southern Rage to Explain* (Baton Rouge: Louisiana State University Press, 1983), 259–260.

18. Cash, *The Mind of the South*, 72–73.

19. *Ibid.*, 353.

20. For a better understanding of southern journalism during Cash's time, see especially John T. Kneebone, *Southern Liberal Journalists and the Issue of Race, 1920–1944* (Chapel Hill: University of North Carolina Press, 1985); Morton Sosna, *In Search of the Silent South: Southern Liberals and the Race Issue* (New York: Columbia University Press, 1977); Charles W. Eagles, *Jonathan Daniels and Race Relations: The Evolution of a Southern Liberal* (Knoxville: University of Tennessee Press, 1982).

21. Cash, *The Mind of the South*, especially pp. 359–362.

22. Lacy K. Ford, Jr., *Origins of Southern Radicalism: The South Carolina Upcountry, 1800–1860* (New York: Oxford University Press, 1988), 19–37.

23. Michael O'Brien, ed., *All Clever Men, Who Make Their Way: Critical Discourse in the Old South* (Fayetteville: University of Arkansas Press, 1982), 420–440; James Oscar Farmer, Jr., *The Metaphysical Confederacy: James Henley Thornwell and the Synthesis of Southern Values* (Macon, GA: Mercer University Press, 1986).

24. James McBride Dabbs, *Who Speaks for the South?* (New York: Funk and Wagnalls, 1964), 380–81; Hobson, *Tell About the South*, 338–352.

25. On this point, see especially King, *A Southern Renaissance*, 146–172.

26. Bertram Wyatt-Brown, "W. J. Cash and Southern Culture," in his *Yankee Saints and Southern Sinners* (Baton Rouge: Louisiana State University Press,

1985), 131–154; Joseph K. Davis, "The South as History and Metahistory: The Mind of W. J. Cash," *Spectrum* 2 (1972), 11–24.

27. Daniel Joseph Singal, *The War Within: From Victorian to Modernist Thought in the South, 1919–1945* (Chapel Hill: The University of North Carolina Press, 1982), 189–190.

28. Garry Wills, *Reagan's America: Innocents at Home* (Garden City, NY: Doubleday and Company, 1987), 378–388.

29. Clayton, *W. J. Cash*, 109.

Notes to W. J. CASH, THE NEW SOUTH, AND THE RHETORIC OF HISTORY
by Edward L. Ayers

1. Cash quoted in Joseph L. Morrison, *W. J. Cash, Southern Prophet: A Biography and a Reader* (New York: Alfred A. Knopf, 1967), 66.
2. W. J. Cash, *The Mind of the South* (New York: Alfred A. Knopf, 1941), 351–3.
3. Cash, *The Mind of the South*, 66.
4. Cash, *The Mind of the South*, 145, 162, 169.
5. Cash, *The Mind of the South*, 173, 184.
6. Cash, *The Mind of the South*, 200, 201, 212.
7. Cash, *The Mind of the South*, 236.
8. Cash, *The Mind of the South*, 243, 356.
9. Cash, *The Mind of the South*, 237, 229; I would like to thank Peter Dimock of Random House for supplying the sales figures.
10. I emphasize these themes in *The Promise of the New South, 1877–1906* (New York: Oxford University Press, 1992).
11. For analyses and critiques of Cash, see C. Vann Woodward, "The Elusive Mind of the South," in *American Counterpoint: Slavery and Racism in the North-South Dialogue* (Boston: Little, Brown, 1971), 261–83; David Hackett Fischer, *Historians' Fallacies: Toward a Logic of Historical Thought* (New York: Harper, 1970); Michael O'Brien, "W. J. Cash, Hegel, and the South," *Journal of Southern History*, 44 (August 1978), 379–98. Bertram Wyatt-Brown offers a penetrating appreciation in "W. J. Cash and Southern Culture," in *Yankee Saints and Southern Sinners* (Baton Rouge: Louisiana State University Press, 1985), 131–54. The most thorough and balanced discussion appears in Bruce Clayton, *W. J. Cash: A Life* (Baton Rouge: Louisiana State University Press, 1991), 192–222; C. Vann Woodward, *Origins of the New South, 1877–1913* (Baton Rouge: Louisiana State University Press, 1951).
12. David L. Carlton, *Mill and Town in South Carolina, 1880–1920* (Baton Rouge: Louisiana State University Press, 1982); Jacquelyn Dowd Hall, James Leloudis, Robert Korstad, Mary Murphy, Lu Ann Jones, and Christopher B. Daly, *Like a Family: The Making of a Southern Cotton Mill World* (Chapel Hill: University of North Carolina Press, 1987); I. A. Newby, *Plain Folk in the New South: Social Change and Cultural Persistence, 1880–1915* (Baton Rouge: Louisiana State University Press, 1989); Allen Tullos, *Habits of Industry: White Culture and the Transformation of the Carolina Piedmont* (Chapel Hill: University of North Carolina Press, 1989).
13. Jonathan M. Wiener, *Social Origins of the New South: Alabama, 1860–1885* (Baton Rouge: Louisiana State University Press, 1978); Dwight B. Billings, Jr., *Planters and the Making of a "New South": Class, Politics, and Development in*

North Carolina, 1865–1900 (Chapel Hill: University of North Carolina Press, 1979); Laurence Shore, *Southern Capitalists: The Ideological Leadership of an Elite, 1832–1885* (Chapel Hill: University of North Carolina Press, 1986); Paul D. Escott, *Many Excellent People: Power and Privilege in North Carolina, 1850–1900* (Chapel Hill: University of North Carolina Press, 1985); Joel Williamson, *The Crucible of Race: Black-White Relations in the American South since Reconstruction* (New York: Oxford University Press, 1984); 1–4; Ted Ownby, *Subduing Satan: Religion, Recreation, and Manhood in the Rural South, 1865–1920* (Chapel Hill: University of North Carolina Press, 1990), 1; Jack Temple Kirby, *Rural Worlds Lost: The American South, 1920–1960* (Baton Rouge: Louisiana State University Press, 1987); Richard H. King, *A Southern Renaissance: The Cultural Awakening of the American South, 1930–1955* (New York: Oxford University Press, 1980); Michael O'Brien, *The Idea of the American South, 1920–1941* (Baltimore: Johns Hopkins University Press, 1979); Fred Hobson, *Tell About the South: The Southern Rage to Explain* (Baton Rouge: Louisiana State University Press, 1983); Daniel Joseph Singal, *The War Within: From Victorian to Modernist Thought in the South, 1919–1945* (Chapel Hill: University of North Carolina Press, 1982), 137–39, 312; Morrison, *Cash*; Clayton, *Cash*.

14. For a more favorable interpretation of Cash on race, see Clayton, *Cash*, 203–7.

15. Clayton, *Cash*; I first heard the concept of historians' "ventriloquism" described in conversation by Jacquelyn Hall and have lifted it without permission.

16. Cash, *The Mind of the South*, 115; Richard King has emphasized the psychological aspects of Cash's portrayal in *A Southern Renaissance*, 146–70.

17. Williamson, *Crucible of Race*, 1–4.

18. On the Populists, see Lawrence Goodwyn, *Democratic Promise: The Populist Movement in America* (New York: Oxford University Press, 1976); on lynching, see Edward L. Ayers, *Vengeance and Justice: Crime and Punishment in the Nineteenth-Century American South* (New York: Oxford University Press, 1984), 238–53; on feuding, see Altina L. Waller, *Feud: Hatfields, McCoys, and Social Change in Appalachia, 1860–1900* (Chapel Hill: University of North Carolina Press, 1988); on segregation, John W. Cell, *The Highest Stage of White Supremacy: The Origins of Segregation in South Africa and the American South* (Cambridge: Cambridge University Press, 1982); on disfranchisement, J. Morgan Kousser, *The Shaping of Southern Politics: Suffrage Restriction and the Establishment of the One-Party South, 1880–1910* (New Haven: Yale University Press, 1974).

19. Eugene Genovese, *Roll, Jordan, Roll: The World the Slaves Made* (New York: Random House, 1974); Paul M. Gaston, *The New South Creed: A Study in Southern Mythmaking* (New York: Alfred A. Knopf, 1970), 11–12; Charles Reagan Wilson, *Baptized in Blood: The Religion of the Lost Cause, 1865–1920* (Athens: University of Georgia Press, 1980); Gaines M. Foster, *Ghosts of the Confederacy: Defeat, the Lost Cause, and the Emergence of the New South* (New York: Oxford University Press, 1987). Hegemony would seem to hold considerable possibilities for the study of the New South, especially if we would adopt the complex vision offered by Raymond Williams in his *Marxism and Literature* (Oxford: Oxford University Press, 1977).

20. This tendency is especially prominent in Goodwyn, *Democratic Promise*.

21. Such a mythology of loss seems deeply embedded in American and Southern culture. It pervades Woodward's *Origins of the New South*, Faulkner's Yoknapatawpha, and much country music. The most influential and sophisticated study in this vein, though too subtle and insightful to fall prey to romanticism for long, is

Steven Hahn's *The Roots of Southern Populism: Yeoman Farmers and the Trans-formation of the Georgia Upcountry, 1850–1890* (New York: Oxford University Press, 1983).

22. On Mencken and Cash, see Fred W. Hobson, Jr., *Serpent in Eden: H. L. Mencken and the South* (Chapel Hill: University of North Carolina, 1974), 111–20; on Woodward and Beard, see John Herbert Roper, *C. Vann Woodward, Southerner* (Athens: University of Georgia Press, 1987), 71–4.

23. Woodward, *Origins*, 449–53; on New South religion, for example, see Rufus B. Spain, *At Ease in Zion: A Social History of Southern Baptists, 1865–1900* (Nashville: Vanderbilt University Press, 1967); John Lee Eighmy, *Churches in Cultural Captivity: A History of the Social Attitudes of Southern Baptists* (Knoxville: University of Tennessee Press, 1972).

24. Gavin Wright, *Old South, New South: Revolutions in the Southern Economy since the Civil War* (New York: Basic Books, 1986).

25. Twelve Southerners, *I'll Take My Stand; the South and the Agrarian Tradition* (New York: Harper, 1930); on the new techniques the Owsleys devised, see Harriet Chappell Owsley, *Frank Lawrence Owsley: Historian of the Old South* (Nashville: Vanderbilt University Press, 1990), 136–59; William Alexander Percy, *Lanterns on the Levee: Recollections of a Planter's Son* (New York: Knopf, 1941); Douglas Southall Freeman, *Robert E. Lee: A Biography* (New York: Scribner, 1934–5); Margaret Mitchell, *Gone with the Wind* (New York: Macmillan, 1936); Howard W. Odum, *Southern Regions of the United States* (Chapel Hill: University of North Carolina Press, 1936); Liston Pope, *Millhands and Preachers: A Study of Gastonia* (New Haven: Yale University Press, 1942); Charles S. Johnson, *Growing Up in the Black Belt: Negro Youth in the Rural South* (Washington: American Council on Education, 1941); John Dollard, *Caste and Class in a Southern Town* (New Haven: Yale University Press, 1937); Hortense Powdermaker, *After Freedom: A Cultural Study in the Deep South* (New York: Viking, 1939); W. E. B. DuBois, *Black Reconstruction: An Essay Toward a History of the Part Which Black Folk Played in the Attempt to Reconstruct Democracy in America, 1860–1900* (New York: Russell and Russell, 1935); Carter G. Woodson, *The Rural Negro* (Washington: Association for the Study of Negro Life and History, 1930); Jean Toomer, *Cane* (New York: Boni and Liveright, 1923); Zora Neale Hurston, *Their Eyes Were Watching God* (Philadelphia: J. B. Lippincott, 1937); Thomas Wolfe, *Look Homeward Angel: A Story of the Buried Life* (New York: Scribner, 1929); William Faulkner, *Absalom! Absalom!* (New York: Random House, 1936).

26. James Agee, *Let Us Now Praise Famous Men* (Boston: Houghton Mifflin, 1941), 7.

27. See Robert F. Berkhofer, Jr., "The Challenge of Poetics to (Normal) Historical Practice," *Poetics Today*, 9 (March 1988), 435–52.

Notes to COMMENTARY
by Linda Reed

1. U. S. National Emergency Council, *Report on Economic Conditions of the South* (Washington: U.S. Government Printing Office, 1938); Linda Reed, *Simple Decency and Common Sense: The Southern Conference Movement, 1938–1963* (Bloomington: Indiana University Press, 1991).

2. Reed, *Simple Decency and Common Sense*, 96–97.

Notes to *THE MIND OF THE SOUTH* AND SOUTHERN
DISTINCTIVENESS
by John Shelton Reed

1. Citations to *The Mind of the South* are to the original edition of 1941, published by Alfred A. Knopf. For the book's thesis, see especially pp. vii–viii.
2. Bertram Wyatt-Brown, "The Mind of W. J. Cash," introduction to new edition of *The Mind of the South* (1941; New York: Alfred A. Knopf, 1991).
3. C. Vann Woodward, "The Elusive Mind of the South," in *American Counterpoint: Slavery and Racism in the North-South Dialogue* (Boston: Little, Brown, 1971), 269–70.
4. See e.g., Michael Skube's article ("Cash and His South," pp. 1J and 5J) and column ("Preening and Posturing about W. J. Cash," p. 4J) on a conference at Wake Forest University, in the Raleigh *News and Observer*, February 17, 1991, and the letters that followed in the issue of March 3 (p. 5J).
5. Michael O'Brien, "W. J. Cash," in Charles Reagan Wilson and William Ferris (eds.), *Encyclopedia of Southern Culture* (Chapel Hill: University of North Carolina Press, 1989), 1130–31.
6. On their declining influence, see Earl Black and Merle Black, *Politics and Society in the South* (Cambridge: Harvard University Press, 1987), 52–57.
7. Woodward, "Elusive Mind," 263.
8. John Shelton Reed, "The Life and Mind of W. J. Cash," *News and Observer* (Raleigh, N.C.), February 17, 1991, p. 4J.
9. O'Brien, "W. J. Cash," 1130.
10. Woodward, "Elusive Mind," 283.
11. *The Mind of the South*, 219.
12. Louis Rubin, "Introduction to the Torchbook Edition," in *Twelve Southerners, I'll Take My Stand: The South and the Agrarian Tradition* (New York: Harper Torchbooks, 1962).
13. V. S. Naipaul, *A Turn in the South* (New York: Alfred A. Knopf, 1989), *passim*.
14. *The Mind of the South*, 7.
15. On the Irishman, see *The Mind of the South*, 14–17.
16. *The Mind of the South*, 429.
17. Bruce Clayton, *W. J. Cash: A Life* (Baton Rouge: LSU Press, 1991).
18. On the marginality of Cash's contemporaries, the Vanderbilt Agrarians, see John Shelton Reed, "For Dixieland: The Sectionalism of *I'll Take My Stand*," in William C. Havard and Walter Sullivan (eds.), *A Band of Prophets: The Nashville Agrarians After Fifty Years* (Baton Rouge: Louisiana State University Press, 1982.)
19. *The Mnd of the South*, 49–50.
20. See also a remarkable four-sentence paragraph (83–84) discussing the slave social type that would later receive considerable attention as "Sambo," in Stanley M. Elkins, *Slavery: A Problem in American Institutional and Intellectual Life* (Chicago: University of Chicago Press, 1959).
21. See, e.g., *The Mind of the South*, 53 ff.
22. Gerald W. Johnson, "The South Takes the Offensive" [1924], in *South-Watching: Selected Essays* (Chapel Hill: University of North Carolina Press, 1983), 97. Johnson may have been being ironic, but I think not here.
23. *The Mind of the South*, e.g. 184, 219–220.
24. Judith Blau, *The Shape of Culture: A Study of Contemporary Cultural Patterns in the United States* (New York: Cambridge University Press, 1989), 25.
25. *The Mind of the South*, 219.

26. *The Mind of the South*, 184.

27. *The Mind of the South*, 31.

28. *The Mind of the South*, 33.

29. *The Mind of the South*, 111.

30. *The Mind of the South*, 33.

31. On Southerners' love of politics, see *The Mind of the South*, 52.

32. Richard M. Weaver, "Two Types of Individualism," in *Life Without Prejudice and Other Essays* (Chicago: H. Regnery Co., 1966).

33. Alasdair MacIntyre, *After Virtue: A Study in Moral Theory*, 2nd ed. (Notre Dame: University of Notre Dame Press, 1984), quotation from 220.

34. Bertram Wyatt-Brown has made a related point, in *Southern Honor: Ethics and Behavior in the Old South* (New York: Oxford University Press, 1982), 45–48, observing that the code of honor vaunts autonomy, but actually implies a fearful sort of dependence, by putting one's standing and even self-esteem at the mercy of others' estimation.

35. On this ethic, see John Shelton Reed, "The Same Old *Stand*," in Reed, *One South: An Ethnic Approach to Regional Culture* (Baton Rouge: LSU Press, 1982).

36. See Durkheim's distinction between "egoistic" and "altruistic" forms, in *Le Suicide: Etude de Sociologie* (Vendome: Presses Universitaires de France, 1960), 149–263.

37. *The Mind of the South*, 33.

38. *The Mind of the South*, 42–43.

39. See, e.g., John W. Roberts, *From Trickster to Badman: The Black Folk Hero in Slavery and Freedom* (Philadelphia: University of Pennsylvania Press, 1989).

40. On these and other white female social types in the South, see John Shelton Reed, *Southern Folk, Plain and Fancy: Native White Social Types* (Athens: University of Georgia Press, 1986), 48–61.

41. Roy Reed, "Revisiting the Southern Mind," *New York Times Magazine* December 5, 1976, 103–4.

42. *The Mind of the South*, 34; see also 35.

43. *The Mind of the South*, 39.

44. *The Mind of the South*, 39.

45. *The Mind of the South*, 41.

46. *The Mind of the South*, 41.

47. *The Mind of the South*, 111.

48. *The Mind of the South*, 212.

49. At least that is true of men; women may be different. James S. Coleman, in *The Adolescent Society: The Social Life of the Teenager and Its Impact on Education* (New York: Free Press of Glencoe, 1961), shows that social-class distinctions matter far more for high-school girls than for boys, whose stratification system is based primarily on athletic ability. In this respect, and maybe others, it could be productive to think of the South as one big open-air high school.

50. *The Mind of the South*, 269.

51. *The Mind of the South*, 269–70.

52. *The Mind of the South*, 270.

53. Bryan Burrough and John Helyar, *Barbarians at the Gate: The Fall of RJR Nabisco* (New York: Harper & Row, 1990), 49.

54. Burrough and Helyar, *Barbarians*, 80, 83.

55. See, e.g., John Shelton Reed, *The Enduring South: Cultural Persistence in*

Mass Society, rev. ed. (Chapel Hill: University of North Carolina Press, 1986), 91–102.

56. Johnson, "Critical Attitudes North and South" [924], *South-Watching,* 91–92.

Notes to COMMENTARY
by Bertram Wyatt-Brown

1. Joseph L. Morrison, *W. J. Cash: Southern Prophet: A Biography and Reader* (New York: Knopf, 1967); Bruce Clayton, *W. J. Cash, A Life* (Baton Rouge: Louisiana State University Press, 1991).

2. This section has been informed by Elizabeth Jacoway, whose essay, kindly sent to the author, will appear in Paul Escott's impending anthology of Cash articles to be published by Louisiana State University Press.

3. See Alfred Lord Tennyson, "Lancelot and Elaine," in *Idylls of the King* in *The Complete Poetical Works of Tennyson* (Boston: Houghton Mifflin, 1898), 381–400; W. J. Cash, *The Mind of the South* (New York: Knopf, 1941), 89.

4. Virginia Woolf, *The Death of the Moth and Other Essays* (1942; New York: Harcourt, Brace and Jovanovich, 1970), 235–42.

5. Cash, *The Mind of the South,* 88.

6. Cash, *The Mind of the South,* 17.

7. Cash, *The Mind of the South,* 204.

8. Katherine Grantham Rogers to Joseph L. Morrison, September 30 [October 2], 1964, Joseph L. Morrison Papers, Southern Historical Collection, Wilson Library, University of North Carolina, Chapel Hill.

9. Cash, *The Mind of the South,* 116–20.

10. Cash, *The Mind of the South,* 87.

11. As reported by Catherine Grantham Rogers to Joseph L. Morrison, September 30 [October 2], 1964, Joseph L. Morrison Papers, Southern Historical Collection, Wilson Library, University of North Carolina, Chapel Hill.

12. *Ibid.*

13. Rogers to Morrison, September 30, [October 5], 1964, Morrison Papers, Southern Historical Collection, Wilson Library, University of North Carolina, Chapel Hill.

14. See Bertram Wyatt-Brown, *Southern Honor: Ethics and Behavior in the Old South* (New York: Oxford University Press, 1982).

15. Michael O'Brien, *Rethinking the South: Essays in Intellectual History* (Baltimore: Johns Hopkins University Press, 1988), 179–80. For greater elaboration, see Bertram Wyatt-Brown, "Introduction: The Mind of W. J. Cash," in W. J. Cash, *The Mind of the South* (1941; New York: Random House, 1991), vii–xli.

16. Peter Novick, *That Noble Dream: The 'Objectivity Question' and the American Historical Profession* (Cambridge: Cambridge University Press, 1988); Simon Schama, *Dead Certainties: Unwarranted Speculations* (New York: Knopf, 1991); Gordon S. Wood, "Novel History," *New York Review of Books,* June 27, 1991, 12–16; and William W. Freehling, *The Road to Disunion: Secessionists at Bay, 1776–1854* (New York: Oxford University Press, 1990).

17. See Bertram Wyatt-Brown, *Yankee Saints and Southern Sinners* (Baton Rouge: Louisiana State University Press, 1985), 131–54. By and large the questions that Cash posed were not ones to engage the academy at all. Except for the last ten years since its publication, *The Mind of the South* did not excite any investigations of the themes that Cash was most concerned to elucidate about race, violence, class

structure, or even the cultural image of Southern women. Indeed there was precious little said about Southern women from 1941 to 1981, and none of Cash's critics even noticed until all of us had our consciences raised in the last few years. So are we any less guilty than Cash himself on that score? See Michael O'Brien, "W. J. Cash, Hegel, and the South," *Journal of Southern History* 44 (August 1978), 379–98.

Bibliography

Works about W. J. Cash and *The Mind of the South*

Clayton, Bruce. "A Southern Modernist: The Mind of W. J. Cash." In *The South Is Another Land*, pp. 171–86. Edited by Bruce Clayton and John A. Salmond. Westport, CT: Greenwood, 1987.

————. "W. J. Cash and the Creative Impulse." *Southern Review* 24 (Autumn 1988): 777–90.

————. "The Proto-Dorian Convention: W. J. Cash and the Race Question." In *Race, Class, and Politics in Southern History*, pp. 260–88. Edited by Jeffrey J. Crow, Paul D. Escott, and Charles L. Flynn, Jr. Baton Rouge: Louisiana State University Press, 1989.

————. *W. J. Cash: A Life*. Baton Rouge: Louisiana State University Press, 1991.

Cobb, James C. "Does *Mind* No Longer Matter? The South, the Nation, and *The Mind of the South*, 1941–1991." *Journal of Southern History* 57 (November 1991): 681–718.

Davis, Joseph K. "The South as History and Metahistory: The Mind of W. J. Cash." *Spectrum* 2 (1972): 11–24. Reprinted in Lewis P. Simpson, ed., *The Poetry of Community: Essays on the Southern Sensibility of History and Literature* (Atlanta: Georgia State University, 1972).

Dean Michael P. "W. J. Cash's *The Mind of the South*: Southern History, Southern Style." *Southern Studies* 20 (Fall 1981): 297–302.

Dearmore, Tom. "The Enigma of W. J. Cash." In *Reporting the News: Selections from Nieman Reports*. Edited by Louis M. Lyons. Cambridge, Mass.: Harvard University Press, 1965.

Downs, Robert B. "Nation within a Nation: W. J. Cash's *The Mind of the South*." In Downs, *Books that Changed America* (New York: Macmillan, 1970), 229–38. Reprinted in Downs, *Books that Changed the South* (Chapel Hill: University of North Carolina Press, 1977), 248–58.

Genovese, Eugene D. *The World the Slaveholders Made*. New York: Pantheon, 1970 (see pp. 137–50).

Grantham, Dewey. "Mr. Cash Writes a Book." *The Progressive* 25 (December 1961): 40–42.

Hobson, Fred. "Wilbur Joseph Cash." In *Southern Writers: A Biographical Dictionary*, pp. 71–2. Edited by Robert Bain, Joseph M. Flora, and

Louis D. Rubin, Jr. Baton Rouge: Louisiana State University Press, 1979.

———. "The Meaning of Aristocracy: Wilbur Cash and William Alexander Percy." In *Tell About the South: The Southern Rage to Explain*, pp. 244–94. Baton Rouge: Louisiana State University Press, 1983.

King, Richard H. "The Mind of the Southerner: Narcissus Grown Analytical." *New South* 27 (Winter, 1972): 15–27.

———. "Narcissus Grown Analytical: Cash's Southern Mind." In *A Southern Renaissance: The Cultural Awakening of the American South, 1930–1955*, pp. 146–72. New York: Oxford University Press, 1980.

Morrison, Joseph L. "The Obsessive 'Mind' of W. J. Cash." *Studies in Journalism and Communications* 4 (May 1985): 1–12.

———. *W. J. Cash: Southern Prophet, A Biography and Reader.* New York: Knopf, 1967.

———. "Found: The Missing Editorship of W. J. Cash." *North Carolina Historical Review* 47 (1970): 40–50.

———. "W. J. Cash: The Summing Up." *South Atlantic Quarterly* 70 (Autumn 1971): 477–86.

O'Brien, Michael. "W. J. Cash, Hegel, and the South." *Journal of Southern History* 44 (August 1978): 379–98.

———. "A Private Passion: W. J. Cash." In *Rethinking the South: Essays in Intellectual History*, pp. 179–89. Baltimore: Johns Hopkins University Press, 1988.

———. "Cash, W. J." In *The Encyclopedia of Southern Culture*, pp. 1130–1131. Edited by Charles Reagan Wilson and William Ferris. Chapel Hill: University of North Carolina Press, 1989.

Rubin, Louis D., Jr. "The Mind of the South." *Sewanee Review* 62 (Autumn 1954): 683–95.

———. "W. J. Cash after Fifty Years." *Virginia Quarterly Review* 67 (Spring 1981): 214–28.

Woodward, C. Vann. "White Man, White Mind." *The New Republic*, December 9, 1967, pp. 28–30.

———. "W. J. Cash Reconsidered," *New York Review of Books*, December 4, 1969, pp. 28–34. Revised version as "The Elusive Mind of the South" in Woodward, *American Counterpoint: Slavery and Racism in the North-South Dialogue*, pp. 261–83. Boston: Little, Brown, 1971.

Wyatt-Brown, Bertram. "W. J. Cash and Southern Culture." In *From the Old South to the New: Essays on the Transitional South*, pp. 195–214. Edited by Walter J. Fraser, Jr., and Winfred B. Moore, Jr., Westport, CT: Greenwood, 1981. Revised version in *Yankee Saints and Southern*

Sinners, pp. 131–54. Baton Rouge: Louisiana State University Press, 1985.

————. "Introduction: The Mind of W. J. Cash." In *The Mind of the South,* vii–xli. By W. J. Cash. New York: Random House, 1991 [1941].

Yoder, Edwin M. "W. J. Cash: After a Quarter Century." In *The South Today: 100 Years After Appomattox,* pp. 89–99. Edited by Willie Morris. New York: Harper and Row, 1965.

Contributors

Edward L. Ayers is a professor of history at the University of Virginia and the author of *Vengeance and Justice: Crime and Punishment in the 19th-Century American South*. His latest work is *The Promise of the New South. 1877–1906* published this year.

Orville Vernon Burton holds a joint appointment as professor of history and sociology at the University of Illinois. His scholarly writings include *In My Father's House Are Many Mansions*, a social history of Edgefield, South Carolina.

Bruce Clayton is Harry A. Logan, Sr., Professor of American History at Allegheny College in Meadville, Pennsylvania. In addition to *W. J. Cash: A Critical Biography*, he has written *The Savage Ideal: Intolerance and Intellectual Leadership in the South, 1890–1914* and *Forgotten Prophet: A Life of Randolph Bourne*.

Don H. Doyle is a professor of history at Vanderbilt University. His work in southern history includes a two-volume history of Nashville and, most recently, *New Men, New Cities, New South: Atlanta, Nashville, Charleston, Mobile, 1860–1910*.

Lacy K. Ford, Jr., is a member of the history department at the University of South Carolina. His *Origins of Southern Radicalism: The South Carolina Upcountry, 1800–1860* won the 1989 Francis B. Simkins Award of the Southern Historical Association.

Anne Goodwyn Jones, a member of the Department of English at the University of Florida, specializes in southern literature. She has written *Tomorrow Is Another Day: The Woman Writer in the South, 1859–1936*, which won the 1980 Jules F. Landry Award.

Michael O'Brien is Phillip R. Shriver Professor of History at Miami University of Ohio. Among his many works in southern intellectual history are *The Idea of the American South, 1920–1941* and *A Character of Hugh Legare*.

John Shelton Reed is a professor of sociology and the director of the Institute for Research in Social Science at the University of North Carolina. His books on the South include *The Enduring South: Subcultural Persistence in Mass Society*, *Southerners: The Social Psychol-*

ogy of Sectionalism, and *Southern Folk, Plain and Fancy: Native White Social Types.*

Linda Reed teaches history at the University of Houston and has written *Simple Decency and Common Sense: The Southern Conference Movement, 1938–1963.*

James L. Roark is Samuel Candler Dobbs Professor of American History at Emory University. He has written *Masters Without Slaves: Southern Planters in the Civil War and Reconstruction,* which won the Allan Nevins Prize in 1974, and *Black Masters: A Free Family of Color in the Old South* (with Michael P. Johnson).

Bertram Wyatt-Brown is Richard J. Milbauer Professor of History at the University of Florida. His books include *Southern Honor: Ethics and Behavior in the Old South* and *Yankee Saints and Southern Sinners.*

Index